T0234434

# Computational Intelligence Methods and Applications

**Founding Editors**

Sanghamitra Bandyopadhyay, Machine Intelligence Unit, Indian Statistical Institute, Kolkata, West Bengal, India

Ujjwal Maulik, Dept of Computer Science & Engineering, Jadavpur University, Kolkata, West Bengal, India

**Series Editor**

Patrick Siarry, LiSSi, E.A. 3956, Université Paris-Est Créteil, Vitry-sur-Seine, France

The monographs and textbooks in this series explain methods developed in computational intelligence (including evolutionary computing, neural networks, and fuzzy systems), soft computing, statistics, and artificial intelligence, and their applications in domains such as heuristics and optimization; bioinformatics, computational biology, and biomedical engineering; image and signal processing, VLSI, and embedded system design; network design; process engineering; social networking; and data mining.

Paul Fergus • Carl Chalmers

# Applied Deep Learning

## Tools, Techniques, and Implementation

 Springer

Paul Fergus
School of Computer Science
and Mathematics
Liverpool John Moores University
Liverpool, UK

Carl Chalmers
School of Computer Science
and Mathematics
Liverpool John Moores University
Liverpool, UK

ISSN 2510-1765          ISSN 2510-1773   (electronic)
Computational Intelligence Methods and Applications
ISBN 978-3-031-04422-9        ISBN 978-3-031-04420-5   (eBook)
https://doi.org/10.1007/978-3-031-04420-5

© Springer Nature Switzerland AG 2022
This work is subject to copyright. All rights are reserved by the Publisher, whether the whole or part of the material is concerned, specifically the rights of translation, reprinting, reuse of illustrations, recitation, broadcasting, reproduction on microfilms or in any other physical way, and transmission or information storage and retrieval, electronic adaptation, computer software, or by similar or dissimilar methodology now known or hereafter developed.
The use of general descriptive names, registered names, trademarks, service marks, etc. in this publication does not imply, even in the absence of a specific statement, that such names are exempt from the relevant protective laws and regulations and therefore free for general use.
The publisher, the authors and the editors are safe to assume that the advice and information in this book are believed to be true and accurate at the date of publication. Neither the publisher nor the authors or the editors give a warranty, expressed or implied, with respect to the material contained herein or for any errors or omissions that may have been made. The publisher remains neutral with regard to jurisdictional claims in published maps and institutional affiliations.

This Springer imprint is published by the registered company Springer Nature Switzerland AG
The registered company address is: Gewerbestrasse 11, 6330 Cham, Switzerland

# Preface

Applied Artificial Intelligence: Mastering the Fundamentals, is aimed at students, academics and industry practitioners to provide them with a conceptual overview of the field. Students can use this book to supplement undergraduate, postgraduate and doctoral studies. Academics who are new to the area can utilise this book to gain a broad understanding of Artificial Intelligence while seasoned academics can use the book as a point of reference. In industry, managers will find this book useful for gaining an understanding of Artificial Intelligence and where it could be integrated into existing business processes. For those primally focused on development and implementation, the book along with its references provides a strong foundation for anyone moving into Artificial Intelligence development. The book discusses key frameworks such as TensorFlow, Dask, RAPIDS, Docker and Kubernetes. What makes this book accessible to a broad range of readers is the conscious decision to minimise both mathematical and programming notation and focus more on the core and practical concepts of Artificial Intelligence and its deployment. Once the reader has a good grasp of the concepts, understanding the theoretical principles becomes much easier.

The first chapter of this book will introduce the field of Artificial Intelligence, Machine Learning and Deep Learning. In the first section following the introduction (Chaps. 2–5) will cover the fundamentals of Machine Learning, supervised and unsupervised learning and performance evaluation metrics. This includes popular algorithms such as Support Vector Machines, Random Forests, Liner Regression and K-Means Clustering. The second section of this book (Chaps. 6–11) will discuss Deep Learning concepts and techniques. This will include an introduction to Deep Learning, image classification and object detection, Deep Learning for time series data, natural language processing, generative models and deep reinforcement learning. This includes algorithms such as Convolutional Neural Networks, Recurrent Neural Networks, Autoencoders and Generative Adversarial Networks. The third section of this book (Chap. 12) will cover accelerated Machine Learning. This includes Spark, Dask and RAPIDS. The forth and final section of the book (Chaps. 13 and 14) will discuss the deployment and hosting of Machine Learning models within enterprise environments using frameworks such as TensorFlow Serving, Docker and Kubernetes.

Liverpool, UK                                                                                          Paul Fergus
                                                                                                              Carl Chalmers

# Acknowledgements

**Paul Fergus:** There have been many contributing factors associated with the completion of this book, the most important being all the people who have helped me. I would first like to thank Dr. Carl Chalmers for his unwavering passion and commitment during the writing of this book. He has had to endure many grumpy moments with me over the last year or so. I would like to thank the Springer team for their help and support and for the excellent guidance they have given us during this project. I would especially like to thank my wife Lorna Bracegirdle for putting up with me over the years and for the support she has given me. I would also like to thank my son Benjamin Fergus, my step-daughter Sasha-Lei Bracegirdle, my mother-in-law Lillian Bracegirdle and my father-in-law Brian Bracegirdle, who sadly passed away before the book was completed, for standing by me and supporting me when I needed it. Lastly, I would like to thank my dog Milo who loves me unconditionally and always makes me laugh when I need it.

**Carl Chalmers:** I would like to thank my wife Rachel and my two sons Joshua and Toby for their patience and support in writing this book. Without their support and encouragement, it would have been impossible to complete. I would also like to thank my friend and colleague Professor Paul Fergus for his support, wisdom and friendship throughout the entire processes. I would also like to thank the inspirational researchers mentioned throughout this book for their tireless dedication to the field of Artificial Intelligence.

# Contents

# List of Figures

# List of Tables

# Part I
# Introduction and Overview

# Chapter 1
# Introduction

We are now beginning to see the widespread use of Artificial Intelligence (AI) in all walks of life. From Alexa in the home to the promise of driverless cars in the future. Many aspects of AI have transitioned from a purely theoretical field to an applied one. Therefore, unlike traditional university courses, this book provides an introductory guide to those wishing to pick up AI and apply it in solving real-world problems. Never before have we seen so many frameworks surrounding the application of AI. With many large organisations such as Google, Microsoft, IBM, Facebook and NVidia offering a wide range of AI technologies, the race is on to capture market share as we continue to see the uptake of AI. This means that businesses both small and large are increasingly looking to use these technologies to start developing solutions to solve their own unique problems. This book is timely as its underlying goal is to bridge the gap between the well-supported frameworks that organisations provide and anyone with a desire to learn applied AI.

This book will provide you with the necessary tools to fast track the development of end-to-end AI solutions. This will help you to build AI systems to address age-old problems and even generate novel products that will have significant and far-reaching impacts. For anyone who is considering a career in AI, there has never been a better time to get started. This book will show you how to develop traditional AI applications using frameworks such as Scikit-Learn and introduce you to Deep Learning (DL) using the TensorFlow framework from Google, TensorFlow Serving and Docker. Traditional machine learning frameworks will be extended using RAPIDS to show how you can accelerate machine learning pipelines to expedite model deployment. This book will introduce in-depth concepts on DL algorithms such as Convolutional Neural Networks (CNNs), Long-Term Short-Term memory (LSTM) networks, Auto Encoders (AE) and Generative Adversarial Neural Networks (GANs). On completion of this book, you will have the necessary knowledge to confidently start a career in applied AI.

Collectively, the authors of this book have over 15 years of industrial experience developing large scale software systems and implementing AI solutions. In addition, the authors have transitioned through the educational system from undergraduate

© Springer Nature Switzerland AG 2022

P. Fergus, C. Chalmers, *Applied Deep Learning*, Computational Intelligence Methods and Applications, https://doi.org/10.1007/978-3-031-04420-5_1

degrees in software engineering and AI right through to PhDs in advanced topics in applied AI. Therefore, they have a unique perspective and understanding of the applied aspects of AI and their deployment in real-world solutions.

## 1.1 Artificial Intelligence, Machine Learning, Deep Learning

Artificial intelligence, machine learning and deep learning, what is the difference? Well AI requires you to hard-code software routines to mimic a specific aspect of human intelligence. This requires writing thousands of lines of code with complex rules and decision trees. Machine learning on the other hand involves feeding huge amounts of data to the algorithm and allowing the algorithm to learn automatically. Deep learning is a subset of machine learning, which is inspired by the structure and function of the brain.

### 1.1.1 Artificial Intelligence

AI can be loosely defined as incorporating human intelligence into machines. Broadly speaking, when a machine completes a task based on a set of predefined rules this behaviour is known as AI. This type of AI is known as symbolic AI. Many AI solutions are designed to solve a particular problem. This is often referred to as narrow AI where machines perform specific tasks well. One of the limitations of narrow AI is that it often fails to generalise to new problems and therefore it can be limited in scope. This is referred to as closed world AI. In modern-day AI, the AI layer acts as an interpretation for non-symbolic ML and DL models. Figure 1.1 provides an overview of the AI family.

There are several reference points as to when AI first emerged. However, it is the work of Alan Turing that is most recognised. This is when Alan Turning proposed the Turing test as a measure of machine intelligence in 1950 [1]. The actual term AI was defined in 1955 which continues to be used today [2]. One of the main programming languages to develop AI was Lisp and was introduced in 1958 [3]. In 1964 languages like Lisp allowed computer scientists to create algorithms

**Fig. 1.1** The AI family

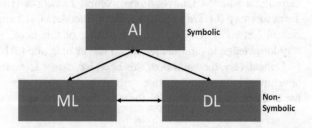

that understood natural language. This was seen as one of the most notable starts in symbolic AI. One of the most famous interactive programs during that time was ElIZA which was programmed to simulate the dialogue of a psychotherapy session [4].

In 1969 a landmark paper called Perceptrons was published which reported the previously unrecognised limits of simple neural network structures [5]. This marked the beginning of the AI winter in the 1970s. Nonetheless, work in symbolic AI continued to grow and was accelerated with the introduction of the Prolog programming language in 1972 [6]. Prolog provided similar rule-based programming functions to Lisp. While Prolog was growing in popularity, systems were still being developed using Lisp. One of the more famous systems in the '70s was MYCIN [7]. MYCIN was able to provide medical diagnosis using a rule-based approach which could make decisions using a small number of facts. This influenced the development of future expert systems. MYCIN was later generalised in 1979 and renamed EMYCIN [8]. EMYCIN provided an expert system shell that captured the knowledge of domain experts and allowed non-expert users to solve particular problems.

While expert systems remained the primary focus of AI development other areas such as game logic started to emerge. The first breakthrough was when Berliner's backgammon program defeated the reigning world champion [9]. As AI progressed through the 1980s more complex computational tasks such as driverless cars were introduced. For exmaple, in 1986 Ernst Dieckmann built the first example of a driverless car that drove at speeds up to 55 mph on empty streets [10]. Developments such as this were directly linked to the emergence of parallel computing and neural networks that utilised backpropagation [11]. During this period other areas of AI were rising to prominence. For example, Marvin Minsky was investigating the use of collaborative AI agents which he later published in his highly acclaimed book the society of mind [12]. At the same time there was a shift towards evolutionary computing with notable work from Rodney Brookes and his subsumption architecture for behaviour-based robotics [13].

During the 1990s AI continued to make significant advancements. This decade saw a continued rise in symbolic AI-based applications such as intelligent tutoring systems, case-based reasoning and multi-agent systems. Interest also grew in new application areas such as planning, scheduling, data mining, Natural Language Processing (NLP), computer vision, virtual reality and games. Perhaps one of the most interesting applications of AI was in gameplay. For example, in 1994 backgammon programs using a Reinforcement Learning (RL) approach were now good enough to play expert level games which later defeated world champion chess players [14]. Success in AI gameplay continued whin in 1997 Deep Blue defeated the world chess champion Garry Kasparov [15].

In the 2000s the use of AI was largely focused in and around robotics and automation. An early example of this was iRobot's Roomba which was capable of automatically vacuuming the floor while successfully navigating and avoiding obstacles [16]. However, the most impressive breakthrough in this domain was the Honda ASIMO robot which was able to mimic complex human tasks such as walking and making deliveries [17]. It was during this period we saw the emergance of modern-day recommender systems in web tracking activity and media usage. One of the earliest adopters of this technology was the TiVo TV service which was used to make program suggestions to viewers [18]. Throughout the 2000s AI continued to advance with algorithms that could exceed human level performance [19].

In 2011 IBM's Watson won Jeopardy defeating the reigning champions Rutter and Jennings [20]. We also witnessed the emergence of smart assistants such as Apple's Siri, Google Now and Microsoft's Cortana which made use of advanced NLP. There were even robots that could perform intricate tasks such as driving a car and climbing a ladder. Returning to gaming, in 2015 Google's Deep Mind AlphaGo defeated three-time European Go champion, Van Hui, 5 – 0 [21]. The following year AlphaGo defeated Lee Sedol 4-1 who in his career won over 27 championship tournaments between 2002–2016 [22]. In the remainder of this chapter we are going to introduce many of the algorithms used in the approaches highlighted above which will be discussed in more detail throughout this book.

### 1.1.2  Machine Learning

So, what is machine learning? Unlike symbolic AI which utilises rules and data to produce answers, machine learning uses answers and data to produce a set of rules automatically. These rules can then be applied to new and unseen data to facilitate a response or action. The key differences between symbolic and non-symbolic approaches can be seen in Fig. 1.2.

This allows algorithms to develop experience in a similar mannar to humans. By exposing algorithms to new data, they learn, adapt and develop on their own. They find insightful information in data without being told where to look. This approach is deep routed in pattern recognition which is designed to learn from previous computations and transactions to produce reliable and informed results.

The concept of machine learning can be traced back to the 1950s with the development of the first neural network machine called SNARC [23]. Around the

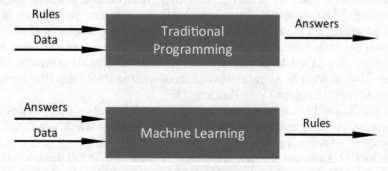

**Fig. 1.2** Difference between the symbolic AI and machine learning approach

same time engineers at IBM also began working on machine learning algorithms to play complex games [24]. One of the first major advancements in machine learning was the invention of the perceptron which is still used extensively today [25]. The era continued to see advancements in the field games particulary with the introduction of reinforcement learning [26]. In 1967 the nearest neighbour algorithm was developed and was largely considered to be the first basic pattern matching algorithm [27].

In the 1970s, a paper was published on Automatic Differentiation (AD). This was widely considered to be the starting point for the modern-day version of backpropagation [28]. In 1979 work describing neocognitron formed the foundation for the development of Convolutional Neural Networks (CNNs) [29] and in 1982 the Hopfield network which is a type of Recurrent Neural Network (RNN) was used as a content-addressable system [30]. NetTalk was developed in 1985 which was able to pronounce words in a similar way to babies [31] and in 1986 one of the most fundamental breakthroughs in the field of Artificial Neural Networks was made when AD was used in a set of experiments to learn internal representations. This work resulted in the development of modern-day backpropagation [32].

1995 saw the introduction of both the Random Forest (RF) and Support Vector Machine (SVM) algorithms [33]. And in 1997 the LSTM RNN was invented to improve the efficiency and practicality of RNNs in time series prediction [34]. Computer vision was also on the rise with the release of the famous MNIST dataset which provides a comprehensive dataset of handwritten digits [35].

In 2002 the Torch machine learning library based on the Lua programming language was released [36]. And in 2006 the Netflix Prize competition was launched which was aimed at using machine learning to outperform their own recommendation software's accuracy in predicting users film ratings [37]. Three years later Bellkors Pragmatic Chaos team beat Netflix's algorithm for predicting ratings by as much as 10% [38]. It was the same year that saw the introduction of ImageNet which at the time of writing had over 14 million images and 20,000 categories [39]. The dataset was envisioned to provide machine learning algorithms with large amounts of real-world image data. ImageNet has since been regarded as one of the most important components for the AI summer which started in 2010. During this year additional datasets were made available through the newly launched Kaggle platform which was the go-to site for machine learning competitions [40]. In 2012 Google Brain developed a neural network to recognise cats using images obtained from YouTube videos [41]. It wasn't until 2014 that a neural network was capable of identifying human faces with over 97% accuracy [42].

### 1.1.3   Deep Learning

Deep Learning (DL) is a subset of machine learning. Machine learning has a specific feature extraction stage in the pipeline. This step is often not required in some DL architectures as features can be automatically learned during the training process. DL uses unsupervised algorithms to extract features and supervised algorithms to classify observations. Figure 1.3 shows the distinction between machine learning and DL approaches.

The DL approach provides several key advantages. Firstly, DL algorithms can build more accurate models from large amounts of data in contrast to traditional machine learning. Secondly, the use of DL can significantly speed up the pipeline as it removes the requirement for expert domain knowledge although training times can be significantly longer. For example, interpreting an Electrocardiograph (ECG) signal would typically require an expert to identify relevant features of the signal and link this to a particular heart condition. However, using DL, the shape of the signal would be automatically mapped to the particular heart condition through the extraction of the most relevant features. Figure 1.4 shows the performance gains achieved when using DL algorithms.

Recently, DL has been primarily applied to the area of computer vision. Not surprisingly the key milestones have focused on the development of neural network architectures to increase the performance of computer vision tasks. There are four

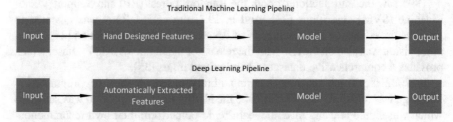

**Fig. 1.3** Machine learning and DL approaches

**Fig. 1.4** DL performance gains

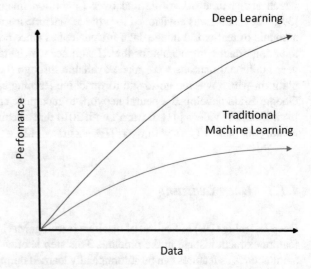

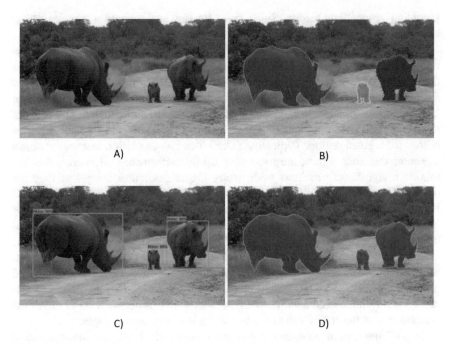

**Fig. 1.5** Different approaches for computer vision which includes (**a**) Image Classification, (**b**) Instance Segmentation, (**c**) Object Detection and (**d**) Semantic Segmentaion

key areas of interest in computer vision as shown in Fig. 1.5. These include, (a) Image Classification—there is a rhino in the image (b) Instance segmentation—classify all the pixels within each distinct object of a rhino (c) object detection—the detection of each rhino in the image and (d) semantic segmentation—classify all the pixels associated with a rhino.

One of the most significant milestones was the introduction of AlexNet in 2012 [43]. At the time AlexNet was one of the most computationally expensive architectures due to its network design which utilised Graphics Processing Units (GPUs) during training. AlexNet competed in the ImageNet Large Scale Visual Recognition Challenge (ILSVRC) and achieved a top-5 error of 15.3%. In 2014 the Visual Geometry Group (VGG) Network architecture was introduced [44]. This network architecture was characterised by its simplicity and become the runner up at ILSVRC in 2014.

2014 also saw the introduction of region-based proposal network (RPN) [45]. The first RPN used a selective search approach. Regions are specific subsections of an image; these images are used by the network to identify objects of interest within them. In the same year, the Fast R-CNN was proposed as a way of speeding up this process and in 2016 [46] the performance was further improved in the Faster R-CNN [47]. Significant advancements were made in 2015 with the introduction of ResNet. ResNet made it possible to train up to hundreds or even thousands of layers while providing compelling results. Since then, ResNet has become a popular object classification network in the research community.

In 2015 the You Only Look Once (YOLO) Unified, Real-Time Object Detection architecture was introduced [48]. The YOLO model is used for the real-time detection of objects within an image. Other types of detection models such as the R-CNN family utilise classifiers or localisers to perform detection. Instead, the YOLO model uses a single neural network to analyse the entire image. The network divides the image into regions and predicts bounding boxes and associated probabilities for a given region. Typically, YOLO uses low-resolution images for object detection therefore significantly speeding up its performance. However, this can introduce significant problems when using higher resolution images as they are downscaled which causes objects to become pixelated and harder to detect. YOLO is typically used to detect close up objects while the R-CNN family are typically implemented with higher resolution images that contain objects of various sizes and those that are occluded. Like YOLO, the Single Shot Detector (SSD) architecture is used for real-time object detection [49]. The SSD speeds up the detection process when compared to the R-CNN family by eliminating the need for a region-based proposal network. The SDD incorporates several features to try and improve accuracies such as multiscale features and default boxes. This allows SSD to match the performance of the R-CNN family when using low-resolution images.

In 2017 the area of computer vision progressed further with the introduction of object segmentation. In particular, the Mask R-CNN architecture was built by the Facebook AI research team [50]. The model is divided into two parts which include a RPN and binary mask classifier. Mask networks have become popular in calculating the volume and dimension of objects for example calculating the food consumption in dementia patients as shown in Fig. 1.6.

Developing neural network architectures is time-consuming and often requires a significant amount of expertise. As a result, this has led to a new area of interest in automatic ML (AutoML). Automating the generation of neural network architectures has many benefits such as removing the need for human involvement. For example, the Neural Architecture Search (NAS) was developed in 2016 to achieve

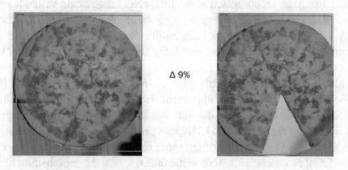

**Fig. 1.6** Monitoring food consumption in dementia patients using Mark R-CCN

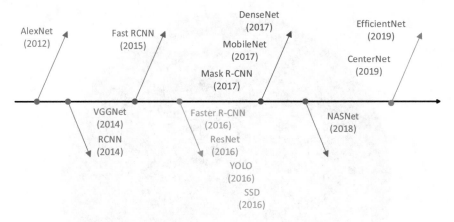

**Fig. 1.7** Key milestones in deep learning development

this [51]. However, training this type of architecture requires significant computational resources which are often unavailable to both researchers and practitioners alike.

Neural networks are not limited to architecture generation but can also be used to generate data. For example, the Generative Adversarial Network (GAN) is a type of alternative learning approach which was first introduced in 2014 that generates synthetic images [52]. GANs trained on photographs can generate new images that look at least superficially authentic to human observers, having many realistic characteristics. There are many areas of research that are investigating the applicability of using GANs to generate synthetic training data for other neural networks. This is particularly useful in applications where training data is not easily accessible or is of poor quality. Fig. 1.7 highlights the significant milestones in DL development over the past ten years.

### 1.1.4 How they Come Together

Hopefully, it is now clear what the differences are between AI, ML and DL and how they are used to address different problems. AI is a broad term used to describe computational intelligence over the last 70 years which has traditionally been grounded in symbolic AI. The new subfields machine learning and DL are extensions of AI that primarily focus on data-driven learning. This is not to say they are used in isolation but are often combined to capture different aspects of intelligence and problem-solving. For example, one of the biggest problems with these complex learning systems is model interpretation and the large amount of data deep neural networks need to learn. By combining some of the symbolic approaches found in AI it may be possible to create explainable models. There is research being conducted

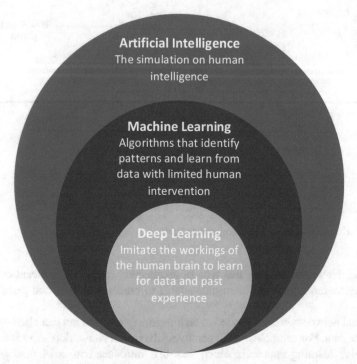

**Fig. 1.8** AI Eco-system

by MIT, Deep Mind and IBM that have shown the power of combining connectionist techniques such as DL with symbolic reasoning.

Choosing the right tool or combination thereof is often part art and part science and can only be learned empirically through experience and experimentation (just like a neural network). This book aims to introduce you to common pitfalls and key considerations when developing real-world AI applications. Figure 1.8 shows an overview of the AI ecosystem.

This book will cover each aspect of the AI family by drawing on real-world examples. This will allow the practitioner to implement all aspects of the AI family and combine them to solve their own unique problems.

## 1.2  Artificial Intelligence Is Driving Innovation

AI is already extensively integrated into everything that we do. One of the most common examples is the modern-day smartphone which provides features such as scene detection, advanced camera features and cognitive assistants such as Siri. AI has recently paved the way for smart cars to enable features such as Tesla's Autopilot, Siri and Alexa integration, so you can ask questions and even monitor a driver's behaviour. Recently large retailers such as Amazon have been developing autonomous drones for automatic parcel distribution and even delivering critical medication to the most remote parts of the world.

With the widespread use of social media everything that we think about and say now has a digital presence. This data is being used by companies such as Twitter, Facebook and Microsoft to create a tailored experience. By using your past behaviour, web searches, and interactions, companies can provide targeted advertising and suggestions. Social media is also being combined with AI and other data to track pandemics such as the recent COVID-19 outbreak as it spreads across the globe. Another great example of the daily use of AI is media streaming platforms. Organisations such as Spotify, Netflix and Amazon use AI to make personalised recommendations and automatic playlists. Google and Apple even embed AI into popular navigation services which incorporate a significant amount of data to provide directions and real-time traffic alerts. The video game industry was one of the earliest adopters of AI which has enabled improved gameplay and a generation of advanced graphical features which was impossible just a few years ago.

While the use of camera systems can be a controversial subject the use of AI is playing a significant role in the automatic identification of objects. It is not feasible for humans to monitor feeds from hundreds or even thousands of cameras at the same time. This is where AI plugs the gap by enabling features such as objects and facial recognition. These features are already being used in many off the shelf systems such as CCTV and other commercial products such as the Ring doorbell. In the upcoming sections, we will discuss some of their applied aspects.

## *1.2.1   Transforming Healthcare*

Healthcare is arguably one of the most active areas where AI is being used. Many industry leaders believe that AI has the potential to revolutionise healthcare and help to solve some of the most difficult health challenges facing humanity. As AI becomes more widely used in the healthcare sector this will lead to better care outcomes and improve the productivity and efficiency of care delivery. One of the most advanced AI health applications is Babylon Health which utilises AI to make healthcare both accessible and affordable. The system is designed to provide healthcare for millions by understanding the unique ways in which patients describe their symptoms. Using this knowledge, combined with a patient's medical history, it is possible to better understand a patient's medical conditions and suggest treatment plans [53].

The diagnosis of conditions through the use of medical imaging has been a longstanding practice within healthcare. In recent years AI has seen rapid use in medical diagnostics and can often outperform clinicians. Radiology for example has seen a significant increase in demand over the last few years and this has led to the use of AI

**Fig. 1.9** Smartphone
classification of a pressure
ulcer

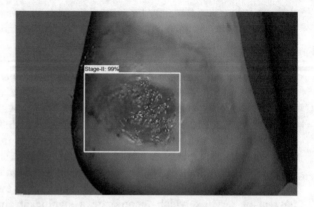

technology to support radiographers in decision making. While much of the theoretical basis for AI in the practice of radiology is extremely exciting, the reality is that
the field has not yet fully embraced it. The most significant issue is that the
technology has not yet matured to work in more general practice. However, this is
a rapidly changing environment that has led to the use of imaging technologies in
many other application domains. For example, mobile systems can now be used to
take photographs of skin damage on people and report back on tissue status using AI
object detection. In a recent clinical trial, researchers used a new and innovative
platform to detect and grade pressure ulcers in vulnerable patients. Using advancements in AI the team was able to create an analytical model that could analyse the
tissue characteristics and automatically report its findings to carers [54]. Figure 1.9
provides an example of a category II pressure ulcer being classified by the model
using a smartphone.

### 1.2.2   Protecting Wildlife

Conservationists are increasingly using AI to gather information about wildlife and
prevent poaching. Many different species are adversely affected by poaching. In
response to this escalating crisis, efforts to stop poaching using hidden cameras,
drones and DNA tracking have been implemented which now generate a significant
amount of data points. These data points are then analysed by AI algorithms to gain
insights into wildlife and support the global conservation effort. A recent study
outlined a flexible and interoperable framework for the automatic detection of
animals and poaching activity to facilitate early intervention practices. The
researchers used object detection algorithms to automatically analyse video data
from various sources including camera traps and drones to track wildlife and
poachers [55]. Figure 1.10 shows an image of a classified frame while Fig. 1.11
highlights object detection and tracking using a drone.

**Fig. 1.10** Object detection of wildlife

**Fig. 1.11** Object detection and tracking using drone footage

Additionally, researchers have been able to classify different species by analysing only audio. Sounds from common animals have been classified to a high degree of accuracy which enables conservationists to monitor wildlife in hard-to-reach places. Figure 1.12 shows a sample bird recording used for training a bird identification algorithm [56].

## 1.2.3   Securing the Environment

As you can imagine AI has been used in a variety of different security applications. Perhaps one of the most controversial areas but one with the most potential is using AI to automatically interpret visual data. One of the most significant domains is facial recognition which has seen widespread use in countries such as China. In Zhengzhou, commuters can use the technology to automatically authorise payments instead of scanning a QR code on their phones. New regulations came into force that

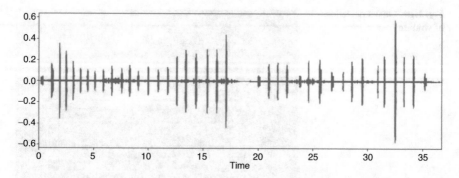

**Fig. 1.12** Bird sound signal used for training

**Fig. 1.13** Thermal camera
for Person detection

requires mobile phone subscribers to have their faces scanned when they sign a new contract with a provider.

Security forces have invested heavily in the use of AI particularly in the use of drones, surveillance, crowd control and search and rescue. Often additional camera technology such as thermal and greyscale images can be used to locate hard to see objects as shown in Fig. 1.13. Combining this technology with some of the AI techniques discussed in this chapter allows processes to be automated and deployed at scale.

Police forces see the use of AI as a solution for falling budgets and reduced manpower. The technology is being utilised to analyse photographs (for preventing child exploitation), CCTV footage (to aid in crime detection), and evidence files (to help analyse key characteristics of evidence and linked crimes). It is also being used to analyse crime logs to identify high-risk areas and the types of crimes being reported. Research is also currently underway to use audio signals as a way of detecting specific noises such as gunshots to help triangulate and target responses.

Using relatively cheap devices it is easy to deploy a network of audio detecting services across large geographical locations which may have much farther identification capabilities.

A significant amount of crime is carried out virtually and this has led to new directions in AI security to identify and stop cyber threats. As cyber-attacks grow in both volume and sophistication new tools are constantly required to stay ahead of the perpetrators. AI is being used to identify new and emerging threats while learning how to respond to novel attacks.

More recently, issues around pandemics have raised serious concerns and there is a significant interest in the use of AI to protect people and the economy. Ideas have been put forward to use the CCTV network to monitor people's temperature using thermal camera extensions while providing support on social distancing. Smart meters also provide significant opportunities to monitor the impact social isolation has on people and communities and the fight against current and future pandemic outbreaks. Smart meters can report the real-time usage of household energy data which has been shown to uncover the daily routine of the occupants. This allows analysts to identify any changes in behaviour as a result of illness or breaking rules such as social distancing. Figure 1.14 shows the relationship between appliance usage and the time of day. The lines between appliances and time-of-day, like ant pheromone trails, show the established routine behaviour for an individual household [57]. For example, it is possible to see that the microwave is mostly used at 06:00 hours and 18:00 hours.

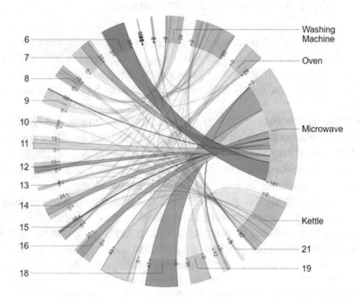

**Fig. 1.14** Relationship between devices usage and hour

## 1.3    Tools, Frameworks and Hardware

As we have seen in this chapter there are some far-reaching and diverse uses of AI to solve a wide-ranging set of problems. During your job, you will likely be faced with many problems where AI might be a useful tool. This book will provide you with all the required skills to solve your real-world problems. In this section we will introduce the tools which are commonly used in research and industry to develop AI applications.

### 1.3.1    Building Intelligent Applications

This book focuses on creating real-world examples using a variety of industry-standard frameworks and tools. The authors build upon their industry and research experience in developing AI solutions using the latest technology. They provide insight for training models and exploiting their benefits using a full end-to-end pipeline. Each of the frameworks and tools will help you to develop enterprise solutions while enabling you to leverage advancements in Central Processing Units (CPU) and GPU hardware.

### 1.3.2    Python, Notebooks and Environments

At the time of writing Python is widely regarded as the go-to language for many data science and AI tasks. Python is a general-purpose programming language that has a significant ecosystem of tools and packages while providing extensive support through forums. Python is easy to learn and is in the top 5 most used programming languages of 2019.

One of the most common ways to write and execute Python code is through the use of Jupyter Notebooks which are run directly in the browser. They are also useful for making notes through the use of markdown and act as an executable document and should be considered as a recipe for your data science task. One advantage of using Jupyter Notebooks is that code can be executed directly in the browser allowing you to instantly see the results in the generated cell. It has an easy-to-use interface that allows you to organise and execute your code using cells. Additionally, Notebooks can be exported as executable Python files which can be used in your development pipeline. This provides a significant advantage over other tools and frameworks as it makes it easier to develop prototypes and deploy end-to-end solutions. One of the most important tasks that Notebooks allow you to do is ensure reproducibility by easily sharing the Notebook and associated data.

Anaconda is a scalable data science platform that allows you to combine and segregate different packages and frameworks to provide canned environments. As these environments are isolated from each other they can be safely modified and

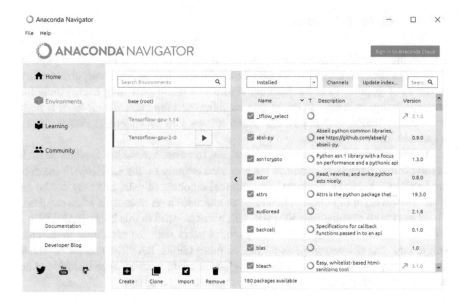

**Fig. 1.15** Anaconda navigator

changed without affecting any other environments used. This is partially useful for managing versions and package dependencies and deployment strategies. One of the key benefits of using Anaconda is the ability to easily share, collaborate on, and reproduce projects. Figure 1.15 shows the Anaconda Navigator, which is a graphical interface for managing environments, installing packages and launching data science tasks.

## *1.3.3 Pre-Processing*

Data often requires a significant amount of pre-processing which is especially true for both machine learning and DL tasks. Lucky there are several Python libraries which include:

- **Pandas** – is a Python library that provides tools for data manipulation and analysis.
- **NumPy** – is a Python library for multi-dimensional arrays and matrices.
- **Seabourn** – is a Python visualisation library for plots and graphing.
- **Matplotlib** – is a Python library for plots and graphs.
- **Plotly** – provides online graphing, analytics, and statistics tools.
- **Pillow** – Python Imaging Library which provides support for processing image data.
- **OpenCV** – is a library for computer vision and image manipulation.
- **SciPy** – is a Python library used for scientific and technical computing.

### *1.3.4   Machine Learning*

For machine learning aspects this book will introduce you to one of the most popular Python machine learning libraries called Scikit-learn. Scikit-learn incorporates many of the most popular machine learning algorithms while providing useful tools for pre-processing, training and evaluating machine learning tasks. Scikit-learn is built on NumPy, SciPy, and matplotlib which allows you to undertake classification, regression and clustering tasks.

Although Scikit-learn has many advantages, there are several key limitations such as long training times as pipelines are executed entirely on the CPU which impacts productivity. In smaller projects with minimal amounts of data, this may not be an issue. However, in big data applications, an alternative set of tools is often required. To support both eventualities RAPIDS will be introduced in this book. RAPIDS is a collection of libraries and API's that provides users with the capability to execute end-to-end data science projects on one or more GPUs. RAPIDS utilises NVIDIA CUDA to expose GPU parallelism and high-bandwidth memory speed which can be accessed through the high-level Python programming language.

### *1.3.5   Deep Learning*

For the DL aspects of this book, we will refer to TensorFlow which includes the high-level Keras API. TensorFlow is the go-to framework for the training, validating and hosting of Artificial Neural Networks (ANNS). TensorFlow provides all the necessary tools for image processing, time series analysis and NLP. TensorFlow integrates seamlessly with the Python programming language to facilitate the rapid development and training of advanced ANNs. Advanced image processing refers to the TensorFlow object detection API for image classification, object detection, and semantic segmentation. Keras offers an API that links to all aspects of the TensorFlow platform. This simplifies the real-world development of applied DL solutions.

### *1.3.6   Inferencing*

The training of a model is a small part of the overall pipeline and is the part where most practitioners tend to struggle due to the complexities of inferencing models in production. While it is relatively easy to get simple end-to-end solutions working, useful algorithms will need to be encased in several different technologies to make them commercially viable. This book will cover the right technologies for the job and will include gRPC, REST, TensorFlow Serving and Docker. To expose model functionality additional tools and frameworks are required. The book will introduce what are considered to be support frameworks in the AI pipeline and will include Flask web development with NGINX. This will allow you to develop and deploy end-to-end enterprise solutions.

## 1.4   How this Book Is Organised

The first section of this book (Chaps. 2–5) will cover the fundamentals of machine learning, supervised and unsupervised learning and performance evaluation metrics. The second section of this book (Chaps. 6–11) will discuss DL concepts and techniques. This will include an introduction to DL, image classification and object detection, DL for time series data, natural language processing, generative models and deep reinforcement learning. The third section of this book (Chap. 12) will cover accelerated machine learning. The forth an final section of the book (Chaps. 13 and 14) will discuss the deployment and hosting of machine learning models within enterprise environments.

This is an applied book and theoretical notation is deliberately kept to a minimum. All of the core concepts are covered with theoretical aspects being provided as references for interested readers. Therefore, this book is primarily targeted towards interested parties that wish to develop and deploy real-world AI applications and solutions.

## 1.5   Who Should Read this Book

This book is intended for people who are interested in learning how to develop and implement AI solutions for practical use. The book is tailored to people who are new to the field and will provide valuable insights to existing software developers and data scientists. Although a programming background is not strictly required it would help you to understand and accelerate the implementation of your own AI solutions. This book would also suit researchers who are primarily focused on the theoretical aspects of AI who want to develop research impact by deploying their solutions to a wider audience.

## 1.6   Summary

In this chapter an overview of AI was presented which provides a brief historical perspective on how the field has developed into what is now known as machine learning and deep learning. This covers over 70 years of innovation ranging from rule-based systems (symbolic) right through to the complex deep neural network architectures (non-symbolic) which feature widely in many advanced applications of

AI. The chapter highlights the differences and relationships between the three primary fields where we are now seeing a shift from systems that use rules and data to generate answers to one where answers and data are used to derive rules. Although the three fields are unique, they are increasingly being used in combination to tackle more complex problems such as explainable AI and model interpretation.

In addition, the chapter provided an overview of how AI is being used to drive innovation and support key transformations within and across many different fields. The impact of AI is already changing how we do things while helping to solve some of the most challenging problems facing society. As a result, the adoption of AI is reshaping and changing how we behave and interact within new technological environments. Most notably we have seen significant impact within healthcare, wildlife protection and security.

Finally, the chapter provides a framework in which the theoretical and applied aspects will be conducted. Guidance was provided for the suggested use of different tools and frameworks to be used alongside this book. We hope that the book provides the reader with the necessary skills and tools to embark on the development and deployment of their own AI solutions to solve the real-world problems they are tasked with.

## References

1. C. Machinery, "Computing machinery and intelligence-AM Turing," *Mind*, vol. 59, no. 236, p. 433, 1950.
2. J. McCarthy, M. Minsky, N. Rochester, and C. Shannon, "A proposal for the dartmouth summer research project on artificial intelligence. Hanover, New Hampshire, USA, Dartmouth College." 1955.
3. J. McCarthy, "History of LISP," in *History of programming languages*, 1978, pp. 173–185.
4. J. Weizenbaum, "ELIZA—a computer program for the study of natural language communication between man and machine," *Commun. ACM*, vol. 9, no. 1, pp. 36–45, 1966.
5. M. Minsky and S. Papert, "Perceptron: an introduction to computational geometry," *MIT Press. Cambridge, Expand. Ed.*, vol. 19, no. 88, p. 2, 1969.
6. A. Colmerauer, H. Kanoui, H. Pasero, and P. Roussel, "PROLOG, Un systeme de communication homme-machine en français," 1973.
7. E. H. Shortliffe, "MYCIN: a rule-based computer program for advising physicians regarding antimicrobial therapy selection.," 1974.
8. W. J. Van Melle, *A domain-independent system that aids in constructing knowledge-based consultation programs*. Stanford University, 1980.
9. H. J. Berliner, "Backgammon computer program beats world champion," *Artif. Intell.*, vol. 14, no. 2, pp. 205–220, 1980.
10. E. D. Dickmanns and A. Zapp, "Autonomous high speed road vehicle guidance by computer vision," *IFAC Proc. Vol.*, vol. 20, no. 5, pp. 221–226, 1987.
11. D. E. Rumelhart, G. E. Hinton, and R. J. Williams, "Learning representations by back-propagating errors," *Nature*, vol. 323, no. 6088, pp. 533–536, 1986.
12. M. Minsky, *Society of mind*. Simon and Schuster, 1988.
13. R. Brooks, "A robust layered control system for a mobile robot," *IEEE J. Robot. Autom.*, vol. 2, no. 1, pp. 14–23, 1986.

14. G. Tesauro, "TD-Gammon, a self-teaching backgammon program, achieves master-level play," *Neural Comput.*, vol. 6, no. 2, pp. 215–219, 1994.
15. F. Hsu, "IBM's deep blue chess grandmaster chips," *IEEE Micro*, vol. 19, no. 2, pp. 70–81, 1999.
16. L. Grossman, "Maid to order," *Time Mag. vol*, 2002.
17. Y. Sakagami, R. Watanabe, C. Aoyama, S. Matsunaga, N. Higaki, and K. Fujimura, "The intelligent ASIMO: System overview and integration," in *IEEE/RSJ international conference on intelligent robots and systems*, 2002, vol. 3, pp. 2478–2483.
18. J. Barton, "From Server Room to Living Room: How open source and TiVo became a perfect match," *Queue*, vol. 1, no. 5, pp. 20–32, 2003.
19. J. Schaeffer *et al.*, "Solving checkers," in *Proceedings of the 19th international joint conference on Artificial intelligence*, 2005, pp. 292–297.
20. J. Markoff, "Computer wins on 'Jeopardy!': Trivial, it's not," *New York Times*, vol. 16, 2011.
21. D. Silver *et al.*, "Mastering the game of go without human knowledge," *Nature*, vol. 550, no. 7676, pp. 354–359, 2017.
22. Y. Chen *et al.*, "Bayesian optimization in alphago," *arXiv Prepr. arXiv1812.06855*, 2018.
23. D. Hillis *et al.*, "In honor of Marvin Minsky's contributions on his 80th birthday," *AI Mag.*, vol. 28, no. 4, p. 103, 2007.
24. A. L. Samuel, "Some studies in machine learning using the game of checkers," *IBM J. Res. Dev.*, vol. 3, no. 3, pp. 210–229, 1959.
25. F. Rosenblatt, "The perceptron: a probabilistic model for information storage and organization in the brain.," *Psychol. Rev.*, vol. 65, no. 6, p. 386, 1958.
26. D. Michie and R. A. Chambers, "BOXES: An experiment in adaptive control," *Mach. Intell.*, vol. 2, no. 2, pp. 137–152, 1968.
27. T. Cover and P. Hart, "Nearest neighbor pattern classification," *IEEE Trans. Inf. theory*, vol. 13, no. 1, pp. 21–27, 1967.
28. S. Linnainmaa, "The representation of the cumulative rounding error of an algorithm as a Taylor expansion of the local rounding errors," *Master's Thesis (in Finnish), Univ. Helsinki*, pp. 6–7, 1970.
29. K. Fukushima, "Neural network model for a mechanism of pattern recognition unaffected by shift in position-Neocognitron," *IEICE Tech. Report, A*, vol. 62, no. 10, pp. 658–665, 1979.
30. J. J. Hopfield, "Neural networks and physical systems with emergent collective computational abilities," *Proc. Natl. Acad. Sci.*, vol. 79, no. 8, pp. 2554–2558, 1982.
31. T. J. Sejnowski and C. R. Rosenberg, "NETtalk: A parallel network that learns to read aloud. Johns Hopkins University Electrical Engineering and Computer Science Technical Report," *EEC*, vol. 86, no. 01, 1986.
32. D. E. Rumelhart, G. E. Hinton, and R. J. Williams, "Learning internal representations by error propagation," 1985.
33. T. K. Ho, "Random decision forests," in *Proceedings of 3rd international conference on document analysis and recognition*, 1995, vol. 1, pp. 278–282.
34. S. Hochreiter and J. Schmidhuber, "Long short-term memory," *Neural Comput.*, vol. 9, no. 8, pp. 1735–1780, 1997.
35. Y. LeCun, L. Bottou, Y. Bengio, and P. Haffner, "Gradient-based learning applied to document recognition," *Proc. IEEE*, vol. 86, no. 11, pp. 2278–2324, 1998.
36. R. Collobert, S. Bengio, and J. Mariéthoz, "Torch: a modular machine learning software library," 2002.
37. J. Bennett, S. Lanning, and others, "The netflix prize," in *Proceedings of KDD cup and workshop*, 2007, vol. 2007, p. 35.
38. A. Töscher, M. Jahrer, and R. M. Bell, "The bigchaos solution to the netflix grand prize," *Netflix Prize Doc.*, pp. 1–52, 2009.
39. J. Deng, W. Dong, R. Socher, L.-J. Li, K. Li, and L. Fei-Fei, "Imagenet: A large-scale hierarchical image database," in *2009 IEEE conference on computer vision and pattern recognition*, 2009, pp. 248–255.

40. J. Carpenter, "May the best analyst win." American Association for the Advancement of Science, 2011.
41. L. Clark, "Google's artificial brain learns to find cat videos," *Wired UK, www. wired. com*, 2012.
42. J. O'Toole, "Facebook's new face recognition knows you from the side," *CNN Money*, 2014.
43. A. Krizhevsky, I. Sutskever, and G. E. Hinton, "Imagenet classification with deep convolutional neural networks," *Adv. Neural Inf. Process. Syst.*, vol. 25, pp. 1097–1105, 2012.
44. K. Simonyan and A. Zisserman, "Very deep convolutional networks for large-scale image recognition," *arXiv Prepr. arXiv1409.1556*, 2014.
45. R. Girshick, J. Donahue, T. Darrell, and J. Malik, "Region-based convolutional networks for accurate object detection and segmentation," *IEEE Trans. Pattern Anal. Mach. Intell.*, vol. 38, no. 1, pp. 142–158, 2015.
46. R. Girshick, "Fast r-cnn," in *Proceedings of the IEEE international conference on computer vision*, 2015, pp. 1440–1448.
47. S. Ren, K. He, R. Girshick, and J. Sun, "Faster r-cnn: Towards real-time object detection with region proposal networks," in *Advances in neural information processing systems*, 2015, pp. 91–99.
48. J. Redmon, S. Divvala, R. Girshick, and A. Farhadi, "You only look once: Unified, real-time object detection," in *Proceedings of the IEEE conference on computer vision and pattern recognition*, 2016, pp. 779–788.
49. W. Liu *et al.*, "Ssd: Single shot multibox detector," in *European conference on computer vision*, 2016, pp. 21–37.
50. K. He, G. Gkioxari, P. Dollár, and R. Girshick, "Mask r-cnn," in *Proceedings of the IEEE international conference on computer vision*, 2017, pp. 2961–2969.
51. B. Zoph and Q. V Le, "Neural architecture search with reinforcement learning," *arXiv Prepr. arXiv1611.01578*, 2016.
52. I. J. Goodfellow *et al.*, "Generative adversarial networks," *arXiv Prepr. arXiv1406.2661*, 2014.
53. K. Middleton, M. Butt, N. Hammerla, S. Hamblin, K. Mehta, and A. Parsa, "Sorting out symptoms: design and evaluation of the'babylon check'automated triage system," *arXiv Prepr. arXiv1606.02041*, 2016.
54. P. Fergus, C. Chalmers, and D. Tully, "Collaborative Pressure Ulcer Prevention: An Automated Skin Damage and Pressure Ulcer Assessment Tool for Nursing Professionals, Patients, Family Members and Carers," *arXiv Prepr. arXiv1808.06503*, 2018.
55. C. Chalmers, P. Fergus, C. Curbelo Montanez, S. N. Longmore, and S. Wich, "Video Analysis for the Detection of Animals Using Convolutional Neural Networks and Consumer-Grade Drones," *J. Unmanned Veh. Syst.*, no. ja, 2021.
56. C. Chalmers, P. Fergus, S. Wich, and S. N. Longmore, "Modelling Animal Biodiversity Using Acoustic Monitoring and Deep Learning," *arXiv Prepr. arXiv2103.07276*, 2021.
57. C. Chalmers, P. Fergus, C. A. C. Montanez, S. Sikdar, F. Ball, and B. Kendall, "Detecting activities of daily living and routine behaviours in dementia patients living alone using smart meter load disaggregation," *IEEE Trans. Emerg. Top. Comput.*, 2020.

# Part II
# Foundations of Machine Learning

# Chapter 2
# Fundamentals of Machine Learning

## 2.1 What Is Machine Learning?

Machine Learning (ML) is a field of AI that utilises historical data and domain knowledge to automatically construct algorithms to solve a given problem. This is in contrast to other methods which construct algorithms through explicit programming and predefined rules. ML can be a lengthy and complex task and is regarded as an iterative process through model training and refinement. The training process is conducted using training data which can be either known or unknown depending on how the algorithm learns. Trained models are evaluated to measure their performance using unseen test data. Depending on the results it may be necessary to retrain algorithms with additional data to increase accuracy over time.

Once a model is trained it can be deployed to receive continuous data. This also allows the model to be evaluated through an iterative learning process. Any test data that is incorrectly identified is added to the training data for future model training. Figure 2.1 shows the end-to-end training, testing and deployment pipeline.

One of the key benefits of using ML is its ability to generalise to new and unseen data. This makes it more flexible than using hard-coded rules known as the closed world problem where applications require redevelopment to express new knowledge. However, one of the key challenges of training an ML model is obtaining a reasonable degree of accuracy while ensuring effective generalisation. Therefore, a big part of ML is the orchestration and management of data (rubbish in/rubbish out) to produce high quality and reproducible models. Data acquisition and processing are key skills that every ML practitioner should learn to master. This book will provide you with a set of best practice tools and techniques for developing your ML solutions.

The approaches to ML which include supervised learning, unsupervised learning and reinforcement learning are the most common techniques that you will find in any ML project. They are all designed to tackle different tasks and problems. Don't

© Springer Nature Switzerland AG 2022
P. Fergus, C. Chalmers, *Applied Deep Learning*, Computational Intelligence Methods and Applications, https://doi.org/10.1007/978-3-031-04420-5_2

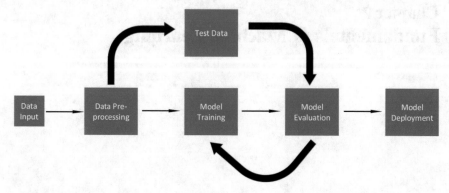

**Fig. 2.1** End-to-end machine learning pipeline

**Fig. 2.2** Mathematical formula for machine learning

$$f([x_1, x_2, x_3, x_4, x_5, x_6, x_7]) = y$$

worry if these are a little vague at this stage as they will be discussed in more detail as we move through the chapter.

### 2.1.1  Formal and Non-Formal Definition

There are two main ways to describe ML:

- **Formal definition:** "A computer program is said to learn from experience **E** with respect to some class of tasks **T** and performance measure P, if its performance at tasks in **T**, as measured by **P**, improves with experience **E**" [1].
- **Non-formal Definition:** "The goal of machine learning is to program computers to use example data or past experience to solve a given problem" [2].

At the most basic level, an ML algorithm tries to create a function (f) through a training process that can take a set of inputs (x) that can predict (y). Figure 2.2 shows a basic mathematical function for training an ML algorithm.

As discussed in Chap. 1, ML is primarily focused on the discovery of patterns within datasets which enables computers to develop intelligence to mimic how complex tasks are solved by humans. ML is good at finding patterns that would remain elusive under human analysis. This is why ML has seen rapid adoption in many areas since the early '90s. For example, ML has been shown to outperform its human counterpart in a wide variety of areas including finance and health where tasks such as time-series analysis, text processing and forecasting are undertaken.

## 2.1.2   How AI and Machine Learning Differs from Conventional Software Development

In computing, some applications are too difficult to construct using software engineering processes alone. For example, writing an application that can identify 90 different objects within and across multiple images would be very complex to achieve using conventual software development tools. If this was possible scaling it up to include additional objects would require significant software changes. For these types of tasks, the use of ML has shown to be much more efficient at tackling these types of problems. Rather than hard-coding software statements, ML is trained to detect patterns and construct object detection algorithms automatically.

It is important to note that software development remains a key component in any ML application. Software development acts as the glue for individual components within the system pipeline facilitating user interfaces, backend data storage procedures and communication between the different ML components. There is a third component however known as symbolic AI that was widely used in the early days of AI that is beginning to see a resurgence. Languages such as Lisp and Prolog are capable of handling the logic and decision-making components using predicate logic and inference. These languages allow facts, rules and inference engines to be implemented to solve different problems. Therefore, you can think of software development as the scaffold and ML as the pattern-matching and generalisation component. While symbolic AI combines the outputs generated by the ML models and other data sources to capture the logic and decision-making processes during the execution of the end-to-end pipeline.

As shown in Fig. 2.3 the software development component requires specific programming to derive an outcome. The symbolic AI component allows new facts

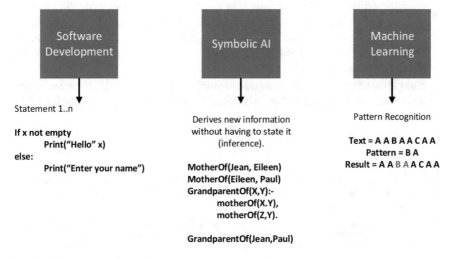

**Fig. 2.3**  Statements, rules and patterns

to be derived without having to explicitly state them. For example, to determine who is the grandparents X and child Y, you can simply traverse the facts (mother of) using a grandparent of rule. In this instance, Jean is the grandparent of Paul because Jean is the mother of Eileen and Eileen is the mother of Paul. For the ML component, it would be able to identify Paul as a man by looking at common attributes such as height, weight and facial hair etc.

### 2.1.2.1  Rewriting the Rules

In conventional software development knowledge is explicitly encoded as a set of rules. This is in contrast to the ML approach whereby algorithms are trained to derive their own set of rules based on the input data and its targeted outcome. A computer program will explicitly follow the rules of a conventional program developed by a software engineer. This means that new information outside the scope of the application can only be included in future software releases. You can think of an application as a closed world problem as briefly discussed in Chap. 1. There are several key advantages to using ML over conventual software development which includes:

- **Generalisation:** firstly, ML gives you the ability to generalise your model to be more flexible to new and similar data. ML practitioners try to regularise ML models as much as possible to prevent overfitting. In contrast software engineering results in extreme overfitting to the problem domain and often requires further development for only minor changes. Figure 2.4 highlights an example of both under and overfitting.
- **Faster Development:** Secondly ML makes it feasible to tackle complex problems significantly faster and with fewer lines of code to achieve the same outcome. Although ML requires you to implement custom code this is only wraparound code to support the ML models. The means that the complexity of rule generation is left to the ML. Therefore, this abstracts from the developer for the rule generation process which significantly speeds up and simplifies the development process.
- **Rule Discovery:** With software development, it is up to the developer to define their own rules in conjunction with customers to tackle a given problem. The

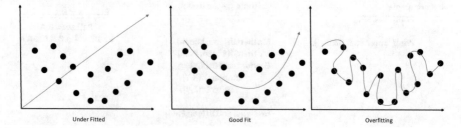

Fig. 2.4  ML vs software engineering

identification and use of these rules are time-consuming and error-prone. This often leads to solutions being delivered that do not fully meet customer expectations. Likewise, the chosen rules might not be the most appropriate for the task. With ML rules are automatically created based on the data you provide. While this can be beneficial, the final model is only as good as the data provided.

### 2.1.2.2   Intelligent Decision Making

The key difference between software engineering and ML is that ML learns and improves over time. This is in contrast to a traditionally developed application that explicitly operates on the provided code. ML continually learns patterns, connections and insights without being programmed to work towards specific conclusions. This learning element is one of the key distinctions between the two methods. One of the key benefits that machine learning offers is the acceleration of the decision-making process. This is achieved by analysing vast amounts of data and drawing intelligent insights that are often difficult to derive from human input. As data volumes continue to significantly increase it becomes more difficult to interpret and process. This is especially true when creating rules to act upon the data and find new insights. What ML allows you to do is to quickly find those important insights and offer them to interested parties for consideration. As a result, ML is now able to provide better business decisions and more intelligent courses of action with minimal human intervention. Therefore, ML does not replace people but enhances and supports them. Figure 2.5 shows a plug and play architecture for ML decision making.

The first stage is to ingest the necessary data sources. Using enterprise technologies, it has now become easier to integrate disparate data sources to solve any number of ML problems. Data is streamed using a wide range of data access technologies and served directly to the analytics models for problem-solving. The analytical models process the acquired data to obtain insights for organisations that provide value. As this is a complete plug and play architecture modules can be quickly inserted, replaced or combined to fit the needs of the organisation.

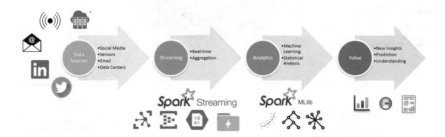

**Fig. 2.5**  ML workflow for decision making

## 2.2   Machine Learning Tribes

There are a variety of different ML algorithms each with their strengths and weaknesses. Choosing the most appropriate algorithm is dependent on a wide variety of factors and the overall goal. However, the selection is guided by the type of data, the computational hardware and the desired outcome. Before we discuss data and computational hardware in this section, we will introduce tribes of the most common ML algorithms you are likely to encounter in your development projects [3]. Although each tribe is different, they have the same objective which is to develop machine intelligence. The five tribes Symbolists, Connectionists, Evolutionists, Bayesians and Analogists are highlighted in Fig. 2.6.

### 2.2.1   Connectionists

Connectionists use neural networks as they are influenced by neuroscience. Essentially connectionists mimic the constructs of the brain to develop machine intelligence. The brain learns by developing strong links between neurons where it leads to a correct outcome. What makes this approach so successful is the brain's ability to determine which connections are responsible for errors in representation and correct them accordingly. The connectionist's role is to transform the brain and its functioning into an associated computational model known as ANNs as seen in Fig. 2.7. Here the biological neuron can be seen on the left-hand side while the synthetic representation can be seen on the right in the input, hidden and output layers. The

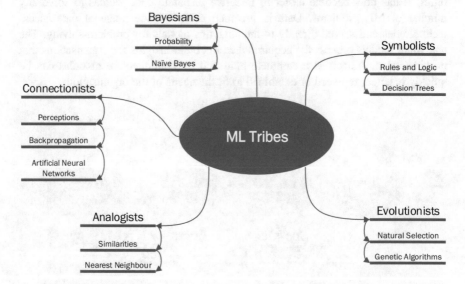

**Fig. 2.6**   The five ML tribes

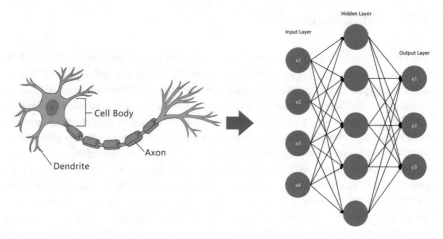

**Fig. 2.7** Biological neuron vs perceptron

**Fig. 2.8** Perceptron with inputs and output

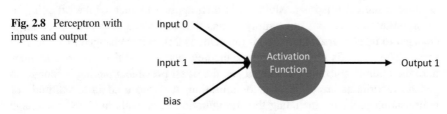

synapses that connect the biological neurons in the left biological image are represented as lines between perceptrons in the image on the right.

In relation to error correction carried out by the brain, ANNs performs similar tasks that propagate errors backwards from the output layer to the input layer, via its hidden layers. This process adjusts the learning of the ANN to minimise its error over time, therefore, increasing the likelihood of obtaining a successful outcome. A neural network consists of many layers of interconnected perceptrons. These perceptrons take a variety of different inputs and contain a processor and a single output. There are four main stages of the process: receive inputs, weight inputs, sum inputs and generate an output. Figure 2.8 highlights a simple perceptron along with its inputs and outputs. If these inputs exceed the threshold of the perceptron it fires (activates) and pulses a value along the output connection to the next perceptron.

Some of the most common algorithms in the connectionist tribe include Multi-layer Perceptron (MLP), Autoencoders, RNNs, LSTMs, CNNs and GANs which will all be discussed in this book.

## 2.2.2  *Evolutionists*

Evolutionists are interested in evolving structures, and they are influenced by biological evolution. These algorithms work by using the principles of natural selection to produce dependants that are the most successful within the environment which contains them. A common example of this is genetic algorithms where the learning process tries to solve an optimisation problem. In genetic programming computer programs are bread to evolve in a similar way nature mates and evolves organisms. Figure 2.9 highlights the process of the genetic algorithm.

The process starts with a population and the fitness of each member in the population is calculated. The members with the highest fitness values are selected and used in the crossover step. This step takes for example 30% of the genetic material from parent A and combines it with 70% of the genetic material from parent B to produce offspring. This process is repeated by combining 70% of the genetic material from parent A is combined with 30% of the genetic material of parent B to produce a second offspring. Mutation is then applied to each of the offspring to incorporate variance and this simply means that one piece of genetic material is changed to its converse value (i.e., if the value is 0 then it is changed to 1 and vice versa). The new offspring then become the new parents and the process continues until the optimal outcome is achieved i.e., the fittest possible offspring is found. As genetic algorithms are efficient at optimisation, they are used in a multitude of optimisation problems including the configuration of weights in CNNs for image processing [4]. Systems can be developed using genetic programming as proposed by John Koza [5].

**Fig. 2.9** Genetic algorithm

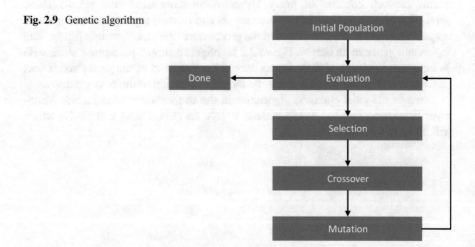

### 2.2.3   Bayesians

Bayesians use probabilistic inference which is influenced by statistics and are concerned with uncertainty. Bayesians focus on using probabilistic inference to test a hypothesis where some outcomes are more likely than others. As more data becomes available the hypothesis is updated. For example, looking at Fig. 2.10 do you know if the person in the image is male or female? Depending on your understanding of hairstyles and fashion you may assume that the person in the picture is a female but without additional information, it may be difficult to say. Now imagine if the person in the image is in a queue for the male toilets. With this additional information, you may now be more confident in assuming that the person in the image is a male. Essentially this is how Bayesian inference works.

Bayesian probability is derived using four main concepts: probabilities (the number of ways that something can happen divided by the total number of things that can happen), conditional probabilities (the same as normal probabilities but they look at a subset of all the examples, I.e. women and women with long hair), joint probabilities (adding two separate probabilities together, I.e., the probability the person is a woman and has long hair) and marginal probabilities (add up the probabilities for all the different ways that something can happen). Some of the most popular Bayesian algorithms include Hidden Markov models [6], Bayesian Networks [7] and Naïve Bayes Classifier [7].

**Fig. 2.10**  Gender probability

### 2.2.4 Symbolists

Symbolists use formal systems. They are influenced by computer science, linguistics, and analytic philosophy. In this paradigm, symbolic rule-based systems are utilised to make inferences. Programming languages such as Lisp and Prolog allow practitioners to encode, in rules, all that we understand about the world. These languages are considered to be first-order logic systems. Unlike many other programming languages, they are declarative programming languages that capture relations that are represented as facts and rules. Once these are defined a user can execute queries over these relations. Not all information or facts need to be explicitly programmed as they can be derived by combining existing facts through inference. This is commonly performed using an inference engine. Fig. 2.11 highlights a symbolic workflow.

Symbolic AI is most often used in Expert Systems, particularly in the medical domain. The general concept is to encode the knowledge of clinicians and use these facts to derive new knowledge based on the symptoms provided by patients. One of the most popular systems used today which incorporates an inference engine alongside other ML techniques is the Babylon Healthcare system. This is a system capable of reasoning on a space of hundreds of billions of combinations of symptoms, diseases and risk factors, per second, to identify conditions that may match the information provided by the patient. There are several applications for implementing symbolic inductive/deductive reasoning which includes CyC [8], Prolog and Decision Trees.

### 2.2.5 Analogists

Analogists are interested in mapping current situations to new situations. They are focused on the identification of similarities between key characteristics of features and inferring similarities. Many people believe that using analogy is a basic building block for human reasoning. When we are faced with a new situation, we draw on our past experience and recall what happened and how we responded. One common use of this approach is online recommendation engines that monitor our interactions and

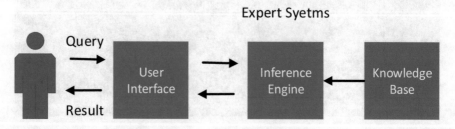

**Fig. 2.11** Symbolic workflow

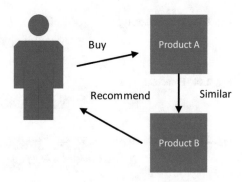

**Fig. 2.12** Recommender system

make new suggestions for similar or closely related products or services. For example, the algorithms learn that if A and B share the same interests, and B likes something that A has not come across before, then A will like that 'something' as well. This is an approach used by big online organisations like Amazon, Spotify and Netflix. Figure 2.12 shows an example of a basic recommender system.

Some example algorithms include Support Vector Machines (SVM) [9] and K-Means [10].

## 2.3  Data Management

The core concept of modern-day ML is to develop algorithms that ingest and learn from data. One of the most important skills to learn in any ML project is to understand different domains and the data they produce. More often than not obtained data will contain missing parts, will be messy, unstructured and imbalanced. It is the role of the practitioner to engineer a pipeline that addresses these issues to produce the most optimal dataset for the ML task at hand. This means that the practitioner will need to utilise many different tools and techniques while drawing on past experience to allow ML algorithms to learn from data and produce the best results. This section will introduce the fundamentals of this process and provide the practitioner with the necessary understanding to deal with data in their ML projects.

### 2.3.1  Data Types and Data Objects

#### 2.3.1.1  Numerical

Numerical data is used to represent information using numbers (integer or floating-point). Data generally needs to be put into a numeric form before it can be used by ML algorithms (even images and text). Primitive numerical data types are one of the

**Fig. 2.13**  Integer data type

```
x = 5
print(type(x))  =  <class 'int'>
```

**Fig. 2.14**  Float data type

```
x = 5.5
print(type(x))  =  <class 'float'>
```

**Fig. 2.15**  String data type

```
x = "hello"
print(type(x))  =  <class 'str'>
```

most common data types used in ML. The base numeric data types you will encounter in this book are Integers (Int) and Floats.

Integers are whole numbers such as 1,2,3,4,5 (Fig. 2.13):

Floats are numbers such as 1.5, 2.5, 3.5, 4.5, 5.5 (Fig. 2.14):

There will be numerous other definitions of primitive data types depending on the programming language that you use. However, the two numerical types mentioned here are the most common ones you will encounter in this book.

### 2.3.1.2  Textual

There are two main types of textual data you will find in this book which are chars and strings. A char is a single character such "a", "b", "c", "1", "2", "3" where a string is a collection of characters stored in a one-dimensional array such ['h','e','l','l','o'] (Fig. 2.15).

### 2.3.1.3  Categorical

In ML, data is nearly always split into two groups: numerical and categorical. In supervised learning, the categorical value is also known as the class label. Class labels are used to describe what an observation is for example "Cat", "Dog", "Car" and "Person". In the example below Fig. 2.16, the class label is shown in the Survived column. In a ML task, this is the value that we would want the algorithm to accurately predict based on the features (non-label columns). Alongside the categorical data, there is a full complement of other data types previously discussed. As ML algorithms only process numerical data, textual data such as Sex would need to be converted into numeric data types using techniques such as one-hot encoding. This is an important step in data preparation as many algorithms can only be trained using numerical data and not text. Techniques such as one-hot encoding work by transforming text to associated numeric values. For example, a,b,c will be converted

| PassengerId | Survived | Pclass | Name | Sex | Age | SibSp | Parch | Ticket | Fare | Cabin | Embarked |
|---|---|---|---|---|---|---|---|---|---|---|---|
| 1 | 0 | 3 | Braund, Mr. Owen Harris | male | 22 | 1 | 0 | A/5 21171 | 7.25 | | S |
| 2 | 1 | 1 | Cumings, Mrs. John Bradley (Florence Briggs Thayer) | female | 38 | 1 | 0 | PC 17599 | 71.2833 | C85 | C |
| 3 | 1 | 3 | Heikkinen, Miss. Laina | female | 26 | 0 | 0 | STON/O2. 3101282 | 7.925 | | S |
| 4 | 1 | 1 | Futrelle, Mrs. Jacques Heath (Lily May Peel) | female | 35 | 1 | 0 | 113803 | 53.1 | C123 | S |
| 5 | 0 | 3 | Allen, Mr. William Henry | male | 35 | 0 | 0 | 373450 | 8.05 | | S |
| 6 | 0 | 3 | Moran, Mr. James | male | | 0 | 0 | 330877 | 8.4583 | | Q |

**Fig. 2.16** Example data

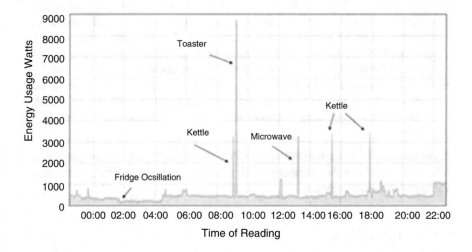

**Fig. 2.17** 24-Hour energy readings

to 1,2,3. Collectively this acts as a data dictionary and mapping component or key-value pairs. It is important to remember that any data transformations undertaken on the training data must also be done on the test data and the live data in the production system.

### 2.3.1.4 Timeseries

Timeseries data is referred to as data points typically taken sequentially over equally spaced time periods. Data points can be either integers or real numbers. For example, these could be energy readings taken from a utility meter in your home as highlighted in Fig. 2.17. Time series data is often used in time series analysis in applications such as financial prediction, earthquake monitoring, electrocardiography, and various types of trend analysis. Time series analysis extracts meaningful statistics or features that characterise the data.

## 2.3.2  Data Structure

Data is stored in a variety of different ways. For example, photographs, news articles and social media all of which fall into one of the groups outlined in Fig. 2.18. How data is stored will affect how it is structured and therefore how you process it.

- **Structured Data:** is data that has a strict set of rules that govern how it is represented, accessed and modified. For example, conforming to schemas in relational databases and associated Database Management Systems (DBMS). Interacting with this data often requires expertise, understanding of the underlying data structure and tools required to interact with it.
- **Semi-Structured:** is a subset of structured data that is less stringent and does not conform to the formal structure of data a model such as those found in a relational database. Semi-Structured data is more about data exchange and is usually accessed through the software layer using an Application Programming Interface (API). For example, the Document Object Model (DOM) and JSON parser.
- **Un-Structured:** does not have any predefined rules and curators have the freedom to develop content however they want. To interface with this type of data often requires proprietary software and a more complex data pre-processing pipeline.

All of the above data formats are used in ML and this requires that data scientists and ML developers have the necessary skills to manage and exploit this data to solve a variety of different problems.

### 2.3.2.1  Data Objects

Data objects are intermediary placeholders that contain imported structured, semi-structured or unstructured data. In these objects, all the necessary data processing is

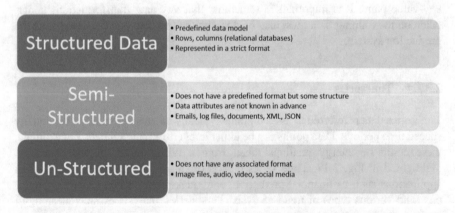

**Fig. 2.18**  Data structure and types

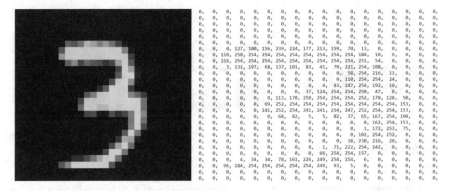

**Fig. 2.19**   Image and numeric representation

In [7] :   `df . head ()`

Out [7] :

|   | country | continent | year | lifeExp | pop | gdpPercap |
|---|---------|-----------|------|---------|-----|-----------|
| 0 | Afghanistan | Asia | 1952 | 28.801 | 8425333 | 779.445314 |
| 1 | Afghanistan | Asia | 1957 | 30.332 | 9240934 | 820.853030 |
| 2 | Afghanistan | Asia | 1962 | 31.997 | 10267083 | 853.100710 |
| 3 | Afghanistan | Asia | 1967 | 34.020 | 11537966 | 836.197138 |
| 4 | Afghanistan | Asia | 1972 | 36.088 | 13079460 | 739.981106 |

**Fig. 2.20**   Pandas Data frame showing tabular data

performed by utilising libraries to prepare the data for use by the ML algorithm. For example, dealing with missing data or performing transformations on data formats such as images and text to produce numerical representations. Figure 2.19 highlights a picture on the left-hand side and its numeric array on the right-hand side.

There are several different data objects which provide a multitude of different ways to store, access and manipulate data. The most common ones you will encounter in ML problems will be a 1-dimensional array and 2 dimensional and 3-dimensional matrices. Many of these will be contained within high-level objects across numerous libraries. For example, with Python, these include Pandas, NumPy, Lists, Dictionaries and Tuples. Depending on the data you use, you will either use a data frame for tabular data or extract data into an appropriate format such as a NumPy array when processing images with DL models. These libraries contain all the required helper functions for manipulating and transforming the data rather than having to write code to loop through the axis and process the data points. Figure 2.20 shows a typical Pandas data frame in tabular format. This type of data object is typically used to train algorithms such as Decisions Forest and SVM's.

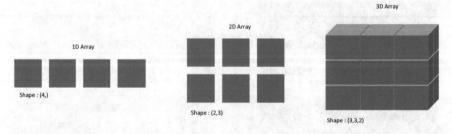

**Fig. 2.21** Different array structures

There may be occurrences where the use of tabular structure is insufficient for the data being used in your project. For example, if you are working with signal data a 1D array would be more appropriate whereas if you are working with images 2D arrays (matrix) will be used for greyscale and 3D arrays for Red, Green and Blue (RGB) images where they represent the ASCII values in each layer. Figure 2.21 highlights the three different array structures for the different types of data you will encounter.

### 2.3.3  Datasets

Data is the fundamental ingredient in the ML recipe. Data is packaged in the form of a dataset, and it is, therefore, important to manage the quality of that dataset to leverage the best performance from ML models—"garbage in garbage out". Datasets are often a collection of dumped information, and it should not be assumed that it is of high quality and in a sufficient state. A key skill of an ML practitioner is to rigorously explore the data and process it using the correct methods and tools. Some of the most common issues you will find is missing data, incorrect data types, fixed and variable-length data and data that provides no use in the learning process. Several different techniques can be used to address these issues such as interpolation for missing values and the removal of data where features or observations are of poor quality or not useful for solving the problem. ML by its nature is data-hungry, therefore there is a constant drive to obtain/generate as much data as possible to ensure the best results. Where this is not possible techniques such as synthetic data generation can be used to mitigate the effects of small datasets.

Websites such as Kaggle have made it easier for ML practitioners to gain access to high-quality data and the support to enable transformations of data for a wide variety of ML tasks. It is, therefore, useful to utilise websites such as Kaggle to provide insights into best practice problem-solving. These platforms are often used by leading experts in data science and ML who compete in data challenges. For example, some of the most pressing challenges in the world are often submitted to these sites to challenge leading practitioners to come up with practical and unique solutions.

**Fig. 2.22**  Imbalanced data

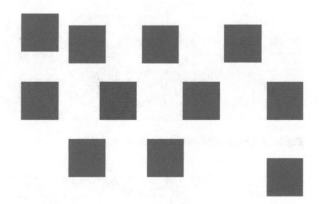

In ML, balanced datasets are the holy grail, but unfortunately, this is rarely the case. This is a particular challenge when dealing with medical datasets where you would naturally expect to see a smaller number of people with a disease as opposed to those that do not have it. In other words, if you were to test 100 people for cancer most people would likely test negative. Imbalanced data poses a challenge for the learning process as the model will typically become sensitive to the majority class (in our example healthy people) as it has more instances to learn from. ML models trained on imbalanced data can introduce bias and limit their ability to tackle real-world problems (generalisation). Figure 2.22 highlights the concept of imbalanced data where a minority is significantly underrepresented.

Another important aspect to consider when dealing with data is scale. Often algorithms such as SVM's are sensitive to scale and can affect the overall performance of the model. Several tools can be used to address the challenges mentioned above which every ML practitioner needs to become familiar with which we will cover throughout this book.

## 2.3.4   Exploratory Data Analysis

It is important to get to know your data to understand and gather as many insights as possible and address the issues outlined above. This process is often skipped by practitioners which can be detrimental to the whole project. In this section, we introduce the concepts, tools and techniques for Exploratory Data Analysis (EDA) to enable you to discover patterns, spot anomalies, test hypotheses and check assumptions.

### 2.3.4.1   What Is Exploratory Data Analysis

EDA is a statistical approach to analysing datasets to uncover their characteristics by using a variety of different methods such as data descriptions and visualisations.

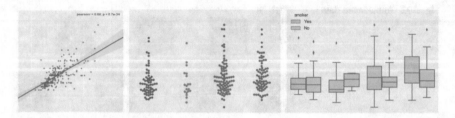

**Fig. 2.23** Common EDA visualisations

```
df.head()
```

| | mean radius | mean texture | mean perimeter | mean area | mean smoothness | mean compactness | mean concavity | mean concave points | mean symmetry | mean fractal dimension | ... |
|---|---|---|---|---|---|---|---|---|---|---|---|
| 0 | 17.99 | 10.38 | 122.80 | 1001.0 | 0.11840 | 0.27760 | 0.3001 | 0.14710 | 0.2419 | 0.07871 | ... |
| 1 | 20.57 | 17.77 | 132.90 | 1326.0 | 0.08474 | 0.07864 | 0.0869 | 0.07017 | 0.1812 | 0.05667 | ... |
| 2 | 19.69 | 21.25 | 130.00 | 1203.0 | 0.10960 | 0.15990 | 0.1974 | 0.12790 | 0.2069 | 0.05999 | ... |
| 3 | 11.42 | 20.38 | 77.58 | 386.1 | 0.14250 | 0.28390 | 0.2414 | 0.10520 | 0.2597 | 0.09744 | ... |
| 4 | 20.29 | 14.34 | 135.10 | 1297.0 | 0.10030 | 0.13280 | 0.1980 | 0.10430 | 0.1809 | 0.05883 | ... |

5 rows × 31 columns

**Fig. 2.24** Pandas head function

EDA is for seeing what the data can tell us beyond formal modelling and hypothesis testing. EDA was introduced by John Tukey who argued that by exploring the data it is possible to formulate a hypothesis that could lead to new data collections and experimentation [11]. Figure 2.23 shows some of the visual representations of EDA which includes scatterplots, line plots and box plots.

Visual representations are often combined with advanced data analysis packages such as Seabourn, Matplotlib, NumPy and Pandas to extract more advanced information and carry out necessary transformations for optimal modelling. For example, using the Pandas data frame head function we can easily get some basic information about our dataset. This includes the columns (features) and rows (observations). Fig. 2.24 shows you how the Pandas head function is used.

By using the Pandas package and functions such as info we can obtain some additional characteristics such as the number of observations, the data types and if there are any missing values (null values) within the dataset. Figure 2.25 shows the Pandas info function and the returned data.

Other functions such as describe allow us to obtain some basic statistical information such as the min and max and standard deviation values for the features contained with the dataset. This can give an insight into the scale of the data and possible normalisation techniques to consider. Figure 2.26 highlights the Pandas describe function.

```
df.info()

<class 'pandas.core.frame.DataFrame'>
RangeIndex: 569 entries, 0 to 568
Data columns (total 31 columns):
 #   Column                  Non-Null Count   Dtype
---  ------                  --------------   -----
 0   mean radius             569 non-null     float64
 1   mean texture            569 non-null     float64
 2   mean perimeter          569 non-null     float64
 3   mean area               569 non-null     float64
 4   mean smoothness         569 non-null     float64
 5   mean compactness        569 non-null     float64
 6   mean concavity          569 non-null     float64
 7   mean concave points     569 non-null     float64
 8   mean symmetry           569 non-null     float64
 9   mean fractal dimension  569 non-null     float64
 10  radius error            569 non-null     float64
 11  texture error           569 non-null     float64
 12  perimeter error         569 non-null     float64
```

**Fig. 2.25**  Pandas Info function

```
df.describe().transpose()
```

|  | count | mean | std | min | 25% | 50% | 75% | max |
|---|---|---|---|---|---|---|---|---|
| mean radius | 569.0 | 14.127292 | 3.524049 | 6.981000 | 11.700000 | 13.370000 | 15.780000 | 28.11000 |
| mean texture | 569.0 | 19.289649 | 4.301036 | 9.710000 | 16.170000 | 18.840000 | 21.800000 | 39.28000 |
| mean perimeter | 569.0 | 91.969033 | 24.298981 | 43.790000 | 75.170000 | 86.240000 | 104.100000 | 188.50000 |
| mean area | 569.0 | 654.889104 | 351.914129 | 143.500000 | 420.300000 | 551.100000 | 782.700000 | 2501.00000 |
| mean smoothness | 569.0 | 0.096360 | 0.014064 | 0.052630 | 0.086370 | 0.095870 | 0.105300 | 0.16340 |
| mean compactness | 569.0 | 0.104341 | 0.052813 | 0.019380 | 0.064920 | 0.092630 | 0.130400 | 0.34540 |
| mean concavity | 569.0 | 0.088799 | 0.079720 | 0.000000 | 0.029560 | 0.061540 | 0.130700 | 0.42680 |
| mean concave points | 569.0 | 0.048919 | 0.038803 | 0.000000 | 0.020310 | 0.033500 | 0.074000 | 0.20120 |
| mean symmetry | 569.0 | 0.181162 | 0.027414 | 0.106000 | 0.161900 | 0.179200 | 0.195700 | 0.30400 |
| mean fractal dimension | 569.0 | 0.062798 | 0.007060 | 0.049960 | 0.057700 | 0.061540 | 0.066120 | 0.09744 |
| radius error | 569.0 | 0.405172 | 0.277313 | 0.111500 | 0.232400 | 0.324200 | 0.478900 | 2.87300 |
| texture error | 569.0 | 1.216853 | 0.551648 | 0.360200 | 0.833900 | 1.108000 | 1.474000 | 4.88500 |
| perimeter error | 569.0 | 2.866059 | 2.021855 | 0.757000 | 1.606000 | 2.287000 | 3.357000 | 21.98000 |

**Fig. 2.26**  Pandas describe function

Another important step is to ascertain the class (dependant variable) distributions to determine if our dataset is balanced as previously discussed. To achieve this visually you can use the count plot function in Seabourn to show the number of observations (rows) that are in each class. As you can see there is a class imbalance

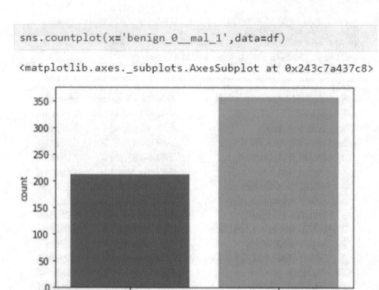

```
sns.countplot(x='benign_0__mal_1',data=df)
```

```
<matplotlib.axes._subplots.AxesSubplot at 0x243c7a437c8>
```

**Fig. 2.27** Seaborn countplot function

in this dataset so we would have to oversample the minority class using a technique such as Synthetic Minority Oversampling Technique (SMOTE) or by removing observations from the majority class [12]. As data is valuable and sometimes scarce it is not always possible to disregard data. Figure 2.27 shows the Seaborn countplot function.

It is also important to obtain some insights into the features (non-dependent variables) and the level of correlation between them. Features that are highly correlated are competing to describe the same thing. Therefore, in this instance having both in your final model would provide limited utility. So, the practitioner would remove one of these features in a manual dimensionality reduction process before modelling takes place. There are other methods for achieving dimensionality reduction (removing features or transforming) which will be introduced later in this book. For example, feature (mean perimeter) is highly collated with feature (worst perimeter) so based on clinical discussions one of these would be removed. Figure 2.28 highlights the Seaborn heatmap function for determining the correlation between features.

### 2.3.4.2  Data Distributions

In ML several algorithms are sensitive to different types of data distributions. Datasets which contain features in the tail end of skewed Gaussian distribution (I.e., skewed to either the left or the right) are likely to be outliners in the data

```
sns.heatmap(df.corr())
```

```
<matplotlib.axes._subplots.AxesSubplot at 0x243c7d46e08>
```

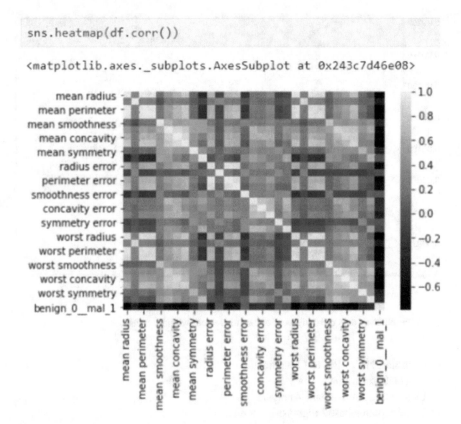

**Fig. 2.28**   Seaborn heatmap Function

which are not representative of the majority of observations. For example, Fig. 2.29 shows that the mean area of a tumour resides between 100 and 1300 mm$^2$. Tumour sizes above 1300 mm$^2$ represent unusual cases (ones less than 100 mm$^2$ are likely to be pre-diagnosis so therefore the cases are not likely to be recorded). If you were to model an ML algorithm that is sensitive to non-Gaussian distributions this would likely reduce the overall detection accuracy. In the case of breast cancer detection, the trade-off is whether you would be happy with the system being correct 68% of the time on 98% of the data or 98% accurate on 95% of the data—I would rather have the latter. One way to overcome this would be to either remove values above a certain threshold or use a power transform to normally distribute the data. Note that not all algorithms are sensitive to non-Gaussian distributions such as an SVM however it is good practice to normally distribute your data as much as possible before the modelling process is performed to minimise the risks associated with skewed datasets. In addition, transforming data distributions can be beneficial to the cost function and help the model to converge correctly and faster.

Algorithms that are particularly sensitive to data distributions include:

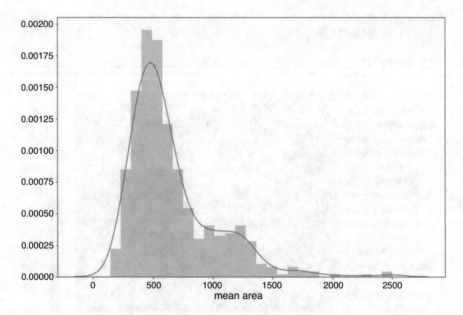

**Fig. 2.29** Skewed data distribution of one of the feature within our dataset

- Gaussian Naive Bayes Classifier
- Linear Discriminant Analysis
- Quadratic Discriminant Analysis
- Least Squares based regression models

In the example dataset, the feature exhibiting the closest Gaussian distribution is mean symmetry which has only minor skewing. Figure 2.30 highlights the distribution of this feature.

There are many different types of data distribution, but in the ML paradigm, we typically focus on Gaussian (normal distribution), Uniform distribution, Bernoulli distribution, binomial distribution, lognormal distribution and Pareto distribution. The Gaussian distribution in ML is based on the 68–95–99.7% rule. Using this rule, we can derive that 68% of the values of the total distribution reside within $\pm 1$ standard deviation of the mean, 95% of the values of the total distribution reside with $\pm 2$ standards deviation of the mean and 99.7% of the values of the total distribution reside within $\pm 3$ standard distributions of the mean. Figure 2.31 shows a Gaussian distribution and associated rules.

To understand this better consider two examples. In the first example, you sell shoes, and you want to know the most common shoe size for both men and women. This would be useful as it would provide you with valuable information on what shoe sizes to stock in your shop. Looking at Fig. 2.31 we could say that the average shoe size for a man would reside within $\pm 1$ standard deviation of the mean. Let's say the mean is size 8 with 68.27% of the region comprising shoe sizes between size

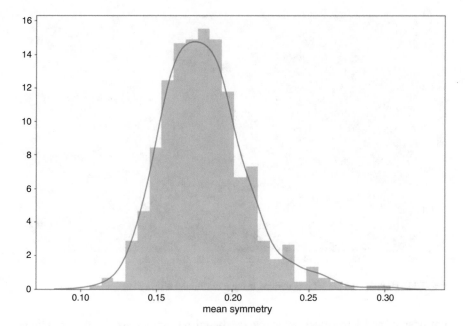

**Fig. 2.30**  Distribution of mean symmetry feature

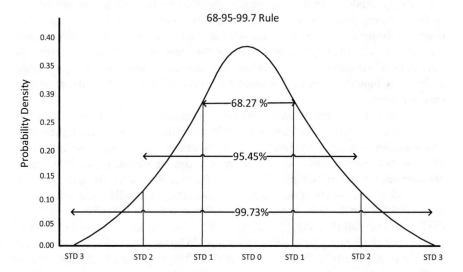

**Fig. 2.31**  Gaussian distribution with associated rules

7 and size 9. As we move towards the tails of the distribution the shoe size would either decrease or increase and would be less common. Therefore, we would not stock equal amounts of shoe sizes as they will not sell at the same rate, I.e., size 11 shoes would be in less demand than say a size 7, 8, or 9. In the second scenario

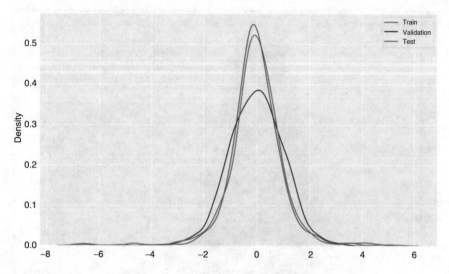

**Fig. 2.32** Highlights three subsets derived using a uniformed distribution

consider a model to detect breast cancer based on tumour size. Again, common tumour sizes will reside within the 68.27% region of the distribution with either increasingly smaller or larger tumours moving outwards towards the end of the tails. In this instance, you may want to create an ML model that is highly accurate at detecting the most common size tumours without being affected by unusual cases. So, for example, training the model using data that resides within ±3 standard deviations of the mean we could deduce that this model would be highly accurate at detecting tumours sizes in that range without being affected by unusual or less common cases.

The next important distribution to consider is the uniform distribution. A uniform distribution tells us if each of the values within our dataset are equally represented and therefore have the same probability of occurrence. In ML using the rules of a uniform distribution allows us to sample our dataset ensuring that its original distribution and the subsample distribution remains the same. For example, the proportion of data points in the histogram's silos remain equally represented. This means that bin 1 in the histogram of the large dataset contains 10% of the values then the bin 1 of the subset should also contain 10% of the values of that subset. This is important when creating your train, validation and test sets whereby they should all have the same probability distribution. Figure 2.32 highlights three identical subsets created from a larger dataset using uniform distributions.

You will encounter two other types of distributions called Bernoulli and the Binomial distribution. The Bernoulli distribution is a discrete probability distribution that covers cases where a single event produces a binary outcome such as 0 or 1, I.e., heads (0) and tails (1) in a coin flip or male (0) and female (1). Where you will most often encounter this type of distribution is in an investigation of binary class label distributions and the results obtained from a single binary classification trial with the first class being (0) and the second class (1). In the case of the Binomial distribution, this can be thought of as a repetition of multiple independent Bernoulli trials (also known as the Bernoulli process). The cumulative outcomes of a Bernoulli process will follow a Binomial distribution. You can also think of a Bernoulli distribution as a Binomial distribution that contains a single trial. In ML you can think of an ML algorithm trained for binary classification as a Bernoulli process, where the prediction made by a model given an input observation is a Bernoulli trial (correct or incorrect). So, the Binomial distribution represents a summary of the k number of Bernoulli trials with a given probability of success.

Log normal distributions represent skewness in your dataset. These types of distributions are heavily weighted towards the left- or right-hand side of the distribution (positively skewed). In other words, unlike your Gaussian distribution, most of the data reside towards the left-hand side of the graph with corresponding large tails that represent the outliers or unusual cases in your data. Depending on the task you would either remove the outliers or you would perform a power transformation to evenly distribute the data. Log normal distributions cannot contain a negative value, for example, imagine plotting the salaries within an organisation. You would expect most people's salaries to be grouped towards the left of the plot and the CEOs to be at the far end of the tail as they will be on significantly more money than most employees. Likewise, you would not expect an employee to have a negative salary. In this instance, ML algorithms are known to perform poorly on skewed data, and we, therefore, would need to normally distribute the data. If your data does not contain a negative number and is positively skewed, you can use a transformation such Box-Cox. If the transformed data resembles a Gaussian distribution, then the data is said to be log-normal. If the data contains a negative number, then you would have to use an alternative transformation such as Yeo-Johnson to normally distribute the data. So, while there may be other reasons to use a log-normal distribution its main use in ML is to normally distribute data. Figure 2.33 shows the different types of skewed data distributions.

So, how do we normally distribute negatively skewed data? You can use transformations such as square root and natural log. The general rule of thumb for ML practitioners is either to remove the observations or use a power transformation.

Poisson distributions ascertain the probability that a given event may or may not happen by determining the normal occurrence of events. In addition, Poisson distributions can be used to predict how many times an event is likely to occur within a given time period. There are essentially two parts which include the Poisson processes and the Poisson distribution.

A Poisson distribution has to meet the following requirements:

- Events are independent (occurrence of one event does not affect the probability that another event will occur).
- The time period between events is constant.
- Two events cannot happen at the same time.

The Poisson process is used to describe randomly occurring events, which is not that useful. We need the Poisson Distribution to do interesting things like finding the

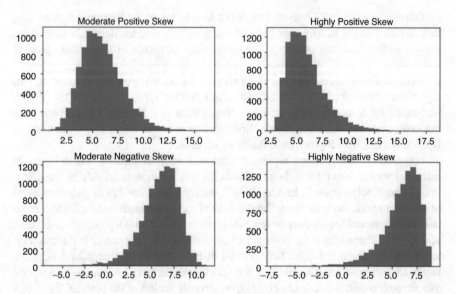

**Fig. 2.33** Data distributions

probability of a number of events in a time period or finding the probability of waiting some time until the next event is derived from an exponential distribution. In ML the distribution of occurrences or the time period of events can be skewed therefore highlighting the presence of outliers within the dataset. Transformations such as the Anscombe transform can be used to transform a Poisson distribution into a Gaussian distribution.

### 2.3.4.3    Validate Assumptions

One of the main functions of EDA is to analyse the data before any assumptions are made. This is important as it allows you to raise questions and validate any prior assumptions you might have made about your dataset. Completing this process will frame the problem, build your dataset and allow you to select appropriate algorithms. This will often be done in conjunction with domain experts, data curators and the client. This step is often missed by ML practitioners and leads to a misrepresentation of the results and poor reproducibility. This can be particularly challenging when we move our models into production.

There are two types of assumptions that need to be considered during the EDA process which includes technical and domain assumptions. Technical assumptions allow us to identify collinearity between variables (two or more variables trying to describe the same thing), variance in the dataset and whether there is any missing or corrupted data values. Without testing your assumptions, you could easily generate a model that performs poorly or gives inaccurate results. EDA also helps during the feature engineering stage by selecting relationships that might be more efficiently encoded when training a model. Before the ML practitioner embarks on the EDA process, they need to discuss the data with domain experts to fully understand the data and the problem you are trying to address. This will help you to better understand the data and allow meaningful information to be extracted for subsequent data modelling. This will improve model accuracy and support the validation results.

#### 2.3.4.4 Feature Engineering

Feature engineering is one of the most important aspects of the ML pipeline and will be covered extensively throughout this book. Feature engineering can be a manual or automatic process depending on the technique and the problem domain. Figure 2.34 highlights the time investment associated with manual and automatic feature engineering processes.

Let us describe what feature engineering is by posing a question. If I said to you what has two wheels and an engine? You would probably tell me a motorbike. Now if I said that its colour was yellow does that make the identification any easier? Probably not so the colour feature could probably be discarded as it does not make the identification any easier. So, looking at the bike in Fig. 2.35 what features would you choose to uniquely identify a motorbike bike?

Based on your extracted features could you use them to identify the object in Fig. 2.36?

The answer is no so congratulations you have identified a set of features to distinguish between two different objects (a bike or a water bottle). So now if I was to ask you what has an engine you could provide a multitude of different answers such as a bike, car or plane. Therefore, we do not have enough information to uniquely describe the different types of objects that have an engine. In this case, we would need more features to give an accurate prediction. What we have described is feature engineering and the challenge is to extract features that uniquely describe all the objects we want to identify in a particular domain while distinguishing between them. Typically, an ML practitioner will extract lots of features and use a

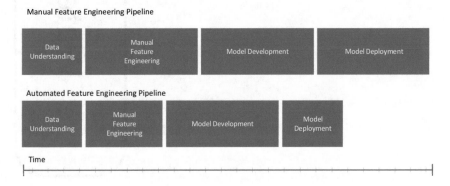

**Fig. 2.34** Manual and automatic feature engineering

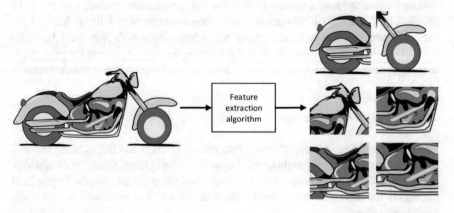

**Fig. 2.35** Bike features

**Fig. 2.36** Bottle features

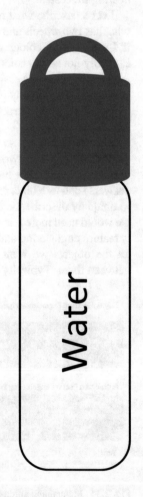

variety of different techniques to decide which ones are best for training the algorithm. This task is often difficult as it requires domain knowledge and empirical analysis of the results. Feature extraction is sometimes regarded as part art and part science and is a skill that is developed with experience. So, don't worry if your models don't perform well initially, ML is an iterative process that will be become easier over time.

## 2.4    Learning Problems

In this section, we will introduce and discuss the three different learning problems you will encounter as an ML practitioner. These are designed to solve specific ML problems which range from the identification of specific outcomes based on a set of features to the identification of outcomes based on how close they are to specific data clusters. The type of problem is dependent on your desired outcome and the type of data available. Figure 2.37 shows the differences between the different learning approaches.

### 2.4.1    Supervised Machine Learning

Supervised learning is probably the most common type of ML task you will encounter as an ML practitioner. Supervised learning is used to predict a target

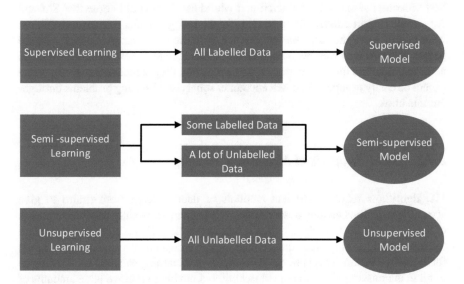

**Fig. 2.37**  Different learning approaches

| PassengerId | Survived | Pclass | Name | Sex | Age | SibSp | Parch | Ticket | Fare | Cabin | Embarked |
|---|---|---|---|---|---|---|---|---|---|---|---|
| 1 | 0 | 3 | Braund, Mr. Owen Harris | male | 22 | 1 | 0 | A/5 21171 | 7.25 | | S |
| 2 | 1 | 1 | Cumings, Mrs. John Bradley (Florence Briggs Thayer) | female | 38 | 1 | 0 | PC 17599 | 71.2833 | C85 | C |
| 3 | 1 | 3 | Heikkinen, Miss. Laina | female | 26 | 0 | 0 | STON/O2. 3101282 | 7.925 | | S |
| 4 | 1 | 1 | Futrelle, Mrs. Jacques Heath (Lily May Peel) | female | 35 | 1 | 0 | 113803 | 53.1 | C123 | S |
| 5 | 0 | 3 | Allen, Mr. William Henry | male | 35 | 0 | 0 | 373450 | 8.05 | | S |
| 6 | 0 | 3 | Moran, Mr. James | male | | 0 | 0 | 330877 | 8.4583 | | Q |

**Fig. 2.38**   Titanic dataset

value (class, dependent variable or label) and as humans, we do this naturally. Taking our motorbike example above we know it's a motorbike by looking at its features and assigning it to a particular value. The input data in a supervised learning problem represents the features extracted from your raw data and are presented in a structured data frame and labelled with an associated class. Figure 2.38 shows raw data with each row representing an observation and each column (independent variable) which represents the associated information collected for each observation (note at this stage they are all not necessarily features). With a supervised learning approach, the columns are mapped to a particular outcome (in our example who survived and who died on the Titanic). The algorithm's job is to identify patterns within the columns that allow it to predict the correct outcome (in our example who lived or died).

The data contained in Fig. 2.38 is not in a state that could be used to train an ML algorithm. Just like our motorbike example, you would need to choose features that best separate the classes (who lived and who dies). You could argue that Sex and Age would be particularly strong features for the task given that women and children were first to leave the ship. As you can see from the small sample in Fig. 2.38 the people who survived were women. Perhaps some of the less useful features would be name and ticket as they are in the wrong format, and they contain unique values that cannot be easily grouped. You will encounter supervised learning problems throughout this book.

### 2.4.2   Semi-Supervised Machine Learning

ML algorithms require sufficient amounts of data to learn from (train) to give accurate predictions on new observations. While there are usually adequate amounts of data available for training not all of it will be labelled. This is a particular problem for supervised learning algorithms which require a dependant variable (class, label) for each observation. This is where semi-supervised learning can help by allowing us to fill in the missing labels in our dataset without having to remove large amounts of data. For example, in our titanic dataset if there were missing labels (who lived and

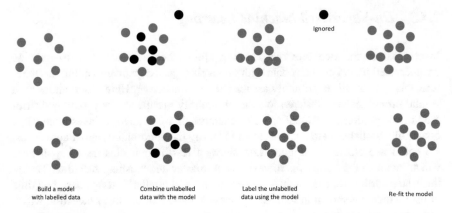

**Fig. 2.39** Semi-supervised clustering method

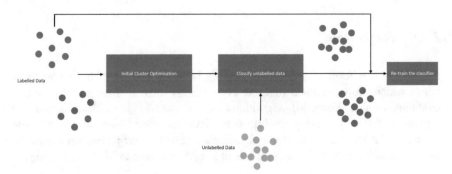

**Fig. 2.40** Semi-supervised predictions

who died) we could use semi-supervised learning to cluster the observations to determine which class they are more likely to belong to based on their features and infer whether they are more likely to have survived or died. You could then take this observation and label it accordingly and add it to your training dataset. While this is a good technique, where possible you would consult with domain experts to verify the results (in our example a historian or a registrar could verify the outcome based upon a death certificate record). Figure 2.39 shows a semi-supervised learning approach by plotting the unlabelled data against model predictions.

An alternative use of semi-supervised learning would be to run unlabelled observations through a trained classifier and use the predicted outcomes to label the data (using domain experts to validate the outcomes) and pass these back into the training data. Figure 2.40 shows a semi-supervised approach that is used to predict against the unlabelled data. The predicted data is then used to retrain the model.

### 2.4.3  Un-Supervised Machine Learning

In contrast to the two previous learning approaches the data used to train an unsupervised model contains data with no labels (class, dependant variable). Therefore, this type of ML is primarily associated with clustering. Here observations with similar properties are clustered together to identify groups and how data is distributed in space (density estimation). For example, if we wanted to investigate when household appliances are being used and identify the abnormal usage of appliances, we could use clustering. Figure 2.41 shows five different clusters of appliances which includes the kettle, microwave, oven, toaster and washing machine. Taking this a step further we can identify outliers (abnormal appliance usage based on time of use) which are shown in red. This process is known as anomaly detection which can also be an unsupervised learning approach.

### 2.4.4  Regression

Regression is a form of supervised learning however instead of having multiple labels which are categorical (discrete class labels) there is a single label with a continuous value. Some ML algorithms can be used for both classification and regression tasks by making modifications. Example algorithms include decision trees and ANNs. However, some algorithms such as linear regression cannot be used for classification tasks. An example of a regression task would be predicting the

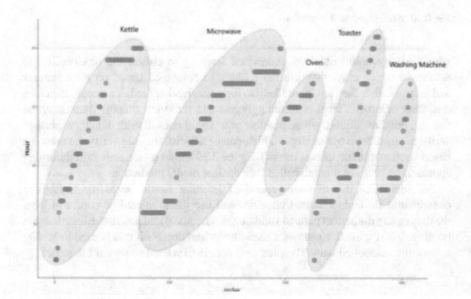

**Fig. 2.41** Clustering of appliances with anomaly detection

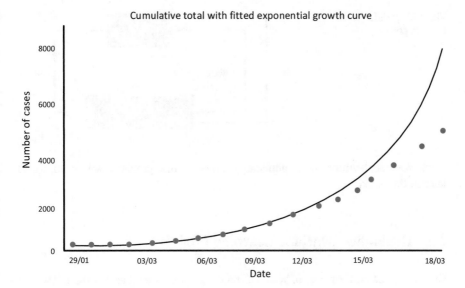

**Fig. 2.42** Linear regression for the prediction of COVID-19 cases

number of future cases that is likely to occur in a pandemic. Take the recent Covid-19 pandemic it would be possible to fit a linear regression model against past data. In Fig. 2.42, we can see the fitted growth curve for the number of cases up to the 15th March and the predicted projected numbers thereafter with a plot of the actual number of cases that occurred. Linear regression will be discussed later in the book.

## 2.4.5   Reinforcement Learning

Reinforcement learning allows you to train an ML model by establishing an end goal and penalising the algorithm for wrong decisions while rewarding it for correct ones. Using an agent, a model learns through trial and error in complex environments. There are key components to the technique which includes:

- **Environment:** The physical world where the agent operates, and models are trained
- **State:** is the current situation of the agent within the environment
- **Reward:** Feedback from the environment
- **Policy:** A mechanism for mapping the agent's state to its actions
- **Value:** A reward that an agent would receive by taking an action in each state

The goal of reinforcement learning is to maximise the total reward using a reward policy specified by the ML practitioner. No prior information is provided to the agent, while the agent starts with random trials and develops sophisticated tactics to solve the problem over time. Figure 2.43 provides a high-level overview.

**Fig. 2.43** Reinforcement
learning process

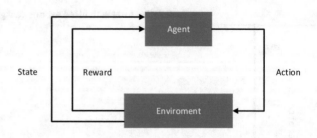

Reinforcement learning and its applications in real-world problems will be discussed later in the book.

## 2.5   Evaluating Machine Learning Models

Evaluating the performance of your ML model is an important aspect when it comes to deploying your model to solve real-world problems. How you evaluate performance and define its success criteria will be wide and varied depending on the customers' expectations and the types of problems to be solved. For example, a system that diagnoses a serious illness would be expected to produce highly accurate results. Where a system used for detecting potholes in a road would not have a serious outcome if one was missed or a misclassification was presented. If done correctly model evaluation will give you a good indication of how your model will perform in production. In this book, evaluation metrics and how to use them correctly will be covered extensively.

## 2.6   Summary

In this chapter, we introduced a high-level overview of the fundamental elements of ML. This has provided you with a conceptual understanding of the most common ML components and terminology you will encounter as you embark on your ML career. A clear definition of ML was provided and how it differs from conventional software development and its unique position within the AI paradigm. ML is a discipline within its own right with several different approaches as evidenced in the ML tribes. Depending on the problem you want to solve and the data you have access too different ML algorithms will be used. Driving the development of good ML models is data management and the numerous techniques provided to produce ML ready datasets for modelling.

The chapter mentioned several ML algorithms each belonging to a distinct learning problem which is categorised as supervised, semi-supervised, unsupervised and re-enforcement learning. The importance of model evaluation was discussed highlighting its use within the ML pipeline. The remainder of this book will dive into these concepts and provide you with more in-depth information which will give you a solid understanding of ML and how it can be used to solve your problems.

# References

1. T. M. Mitchell, "Textbook," *Biochem. McGraw Hill, London*, 1950.
2. E. Alpaydin, *Introduction to machine learning*. MIT press, 2020.
3. P. Domingos, *The master algorithm: How the quest for the ultimate learning machine will remake our world*. Basic Books, 2015.
4. T. Kozek, T. Roska, and L. O. Chua, "Genetic algorithm for CNN template learning," *IEEE Trans. Circuits Syst. I Fundam. Theory Appl.*, vol. 40, no. 6, pp. 392–402, 1993.
5. J. R. Koza and J. R. Koza, *Genetic programming: on the programming of computers by means of natural selection*, vol. 1. MIT press, 1992.
6. L. E. Baum, T. Petrie, G. Soules, and N. Weiss, "A maximization technique occurring in the statistical analysis of probabilistic functions of Markov chains," *Ann. Math. Stat.*, vol. 41, no. 1, pp. 164–171, 1970.
7. J. Pearl, "Bayesian networks: A model cf self-activated memory for evidential reasoning," in *Proceedings of the 7th conference of the Cognitive Science Society, University of California, Irvine, CA, USA*, 1985, pp. 15–17.
8. D. B. Lenat, "CYC: A large-scale investment in knowledge infrastructure," *Commun. ACM*, vol. 38, no. 11, pp. 33–38, 1995.
9. C. Cortes and V. Vapnik, "Support vector machine," *Mach. Learn.*, vol. 20, no. 3, pp. 273–297, 1995.
10. S. Lloyd, "Least squares quantization in PCM," *IEEE Trans. Inf. theory*, vol. 28, no. 2, pp. 129–137, 1982.
11. J. W. Tukey, *Exploratory Data Analysis*. 1977.
12. N. V. Chawla, K. W. Bowyer, L. O. Hall, and W. P. Kegelmeyer, "SMOTE: Synthetic Minority Over-sampling Technique," *J. Artif. Intell. Res.*, vol. 16, pp. 321–357, 2002.

# Chapter 3
# Supervised Learning

Following on from Chap. 2 we will now begin to explore the supervised learning problem in more detail. We will discuss some of the key supervised learning tasks and describe how they work and fit into a supervised learning pipeline. These tasks provide a scaffold to support the development of supervised learning models. This chapter will include data processing, feature engineering and model selection along with example algorithms. The two strands of supervised learning which includes classification and regression will also be discussed.

## 3.1  Basic Concepts

Supervised learning is a form of ML for learning a function which maps a given set of inputs to one or more outputs. This process creates a function that is inferred from labelled training data which consists of a set of examples (observations) and a set of corresponding target values (classes, dependent variables). The trained model (the function) is then evaluated using unseen test data (with the same feature structure but without the label) to determine the overall performance of the model. In other words, given a set of features, you are asking the trained model what class it thinks the observation belongs to.

Note we have discussed both training and test data however there is a third dataset called validation data which is used for tuning the model during training. Don't worry about this for now as it will be discussed in detail later in this chapter. The validation dataset is a way of improving an ML model during training without giving it an unfair advantage when it is presented with unseen test data.

Each of the ML types is suited to a particular task and the type of data available. Choosing the right learning approach for the problem is a key stage in the successful development of an ML solution. Supervised learning is primarily used for two types of tasks which includes classification and regression. Figure 3.1 highlights each of the ML types and their associated uses.

© Springer Nature Switzerland AG 2022                                                      63
P. Fergus, C. Chalmers, *Applied Deep Learning*, Computational Intelligence
Methods and Applications, https://doi.org/10.1007/978-3-031-04420-5_3

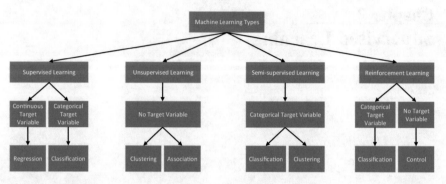

**Fig. 3.1** ML types

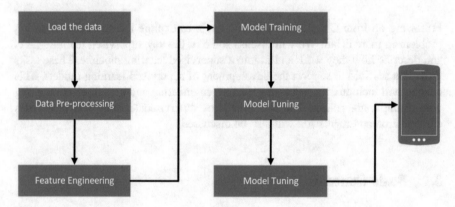

**Fig. 3.2** ML training pipeline

The remainder of this chapter will discuss the main supervised learning tasks that you will encounter when developing your ML models.

## 3.2   Supervised Learning Tasks

The supervised learning pipeline is typically broken down into six key steps as highlighted in Fig. 3.2. Before we begin there are several assumptions:

- There is a clearly defined problem to solve
- There is adequate data
- It makes sense to model the problem
- You can manage the lifecycle of the model (it is very rarely a success on the first attempt) and will require continuous improvement over time
- The assumption is that using simple models provide a baseline of reasonable performance

- You have the computational capacity to train and host the model
- You have the relevant domain expertise to validate the model

Assuming that the above assumptions are true the ML process adheres to the following steps data extraction, data pre-processing, feature engineering, model training, evaluation (iterative process) and deployment as shown in Fig. 3.2.

## 3.2.1   Data Extraction

As discussed in Chap. 2 data comes in several different forms which means that it is often stored in a variety of formats. Note you will need to engineer your dataset. Depending on the data format you will need to use tools to access the given data storage technology. For example, consider Fig. 3.3 the collective data you require might reside across multiple data storage technologies (excel, SQL and HDFS) which will require you to perform Extract Transform and Load (ETL) using different tools. You will have encountered this in the supporting material in the previous chapter where data is loaded into data frames using libraries such as Pandas.

The end goal of the data extraction phase is to load data into a compatible and structured object to facilitate the various data processing steps required before modelling. Figure 3.4 shows an example of the data extraction process using Pandas. Here the read_csv method is parsing a CSV file into Pandas DataFrame object (which you will be familiar with as it has a similar structure to excel e.g., rows and columns).

A single dataset is unlikely to contain all the information required to perform data analysis to model ML algorithms. You will often need to introduce data components from different sources to capture the full context of the given problem. Once you have a full understanding of the given problem it is a good idea to clearly define both the central question and measurable outcomes. This will give you an understating of what additional peripheral information is required. This structure will guide the development of your dataset and provide a framework to test your assumptions. The final data structure will be a composition of information from different data

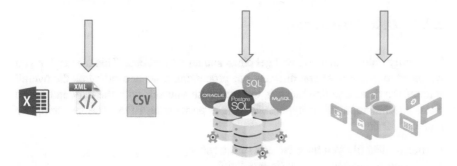

**Fig. 3.3**  Data storage technologies

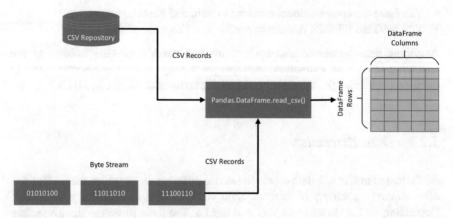

**Fig. 3.4** Reading a CSV into a Pandas DataFrame

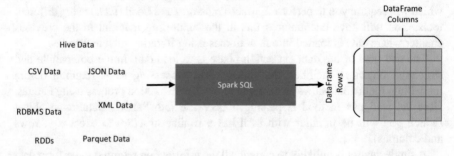

**Fig. 3.5** Different datasets for modelling

formats and structures. Typically, you would develop a data layer that provides an interface to the sources which results in a DataFrame for ML tasks. Figure 3.5 highlights a DataFrame which is constructed from a variety of different datasets using a data layer.

### 3.2.2   Data Preparation

It is highly unlikely that you will get clean and structured data. This means that you will need to perform several different pre-processing tasks depending on the overall state of the data. The first stage is to familiarise yourself with the data and not to make any assumptions or hypotheses before performing EDA. The key things to look out for are:

- Size of data (do you have enough or too much)
- Missing or incomplete data (interpolation)
- Textual data (not good for ML)

- The range of values (normalisation)
- Its distribution (depending on the task)
- Class balance
- Correlation between features

### 3.2.2.1   Data Size

The amount of data required for training an ML algorithm depends on a wide range of factors. Two key things to consider are the complexity of the problem and the complexity of the learning algorithm itself. If possible, it's a good idea to have a look at what other people have done and the results they attained in similar scenarios. A good set of recourses to find such material is Google Scholar, Arxiv and Kaggle.

Using domain expertise will provide you with an insight into the scale of data required to capture the complexity of the problem. The key point to remember is that we are trying to map a function based on input data to the output data. The mapping function is only as good as the data provided so it is important to ensure that there is enough data to map the relationship effectively. You will need to liaise closely with the domain expert to understand the problem and the scale of the data required to sufficiently capture and map the input-output relationships.

Furthermore, when considering data size, it is important to also consider the number of classes and observations. You must have enough observations to represent each of the classes that you wish to model. You will need to have enough features to sufficiently describe the class, however you need to ensure that the number of features does not exceed the number of observations this is known as the curse of dimensionality. When we have too many features, observations become harder to classify due to data sparsity (the closeness of data) which can lead to overfitting. Data sparsity occurs when we move to higher dimensions. Dimensionality and associated mitigations are discussed later in the chapter. Figure 3.6 highlights the effect of dimensionality. In the first image (low number of features) the distance between them is small while the sparsity between observations is less. As you increase the number of features the sparsity (the distance between observations

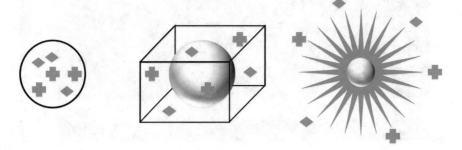

**Fig. 3.6** Dimensionality

increases) which makes it hard to cluster or classify the data (placing a decision boundary between classes).

Typically, non-linear algorithms require more data as they need more tuning than their linear counterparts. If a linear algorithm achieves good performance with hundreds of observations per class, you will more than likely need 10x that for non-linear algorithms. Both these approaches will be discussed in more detail later in the chapter.

Over time you will become more experienced in the different types of problems you encounter, and you will therefore be better equipped to estimate the amount of data you will require to solve a given problem.

### 3.2.2.2  Missing Data

The data collection process is far from perfect, and you are likely to see inconsistencies within the data, one of which is missing values. There are several potential reasons for this which include human error, incorrect sensor readings and bugs in software. Missing values in ML can be a significant problem and adversely affect the overall performance of your model. To solve the problem there are two primary methods which include imputation and removing data. Simply removing the missing data can significantly reduce the amount of data you have which arguably is something you do not want to do in ML. Figure 3.7 highlights the missing values in an example dataset. The white lines represent missing data (e.g., NAN's, NA, None, Null and ?).

The easiest method for addressing missing data is to simply drop the missing values. This would be fine when the proportion of missing values is relatively low (typically less than 10%). However, most of the time this technique will likely result in significant amounts of data loss. The missing values might reside within a single feature therefore you would not want to remove all of the other complete features. In

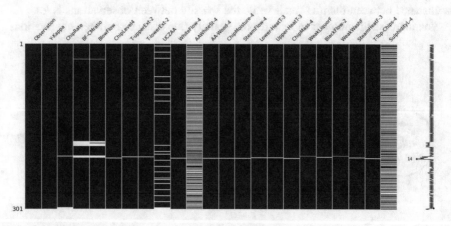

**Fig. 3.7** Missing data

this case, you might simply remove the poorly represented feature from the dataset. A common mistake is to also replace missing values with 0's. This would allow the model to run but would produce misleading results.

There are a variety of different imputation methods which replace the missing values with statistically derived values. For numeric NAN's you can use statistical replacement methods such as:

- **Mean, and Median:** this technique is easy to implement and typically works well with small numerical datasets. However, it does not consider the correlations between features (works only on the selected column). It cannot be used for encoded categorical features.
- **Most Frequent:** works by replacing missing data with the most frequent values within each column and works with categorical features (strings or numerical representations). However, it doesn't factor in the correlations between features and can introduce bias into the data.
- **Imputation Using K-Nearest Neighbour (K-NN):** which works by creating a mean impute of k selected neighbours. In this instance, k can be an application-specific covariant. It can be more accurate than using the mean and median of the whole feature as it is more localised. However, it's more computationally expensive and is sensitive to outliers in the data.

Similar approaches have been proposed using Linear Discriminant Analysis (LDA) and deep learning. For example, Datawig works with both categorical and non-numerical features and can be used on either a CPU or GPU during training. You will also see in this book the use of Generative Adversarial Models (GANs) that can learn to generate new data with the same statistics as the training data.

### 3.2.2.3   Textual Data

Many ML algorithms are not able to process textual data. They require all input and output variables to be numeric. Example categorical labels, such as a pet, cat and dog would need to be converted into numerical representations. Some algorithms such as decision trees can learn directly from categorical data with no transforms required. There are a variety of different methods you can choose to transform categorical data into number representations:

**Label Encoding (Integer Encoding)**   Label encoding converts each column within the DataFrame to a corresponding number value as shown in Fig. 3.8.

While label encoding is straightforward the numeric representations will increase based on the number of distinct categorical values within the DataFrame. For example, you had a dataset containing a variable sex with corresponding values

**Fig. 3.8**  Label encoding

- convertible -> 0

- hardtop -> 1

- hatchback -> 2

- sedan -> 3

- wagon -> 4

| Colour | | Red | Yellow | Green |
|--------|---|-----|--------|-------|
| Red    | | 1 | 0 | 0 |
| Red    | | 1 | 0 | 0 |
| Yellow | | 0 | 1 | 0 |
| Green  | | 0 | 0 | 1 |
| Yellow | | 0 | 1 | 0 |

**Fig. 3.9**  One hot encoding

male and female numbers 0 and 1 would be sufficient for label encoding. However, if you were converting a dataset containing car colours you could end up with 100's of values. Even 20 different colours would create a range of 0–19. If all other remaining features were between 0 and 1 this feature would pose a problem where algorithms are sensitive to scale.

One Hot Encoding

To overcome the issue where data ranges are large, we can utilise a technique called one-hot encoding. It works by converting each category value into a new column and assigning it a 1 or a 0-value representing (Ture/False). This means it overcomes the issues where models are sensitive to scale. However, the technique adds new columns to your dataset, therefore, increasing its dimensionality. Figure 3.9 high-lights the one-hot encoding process.

### 3.2.2.4   Value Ranges (Normalisation and Scaling)

Normalising and scaling data ensures that it is centred (I.e., a gaussian distribution) and within a standardised range (I.e., between 0 and 1). If features have largely different values, it can negatively affect algorithms that are sensitive to scale (exploits distances or similarities) such as SVM's, KNN's and ANN's. Example algorithms that are invariant to feature scaling include Naive Bayes and Decision Forests. Although these models are not sensitive to scale it is good practice to normalise/re-scale and standardise your data. Making sure that all your features are normalised or scaled ensures that each feature is equally weighted in its representation. There are two primary techniques to address this issue which are normalisation and scaling. Both approaches are similar however with scaling you are changing the range of your data while with normalisation you are changing the shape of the distribution.

Scaling

Scaling transforms your data so that it fits within a specific scale for example between 0–1. It is a useful tool when you are using methods that measure the distance between data points. Scaling does not alter the distribution of your data just the scale of the values contained within it as shown in Fig. 3.10.

One of the most common methods for scaling your data is MinMax. Here you transform the data such that the features are within a specific range e.g. [0, 1]. With scaling each feature is scaled individually rather than the whole dataset. In other words, the MinMax values are obtained from the individual feature, not across all features. As you can see in Fig. 3.10 scaling each feature individually retains the original distribution.

Normalisation

In scaling, you're changing the range of your data one feature at a time while in normalisation you're changing the range and the shape of the distribution of your data using all your features at once. In other words, you are taking the minimum and

**Fig. 3.10** Scaling effect

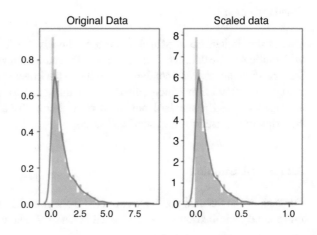

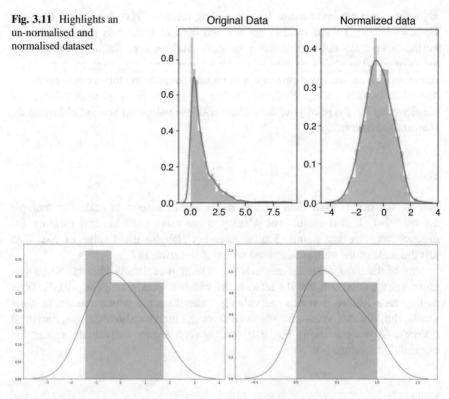

**Fig. 3.11** Highlights an
un-normalised and
normalised dataset

**Fig. 3.12** Standardisation on the left vs Min-Max normalisation on the right

maximum values from the full complement of features. Figure 3.11 shows a dataset
that has been scaled and normalised.

Standardisation

One of the limitations of MinMax normalisation is that it does not effectively deal
with outliers in the data set. This means that the maximum value is determined by the
larger outlier and causes a condensing effect on the lower value. Standardisation uses
Z-Score normalisation which converts all data points to a common scale with an
average of 0 and a standard deviation of 1. Figure 3.12 highlight the effects of
MinMax normalisations and standardisation.

### 3.2.2.5  Distribution

For each of the features you have extracted from your data you will need to plot and
understand their distribution as discussed in Chap. 2. Skewed data distributions will

be a common occurrence in your ML projects. As you will recall, skewed distributions represent the degree of distortion in your data from a normal distribution. If the values in your features are skewed, then they may violate model assumptions depending on the model or impair the interpretation of feature importance. The previous section focused on normalisation, and you will have seen references to techniques to transform your data into Gaussian distribution using box-cox and min-max normalisation. These methods were also discussed in detail in Chap. 2.

When developing your data preprocessing pipelines, it is therefore considered good practice to explore each of your features using EDA techniques and uniformly transform your features into a common range and gaussian distribution where possible. While not all algorithms will be sensitive to data distribution you are likely to evaluate models that are. Therefore, standardising your data preprocessing pipeline to include tasks to normally distribute data will prove valuable in your ML projects.

### 3.2.2.6 Class Balance

In ML many datasets that you use/create will have imbalanced classes (dependent variables). This describes a disproportionate ratio of observations in each class and poses a significant problem in ML. This is because ML algorithms will become more sensitive to the majority class as the algorithm has more examples to learn from. Examples where you might encounter class imbalance are widespread and will include medical diagnosis (e.g., patients that have tumours are more likely to be benign than malignant as shown in Fig. 3.13), spam filtering, and credit card fraud.

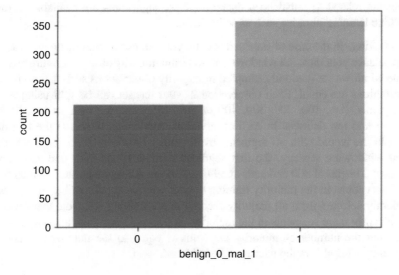

**Fig. 3.13** Class distributions for a given dataset

There are several different methods for addressing the class imbalance. A slight class imbalance does not usually require any attention where the ratio is around 4:6. A severe class imbalance is regarded as 1:100. Some real-world datasets can however have much larger class imbalances, I.e., 1:1000 or 1:5000, such as in credit card fraud. One of the most common metrics you will see for assessing model performance is accuracy. Accuracy is not a good indicator of performance where you have a class imbalance. This is because statistically, it has more of a chance of selecting the majority class rather than the minority one. Some of the common methods for addressing class imbalance are:

**Collect More Data**  If possible, it's always better to try and collect more data to supplement the minority class.

**Remove Majority Observations (Under-sampling)**  This approach is the easiest to do however you might be removing important or unique observations from your data. Data is often difficult to collect so simply discarding it in many instances is not an option.

**Oversample the Minority**  Generating synthetic samples by randomly sampling the attributes (features) of the observations contained in the minority class to generate new synthetic observations. There are a variety of different synthetic oversampling algorithms with the most common being the Synthetic Minority Over-sampling Technique (SMOTE) [1]. Using SMOTE the minority class (cases) is oversampled using each minority class record, to generate new synthetic records along line segments joining the k minority class nearest neighbours. This forces the decision region of the minority class to become more general and ensures that the classifier creates larger and less specific decision regions, rather than smaller specific ones. In [2] the authors indicated that this approach is an accepted technique for solving problems related to unbalanced datasets. These algorithms are available in most machine learning libraries such as scikit-learn.

**Windowing**  In the case of time series data, you can use a windowing approach to help balance your data. All windows derived from minority observations are retained while windows are randomly sampled in majority observations such that both class distributions are equal. Each observation in your dataset can be split using n-size data points, (i.e., 100, 200, 300, 400 or 500) [3]. First, the data set is split into training and test datasets. In each observation, windowing begins at the first data point in the record with no segments overlapping. For example, using a 300 data point windowing strategy, the first segment starts at 0 and ends and 299, while segment 2 begins at 300 and ends at 599, and so on. All segments are retained from all observations in the minority training dataset with an equal number of segments randomly selected from all majority records in the training set. Note there will be significantly more segments in the majority. We do not need them all, only enough such that the number of minority segments is equal to the number of majority segments—this allows the dataset to be balanced.

**Algorithm selection** Certain algorithms perform well on imbalanced data. So, if none of the above techniques are feasible you could try algorithms such as decision trees and random forests. If your problem is binary (two classes) and the minority is significantly lower than the majority, you could use anomaly detection by training the algorithm on the majority and reporting anything that's different.

**Penalisation** Penalised classification allows us to impose a cost on the model for making incorrect predictions on the minority class which essentially uses the model's performance as a hyperparameter that can be tuned over the learning process. Example algorithms include penalised-SVM and penalised-LDA.

### 3.2.2.7 Correlation Between Features

As we have previously discussed ML models are only as good as the data used to train them. As part of the data pre-processing stage, it is also important to select the features that contribute the most to the performance of the ML model. Often it is common for features to compete to describe the same thing. Therefore, an important step is to perform data and feature correlation analysis to detect competing features and select the appropriate one. Feature correlation describes the relationships that exist between your variables (features) and attributes (values) in your dataset. Some interesting insights from this analysis include a better understanding of attributes and the dependence on other attributes in the data. For example, height is likely correlated with weight (the taller you are the heavier you will be). Another insight might be the detection of multiple attributes and their association with other attributes. Some useful aspects of correlation analysis are being able to predict one attribute from another (this can help to impute missing values). Correlation can also highlight causal relationships between attributes. There are three types of correlation which include:

- **Positive correlation:** means that there is a direct relationship between features. For example, if the value of feature 1 increases, then so does feature 2. Likewise, if the value of feature 1 decreases so does feature 2.
- **Negative correlations:** with a negative correlation if the value for feature 1 increases, then the value for feature 2 decreases. Likewise, if the value for feature 1 decreases the value for feature 2 increases.
- **No correlations:** means that there is no relationship between the features.

The correlation between features is measured on a scale between 0 and 1. A value of 0 would indicate no correlation whereas a value between 0.5 and 0.7 would describe a slight highly positive correlation between features. Therefore, a value of 0.9 or 1 would indicate a strong or perfect positive correlation. As you would expect negative values would represent negative correlations along the same scale. Figure 3.14 highlights a correlation matrix between features using a heatmap (colour intensity) and associated values to visually capture the correlation of features in a DataFrame.

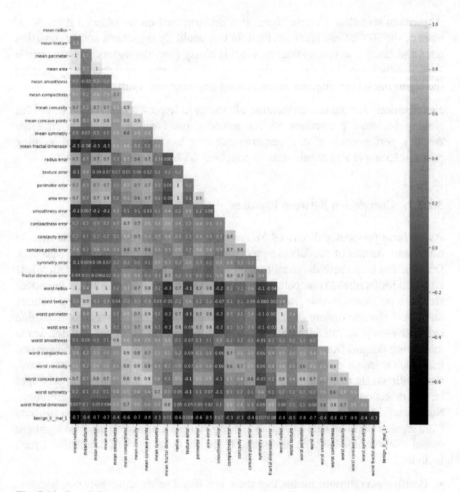

**Fig. 3.14** Correlation matrix

Perfectly positive or negative features can impact the performance of a model this is known as multicollinearity. Some ML algorithms, such as linear regression, are sensitive to this while other algorithms such as decision trees are not. Multicollinearity essentially means that the features are all competing to describe the same thing. For example, if one person is singing a song in an audition you would be able to decide if the singer is good or not. However, if you audition five people at the same time all singing at once it's much harder to decide which of the singers is the best. To solve this problem, you would have to audition each singer in turn and score them independently. This would allow you to determine and retain the best singer. Similarly, you would undertake a similar task where multicollinearity is present and remove competing variables. There are other methods such as Principal Component Analysis (PCA) which transforms the data to achieve the same result. These techniques will be covered later in the chapter.

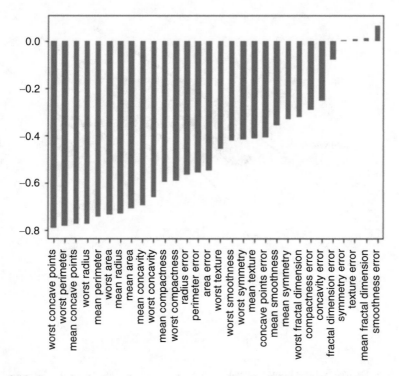

**Fig. 3.15**  Correlation between features and corresponding classes

In addition to checking the correlation between features is it also useful to check the correlation of each feature in relation to the class. Figure 3.15 highlights the correlation between each feature and the corresponding class.

As shown in Fig. 3.15, more positive features have a higher correlation with the target class. Conversely, features with negative values have less of a correlation with associated classes. You would aim to train your model using features that show a strong correlation to the class.

### 3.2.3  Feature Engineering

Feature engineering enables you to get the most out of your data and in many instances improves the overall performance of your model. The features in your data will influence your ML models and the result that you can attain. In the case of tabular data, your columns will already represent features such as age, sex and height. However other data formats such as time series (ECG) signals and images are comprised of raw data and at this stage, no features have been extracted. For example, in ECG data counting the amplitudes over a given threshold for 60 seconds would provide a new feature called beats per minute. In the case of images, you

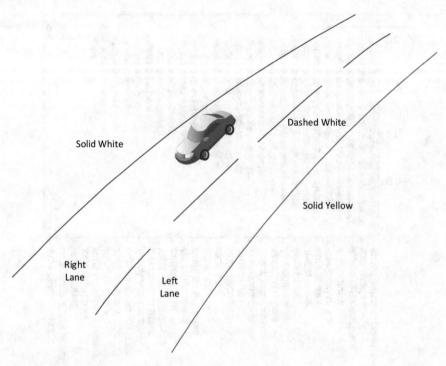

**Fig. 3.16** Derived features from an image

could use a set of derived features (these would have to be calculated in a similar way to beats per minute) within an image to describe a scene (I.e., road or street). For example, as shown in Fig. 3.16 using the features left lane, right lane and solid yellow you could infer that the scene is of a road. As you can see from this example, we don't need a full image and all its features, just a subset to predict what the scene is. This is the key benefit of feature engineering where you don't need all the original data just the derived features which can then be used to make predictions on new images.

Following the feature engineering task, it may result in many features—you will not need all of these to describe a particular data component and many of the features may even be redundant or useless. Therefore, the trick is to find the optimal set of features to uniquely describe each of the classes within your dataset. There are two primary techniques for achieving this which are feature selection and dimensionality reduction as shown in Fig. 3.17.

Feature engineering typically provides more flexibility and allows you to utilise less complex models that run faster and are easier to understand and maintain. This is an important aspect of ML deployment where complex computational models are often expensive and difficult to manage.

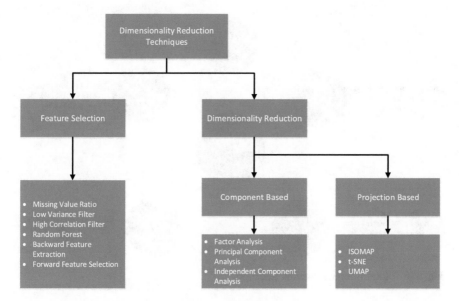

**Fig. 3.17** Feature selection and dimensionality reduction

### 3.2.3.1  Feature Selection

Not all features have the same discriminative capabilities therefore feature selection techniques are needed to automatically select a subset of features that best describes the target class. There are several different techniques available which utilise a scoring mechanism to rank and choose features based on their predictive power. Some methods use metrics such as correlation to determine the best features while other methods use a subset of features using a trial-and-error approach (modelling subsets of features and measuring the classification performance to ascertain the best feature combination). Some algorithms automatically perform feature selection as part of the training process for example stepwise regression. Some of the most common feature selection processes you are likely to find are described in Fig. 3.18.

There are several different feature selection techniques which include univariate filter methods (F-Score, Chi-2 Square and mutual information), Multivariate filter methods (minimum redundancy maximum relevance), Wrapper Methods (forward selection/backwards selection), Embedded Methods (L1 Regularisation), and Feature importance in tree base models (Random Forest, XGBoost, and SHapley Additive exPlanations SHAP).

### 3.2.3.2  Dimensionality Reduction

In the previous section, we talked about the scores and selection of pre-existing features. This section however focuses on transforming existing features into a

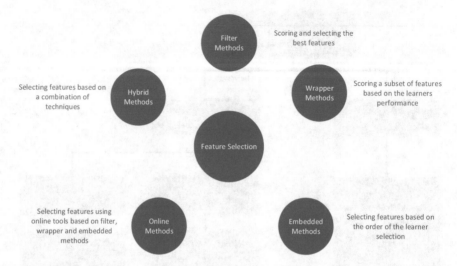

**Fig. 3.18** Different feature selection techniques

**Fig. 3.19** PCA plot

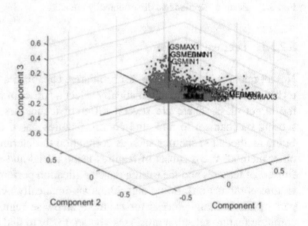

subset of new features which captures most of the variance contained within the data. One of the most common techniques for performing dimensionality reduction is PCA [4]. PCA works by creating uncorrelated variables that collectively maximise the variance within a dataset. These variables are known as the principal components which are used to train the model. Figure 3.19 highlights PCA undertaken on a dataset. Here you can see the three principal components mapped in a 3D space. It is clear to see that component 1 captures most of the variance while component 2 capturing slightly less with component 3 capturing the least. Note that in this technique once the original features are transformed, they are no longer used for training the model. It is the principal components that become the new features in model training.

Both feature selection and dimensionality reduction help to combat the previously discussed curse of dimensionality which are efficient ways of reducing the number of features (dimensions) in your observations. These strategies are none competing, and you would likely evaluate multiple techniques to determine which approach produces the best results.

This is a manual process that is often time-consuming and requires input from experts within the domain you are trying to model. Later in this book, we will walk you through automatic feature engineering and selection in the topics on DL which will demonstrate how this process can significantly reduce time and produce more accurate ML models.

### 3.2.4   Selecting a Training Algorithm

When selecting the correct training algorithm there are seven key considerations:

**Type of Problem** Machine learning algorithms are designed to solve a specific problem. For example, classification, regression, clustering or anomaly detection. If you want to classify labelled categorical data, you will use a classification algorithm such as logistic regression or an SVM. An example classification problem is the titanic dataset where we are trying to classify who lived and who died. If you would like to categorise unlabelled data, you would use a clustering algorithm such as K-Means. For example, in Chap. 2 we discussed how household appliances can be clustered together based on their electrical usage properties. If you want to predict a quantity, you will use a regression algorithm such as linear regression (not to be confused with logistic regression which is a binary classifier and is discussed later in this section). An example regression problem is trying to predict the value of a property based on the number of rooms the property has. For anomaly detection, we would use an algorithm such as z-score anomaly detection to identify observations that reside outside of well-defined clusters. For example, again looking at appliance usage you can detect when appliances are being used at abnormal times of the day.

**Size of Dataset** The size of your dataset will greatly influence the type of algorithm you can use. That said there is no golden rule to the amount of data required to train an ML model. However, some ML algorithms cope better where there is less available data. For example, an image classification task can require tens of thousands of images. Regression tasks require many more observations than features ($10\times$ as much) while NLP can require 1000's of examples due to a large number of words and complex phrases. Some algorithms such as neural networks can be extremely data-hungry while other algorithms such as a random forest can produce reasonably good results with limited amounts of data. The process of finding the correct model based on the size of available data is an empirical one.

**Accuracy** The required model performance is largely application-specific and based on the recommendation of the domain expert. For example, the correct classification of a cancer diagnosis would arguably need to be very accurate. However, counting the number of cars entering a city centre for traffic control might not need to be as accurate. There is a trade-off between more computationally expensive models, the amount of data needed, and the required accuracy. The rule of thumb is to decide on the performance requirement and start with simpler algorithms and slowly introduce more complex algorithms until the requirement is met.

**Training Time** Using more complex models and a higher data size will introduce longer training times. This will also be dependent on the type of hardware available not just for training but also for inferencing. In later chapters, you will see how training times can be significantly reduced by using the GPU.

**Linearity** Some algorithms make assumptions about the data. For example, linear regression and logistic regression make use of linearity to learn. While they are simple and relatively fast to train, data may not be linear or linearly separable. As a result, different algorithms such as a decision forest will improve model performance. Most ML practitioners start with linear algorithms. If the desired results are not obtained more complex or non-linear algorithms are considered.

**Number of Parameters** Most ML algorithms have several different parameters which tend to increase with model complexity. Algorithms with many parameters typically provide more flexibility however it often requires trial and error to ascertain the optimal configuration. There is often a correlation between model flexibility and the time taken to train models. However, it is often worth spending the time to configure these parameters as they often yield better performance.

**Number of Features** Having many features (as is common with textual and genetic data) runs the risk of overfitting the model. The idea is to train a model with a minimal number of features that sufficiently describe each of the classes in your model and produce the required performance. Note that adding more features will not necessarily improve the performance of a model. The only time you would consider adding more features is if the required performance has not been met and the additional features are statistically significant. If adding more features does improve the model performance to the desired level, you may need to consider a different algorithm. Figure 3.20 highlights some of the common decision points which will help you in choosing your algorithms for the given problem.

## 3.3  Supervised Algorithms

There are a wide variety of different supervised learning algorithms each suited to a particular task and corresponding data characteristics. They are split into four distinct categories which include linear regression, non-linear regression, linear classification and non-linear classification. Some of the more common algorithms you will come across are shown in Fig. 3.21.

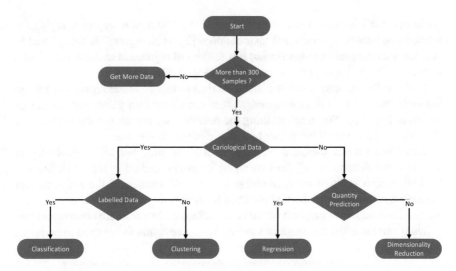

**Fig. 3.20** Training decisions point for selecting an appropriate ML algorithm

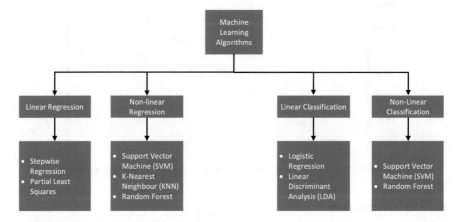

**Fig. 3.21** Different supervised learning algorithms

In this section, we are going to take you through the most common supervised learning algorithms across all four categories. Note some of these algorithms below can straddle multiple categories as shown in Fig. 3.21 depending on the algorithm's parameter configuration.

## 3.3.1 Linear Regression

Linear regression is used to make predictions on real values such as the cost of a house or the number of likely infections. Linear Regression is used in many fields for predictive analytics and was first conceived in the 1800s as a way of studying the relationship between parents and their children [5]. With regression, things tend to drift towards the mean or average and it is the aim of regression to draw a line that's as close to every dot as possible as shown in Fig. 3.22.

Real-world data contains more than two data points so linear regression tries to minimise the vertical distance (variance) between all the data points and our line as shown in Fig. 3.23. So, in determining the best line, we are attempting to minimise the distance between all the points and their distance to our line.

There are several different methods to achieve this, but all methods try to minimise the distance of all data points. A common method is the Least Squares Method, which is fitted by minimising the sum of squares of the residuals (for example a residual is r2 which is obtained by subtracting y2 from y2 hat). In other words, the residual for an observation is the difference between the observation (the y-value) and the fitted line as shown in Fig. 3.24. The residuals are used to derive an

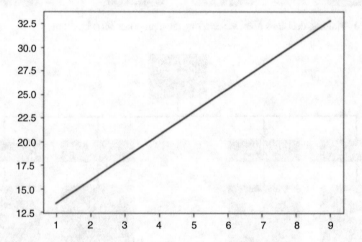

**Fig. 3.22** Regression line

**Fig. 3.23** Linear regression

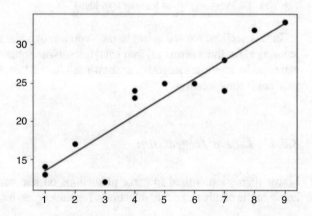

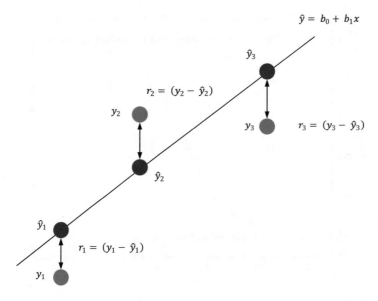

**Fig. 3.24** Least mean squares for minimising the residuals

optimal line through observations such that all residuals are minimised as much as possible. If you were to look at this visually the line in Fig. 3.24 would be constantly moving until the optimum residual value is achieved for each data point. You can now see why outliers in linear regression pose a big problem when fitting the line to the data points.

### 3.3.2 Logistic Regression

As discussed earlier logistic regression is not to be confused with linear regression. Logistic regression is a classifier that is used to estimate the dependant variable (class) based on a set of independent variables (features) [6]. It works by predicting the probability that an event will occur by fitting data to a logit function (this is the S shape shown in Fig. 3.25). This means that if we were trying to predict the gender using a single feature, height, we would calculate the likelihood of that value being either male or female.

The probability of a given output sits between 0 and 1. The threshold for logistic regression is set at 0.5. If the likelihood of seeing a given value is higher than 0.5 it is assigned to 1. In contrast, if the likelihood of seeing a given value is less than 0.5 is assigned to 0. When training a logistic regression model, the shape of the s function changes around the 0.5 threshold. In other words, the tails on either side of the threshold are either stretched or shrunk depending on the variables in each class. The

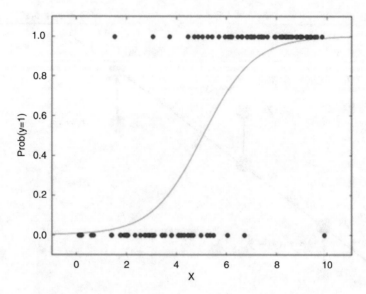

**Fig. 3.25** Logit function in logistic regression

curve with the maximum likelihood is selected (several different shaped curves are produced during training to find the maximum likelihood).

### 3.3.3   Linear Discriminate Analysis

Linear Discriminant Analysis (LDA) is a generalisation of Fisher Linear Discriminant Analysis (FLDA) which uses a linear combination of features to find the direction along which the two classes are best separated [7]. Data is projected onto a line in such a way that it maximises the distance between the means of the two classes while minimizing the variance within each class. Classification is performed in this one-dimensional space. FLDA and its decision boundary is shown in Fig. 3.26. In the left side of the image, the decision boundary has significant overlap between the two classes. FLDA addresses this by moving the decision boundary along the axis to reduce the overlap of the two classes as shown in the right side of the image. FLDA is a good technique to identify linearity in your data. If your data is linearly separable you may consider FLDA as it is simple to implement and less computationally expensive to run. If there is no linearity you will have to consider more complex models which we will see later in this book.

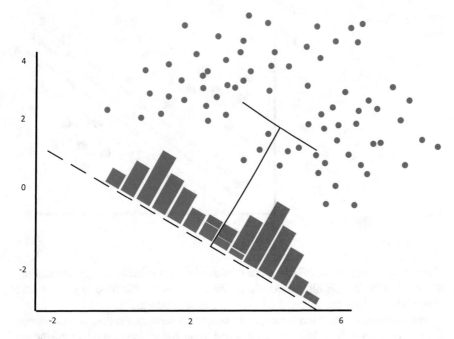

**Fig. 3.26** FLDA decision boundaries

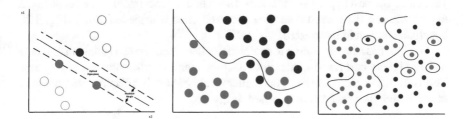

**Fig. 3.27** SVM decision boundaries (linear, quadratic and polynomial)

### 3.3.4   Support Vector Machine

Support Vector Machines (SVMs) try to separate two or more classes using an optimal hyperplane [8]. They work on either binary or multiclass problems by using a one vs all approach. The hyperplane can be altered from linear, quadratic or polynomial shapes by altering the kernel of the algorithm as shown in Fig. 3.27. While altering the kernel can improve class separation, complex hyperplanes can lead to overfitting. If your data exhibits linearity the image on the left would best describe the optimal hyperplane required. If your data is none linear you would be better using the hyperplane described in the middle image as opposed to the far-right which can lead to overfitting. Ideally, you want your hyperplane to be pliable like a

**Fig. 3.28** Optimal
hyperplane

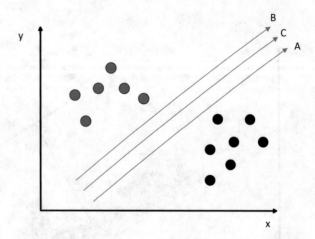

piece of bamboo as opposed to a piece of string to appropriately manage overfitting. SVMs work well with high dimensional data and can be effective in cases where several dimensions are greater than the number of samples.

Hyperplanes are decision boundaries that help to separate the data points belonging to a particular class. Data points that reside on either side of the hyperplane are then attributed to different classes. SVMS allow you to fit multiple hyperplanes to your data. The best hyperplane is selected such that the maximum value between the hyperplane and the nearest data point for each class is achieved. So, in Fig. 3.28 hyperplane C would be selected.

An SVM has a handy feature to deal with outliers. Here we can simply instruct the SVM to ignore outliers so it does not affect the margin in the optimum hyperplane. This is shown in Fig. 3.29 where the outlier would ordinarily affect the calculation of the optimal hyperplane but in this case, is ignored.

### 3.3.5   Random Forest

Random forests are a supervised learning algorithm that can be used for both binary and multiclass problems as well as regression [9]. Random forests are based on the construction of several predefined decision trees. In classification, the output is the mode of the classes and for regression, it is the mean prediction of the individual trees. Today the random forest algorithm is based on bagging and a random selection of features to construct a collection of decision trees with controlled variance. Each tree in the forest outputs a class prediction and the class with the most votes becomes the model's prediction as shown in Fig. 3.30.

Each tree is constructed of a set of nodes, edges and leaves as shown in Fig. 3.31. Nodes split for the value of a certain attribute while edges are the outcome of a split to the next node.

**Fig. 3.29** SVM outlier

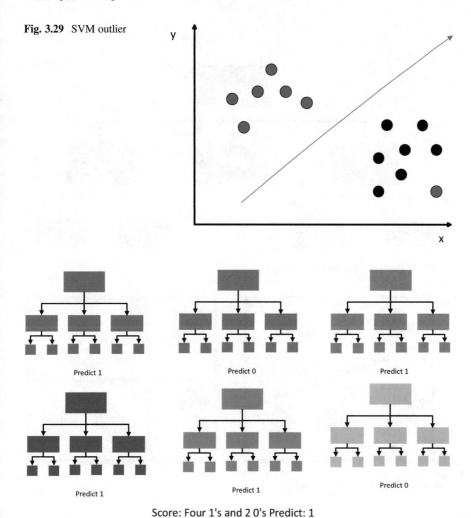

Score: Four 1's and 2 0's Predict: 1

**Fig. 3.30** Random forest with voting

There are cases where it is impossible to achieve a 0-error using a linear model. However, by using a decision tree we can achieve a 0 error by adding more splits (axis-aligned portioning) but can lead to extreme overfitting as shown in Fig. 3.32. However, because trees are axis-aligned, they cannot easily model diagonal boundaries. With more data points the splitting can become more complicated.

A decision forest can be configured using several different parameters which include the following:

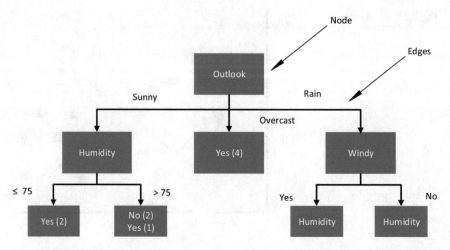

**Fig. 3.31** Decision trees nodes and edges

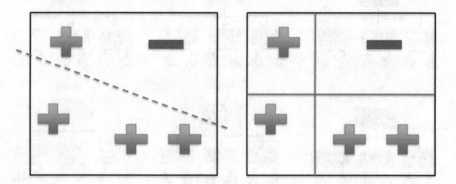

**Fig. 3.32** Axis aligned partitioning

- **Maximum depth of the decision trees:** limits the maximum depth of any decision tree within the forest. Increasing the depth of the tree might increase precision, at the risk of some overfitting and increased training time.
- **Number of random splits per node:** is used when building each node of the tree. A split means that features in each level of the tree (node) are randomly divided.
- **Minimum number of samples per leaf node:** is the minimum number of cases that are required to create any terminal node (leaf) in a tree.

Getting the optimal configuration for a random forest is an empirical one however we suggest starting with the following configuration depth of trees 32, number of trees 8, number of random splits 128.

### 3.3.6   Naive Bayes

A Naive Bayes classifier is a probabilistic machine learning algorithm that works on the principles of Bayes theorem [10]. Bayes theorem allows you to find the probability of something occurring based on something that has historically occurred. For example, we could determine the probability of someone paying back a loan based on whether they have successfully paid back a loan in the past. Figure 3.33 shows the probability of a Naïve Bayes classifier.

Navies Bayes makes certain assumptions regarding the data. Firstly, one feature does not affect another (Naïve) secondly each feature has an equal effect on the outcome. There are three types of Navies Bayes classifier which includes:

- **Multinomial Naive Bayes:** works by determining the frequency of a given feature value. For example, how many times the word male comes up in the titanic data associated with survived or died.
- **Bernoulli Naive Bayes:** is similar to multinomial naive Bayes but in this scenario, the features are a Boolean value (true/false). Here Boolean values are used to predict the class. For example, concluding that a customer was unhappy based on a Twitter post containing the word "rubbish".
- **Gaussian Naive Bayes:** uses features with a continuous value (non-discrete) to predict the class. The algorithm assumes a Gaussian distribution—for example predicting someone income based on their age.

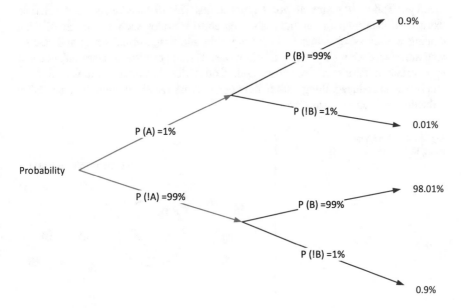

**Fig. 3.33**  Probability calculations using a Naïve Bayes classifier

### 3.3.7   K-Nearest Neighbours

k-nearest neighbours (KNN) algorithm is one of the simplest algorithms and is easy
to implement. KNN is a supervised machine learning algorithm that can be used to
solve both classification and regression problems [11]. With KNN there is no need to
build a model, tune parameters or make any assumptions. The entire dataset is loaded
into memory and new observations are plotted to determine the distance using
Euclidean distances calculation. A prediction is made by averaging the labels of
the KNN to the observation. For regression, the k number of observations closest to
the new observation are averaged. In classification, the mode is used to determine the
class. Figure 3.34 shows a classification of a new observation ($k = 1$) using KNN.

## 3.4   Summary

In this chapter, we introduced the basics of supervised learning and its application
within the ML paradigm. Supervised learning is used to determine an observation
based on a predefined set of labelled features used to describe it. Depending on what
you are trying to predict or classify you can use either regression (predicting a
continuous value) or classification (classifying a discrete value or class). The chapter
introduced and discussed the supervised learning pipeline which the authors recom-
mend you follow in your real-world applications. This included a discussion on data
extraction, data preparation and associated considerations such as the size of data,
dealing with missing values and data types. In addition, normalisation and scaling
was introduced along with data distributions. The importance of class balance and
appropriate mitigations were discussed. Correlation between features and class
labels was introduced along with feature engineering which covered dimensionality
reduction and feature selection.

**Fig. 3.34** Classification
using KNN

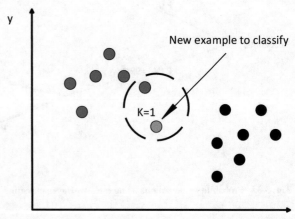

The chapter also discussed how to select an appropriate training algorithm before a discussion on some of the most common supervised algorithms you will encounter was provided. These included linear regression, logistic regression, linear discriminant analysis, support vector machine, random forest and decision trees, naïve Bayes and k nearest neighbours.

The following chapter will discuss supervised learnings counterpart un-supervised learning. This will include clustering, principal component analysis and association rule mining.

# References

1. N. V. Chawla, K. W. Bowyer, L. O. Hall, and W. P. Kegelmeyer, "SMOTE: Synthetic Minority Over-sampling Technique," *J. Artif. Intell. Res.*, vol. 16, pp. 321–357, 2002.
2. J. Bennett, S. Lanning, and others, "The netflix prize," in *Proceedings of KDD cup and workshop*, 2007, vol. 2007, p. 35.
3. P. Fergus, C. Chalmers, C. C. Montanez, D. Reilly, P. Lisboa, and B. Pineles, "Modelling segmented cardiotocography time-series signals using one-dimensional convolutional neural networks for the early detection of abnormal birth outcomes," *IEEE Trans. Emerg. Top. Comput. Intell.*, 2020.
4. K. Pearson, "LIII. On lines and planes of closest fit to systems of points in space," *London, Edinburgh, Dublin Philos. Mag. J. Sci.*, vol. 2, no. 11, pp. 559–572, 1901.
5. F. Galton, "Kinship and correlation," *North Am. Rev.*, vol. 150, no. 401, pp. 419–431, 1890.
6. D. W. Hosmer Jr, S. Lemeshow, and R. X. Sturdivant, *Applied logistic regression*, vol. 398. John Wiley \& Sons, 2013.
7. R. A. Fisher, "The statistical utilization of multiple measurements," *Ann. Eugen.*, vol. 8, no. 4, pp. 376–386, 1938.
8. C. Cortes and V. Vapnik, "Support vector machine," *Mach. Learn.*, vol. 20, no. 3, pp. 273–297, 1995.
9. L. Breiman, "Random Forests," *Mach. Learn.*, vol. 45, no. 1, pp. 5–32, 2001.
10. T. Bayes, "LII. An essay towards solving a problem in the doctrine of chances. By the late Rev. Mr. Bayes, FRS communicated by Mr. Price, in a letter to John Canton, AMFR S," *Philos. Trans. R. Soc. London*, no. 53, pp. 370–418, 1763.
11. E. Fix and J. L. Hodges, "Discriminatory analysis. Nonparametric discrimination: Consistency properties," *Int. Stat. Rev. Int. Stat.*, vol. 57, no. 3, pp. 238–247, 1989.

# Chapter 4
# Un-Supervised Learning

Following on from Chap. 3 where we discussed supervised learning, we will now begin to explore an alternative approach called unsupervised learning. The supervised learning aspect of the previous approach is reliant on labelled data to train a model. In unsupervised learning, the algorithms are designed to look for patterns within a dataset with no predetermined labels. There are two primary types of unsupervised learning which includes cluster analysis and principal components. Additionally, in this chapter, we will provide an overview of association rule mining which allows us to understand the relationships between clusters.

## 4.1 Basic Concepts

With unsupervised learning, the class label (dependent variable) is not known. Unsupervised learning problems can be further grouped into clustering and association problems. Instead, the features (independent variables) are used to find similarities between observations as shown in Fig. 4.1.

The emergent property of an unsupervised learning approach is the creation of one or more clusters as shown in Fig. 4.2. A clustering problem is where you want to discover the inherent groupings in the data, such as grouping customers by purchasing behaviour. It is up to the domain expert to interoperate what each cluster means and what they represent. This can be a useful technique to help decide what the labels should be to facilitate a supervised learning approach. You can think of it as an attempt to create labels.

In clustering, it can be difficult to evaluate the groups or clusters for correctness. A large part of unsupervised learning is being able to interpret the assigned clusters which often requires domain knowledge. As an ML practitioner, you will need to decide what each of the groups represent. Sometimes this is easy, sometimes it is difficult. Also depending on the clustering algorithm, it may be up to you to decide beforehand how many clusters you expect to create. This type of ML is beneficial as

© Springer Nature Switzerland AG 2022
P. Fergus, C. Chalmers, *Applied Deep Learning*, Computational Intelligence Methods and Applications, https://doi.org/10.1007/978-3-031-04420-5_4

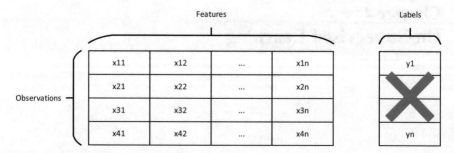

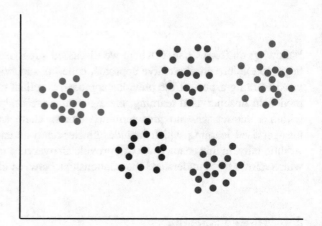

**Fig. 4.1** Unsupervised learning approach

**Fig. 4.2** Clustering

annotating large datasets is both time-consuming and expensive. There may also be
cases where the number of classes is not apparent. You may also want to use
clustering to help you understand the structure of your data, in particular knowing
whether your data is linearly separable. Unsupervised learning is a useful tool for
achieving many of these objectives which you will encounter and likely use to solve
your ML problems.

As previously discussed in supervised learning many of the steps defined in the
ML pipeline are applicable in unsupervised learning. These will include data collection, pre-processing and feature engineering. If you are unfamiliar with these
concepts, please refer to Chap. 3 for full details before exploring the different
unsupervised learning approaches below.

## 4.2 Clustering

### *4.2.1 Hierarchical Clustering*

Hierarchical clustering is one of the most popular techniques in ML [1]. In Hierarchical Clustering, we begin by assigning each data point to a unique cluster. As shown in Fig. 4.3 we have four data points and four clusters.

The next step is to iterate and merge the closest pair of clusters to create a new cluster. This iterative process continues until we have one single cluster as shown in Fig. 4.4 that contains all the observations in our dataset. To use an analogy, you can imagine that this is like a taxonomy of animals, where the light blue cluster is the most general and the dark blue cluster the more specific species. For example, light blue could represent all mammals and the dark blue cluster represents a specific species of dog, such as a German Shepperd.

**Fig. 4.3** Starting clusters

**Fig. 4.4** Amalgamation into a single cluster

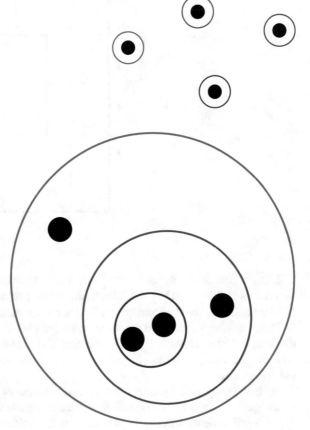

**Fig. 4.5** Proximity matrix

| ID | 1 | 2 | 3 | 4 | 5 |
|----|---|---|----|----|----|
| 1 | 0 | 3 | 18 | 10 | 25 |
| 2 | 3 | 0 | 21 | 13 | 28 |
| 3 | 18 | 21 | 0 | 8 | 7 |
| 4 | 10 | 13 | 8 | 0 | 15 |
| 5 | 25 | 28 | 7 | 15 | 0 |

**Fig. 4.6** Dendrogram for
cluster groupings

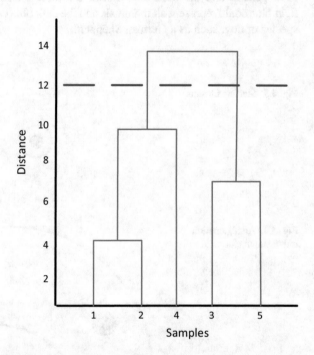

Hierarchical clustering uses a proximity matrix to determine the distance between two clusters as shown in Fig. 4.5. This figure shows that we have clusters 1,2,3,4 and 5. The values on the diagonal are all 0 as a cluster against itself will always be a 0. The remaining values describe the distance between all clusters. For example, the distance between clusters 1 and 2 is 3 and this represents a closer relationship whereas the value between clusters 1 and 5 is much larger therefore the clusters are further apart.

By using the proximity matrix and the derived clusters you will need to generate a dendrogram. A dendrogram is used to record the sequence of merges as illustrated in Fig. 4.6 and to define thresholds or cutoffs to determine the number of clusters you would like to consider and as represented by the horizontal dashed line. The threshold would be an application-specific requirement. For example, in the case of tumour analysis, you would expect the threshold to be lower to include as many clusters as possible (different tumour types). This would allow you to analyse the specifics of individual clusters and the prognosis outcomes if you were interested in determining optimal treatments. If your threshold was too high you would have fewer clusters (fewer tumours) therefore the analysis would be more general and in the case of tumours generalised treatments may lead to adverse outcomes.

The hierarchical clustering algorithm undertakes the following steps to assign clusters:

- **Step 1:** assign each data point to a cluster as shown in Fig. 4.3
- **Step 2:** merge the data point using the proximity matrix method shown in Fig. 4.5 by calculating the distances between clusters as shown in Fig. 4.4.
- **Step 3:** repeat step two until there is a single remaining cluster I.e., the light blue cluster shown in Fig. 4.4.
- **Step 4:** create a Dendrogram to record the sequences of mergers as shown in 4.6.
- **Step 5:** define a threshold to determine the number of clusters as represented by the horizontal dashed line in Fig. 4.6 for which there are two clusters. Moving the threshold lower would increase the number of clusters depending on your data.

This type of clustering is an agglomerative version of hierarchical clustering. However, other approaches work oppositely (by starting from a single cluster and iterating through to individual clusters). This is known as divisive hierarchical clustering.

## 4.2.2   K-Means

K-Means Clustering is an unsupervised learning algorithm that will attempt to group similar clusters in your dataset [2]. Typical clustering problems include clustering similar documents, clustering customers based on features, market segmentation, and identifying similar physical groups. K-Means works in the following way:

- **Step 1:** Set the number of desired clusters "K". Randomly assign each point to a cluster as shown in Fig. 4.7.
- **Step 2:** Calculate the distance of all the observations in relation to all the cluster centroids and assign it to the cluster that has the shortest distance as shown in Fig. 4.8.
- Once every datapoint in the dataset has been calculated you will end up with the clusters shown in Fig. 4.9.
- **Step 3:** For each cluster, compute the cluster centroid by taking the mean vector of points in the cluster as shown in Fig. 4.10.
- Repeat steps 2 and 3 until each of the clusters stop changing.

**Fig. 4.7** Random
assignment of clusters

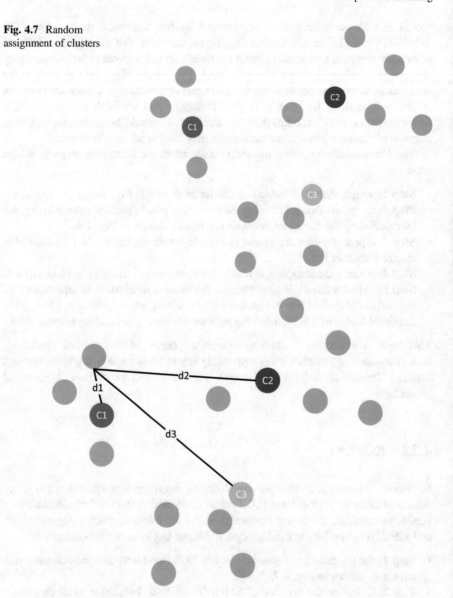

**Fig. 4.8** Distance calculation

The K-Means algorithm is widely used because; it is easy to use, scales well to large
datasets, and has good generalisation characteristics. You can use K-Means in the
initial stages of the ML projects to gain a robust understanding of your data.

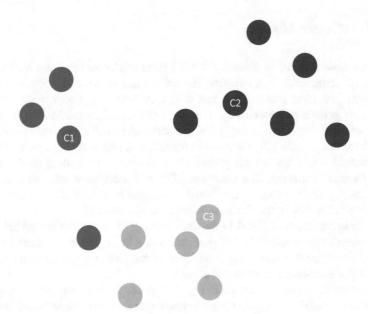

**Fig. 4.9**   Initial clusters

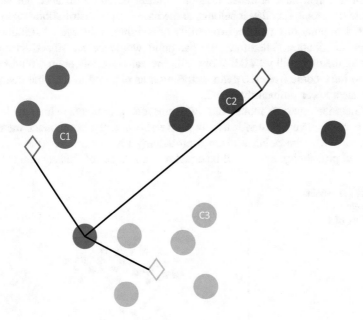

**Fig. 4.10**   Mean vector

### 4.2.3  Mixture Models

In the previous section, we discussed the K-Means clustering algorithm which works well at grouping datapoints together. However, there are several limitations to this approach. The most important is that it utilises hard assignment when grouping datapoints as discussed previously. Therefore, Gaussian Mixture Models have been proposed as an alternative as they provide a soft assignment approach [3]. Instead of using hard assignment and when we are uncertain in which cluster a particular data point should reside, we can use probability to determine the correct cluster assignment for our data point. The Gaussian Mixture Model approach can extend the K-Means algorithm and utilise the clusters generated by K-Means as a starting point for data point tuning in the Gaussian Mixture model method.

For example, consider Fig. 4.11 the probability of the data point circled belonging to the blue cluster would be 1. The probability of it belonging to the green and cyan clusters would be 0, respectively. Therefore, in this case, we can conclude that the blue cluster datapoint assignment is correct.

However, the circled data point in Fig. 4.12 is not so clear. We can conclude that the probability of the circled data point belonging to the green cluster would be 0 as it does not reside anywhere near that cluster. The K-Means algorithm using hard assignment might have assigned it to blue cluster based on distance but when we calculate the probability that it belongs to the blue or cyan distribution you may find that the data point has a higher probability of residing in the cyan distribution than the blue distribution. Therefore, the datapoint would be reassigned to the cyan cluster as the probability of 0.8 shows that the value for this point would be more likely to have come from the cyan distribution as opposed to the blue distribution which has a lower probability of 0.2.

A Gaussian mixture model has two tuneable parameters which include the mixture component (cluster/distribution) weight, and the component means and variances. Each data point is given a probability for each cluster (the number of individual probability values will be equal to the number of clusters defined by the

**Fig. 4.11** Datapoint assignment with a probability of 1

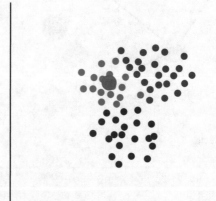

**Fig. 4.12**  Value with an
associated probability

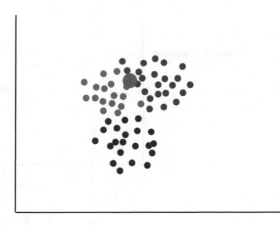

user) which defines its membership. All probabilities for a given data point must total 1, as shown in Fig. 4.12 where there are three clusters and three probability values. The common way of using the Gaussian mixture model is to use K-Means to first define the initial clusters. In this instance, the clusters are not learned, I.e., the component means and variances. If the component weights are not learned (K-Means has been used) the probability x was generated by a particular cluster will be equal to the proportion of the probabilities assigned across all clusters. If they are learned (the clusters are not predefined by another algorithm such as K-Mean) the mean and the variance for each cluster are initialised based on your data.

With K-Means you select several K components (where K-Means has been used the number of K-components weights will be used instead). Where K-Means has not been used to initialise the model it is typical to guess the number of components and try to fit the model using the Expectation Maximisation (EM) algorithm. It may be necessary to set a number of different values for K to determine the best trade-off between fit and the number of components (ideally you should aim for simpler models with fewer components). When training the model, it utilises the EM algorithm to estimate the mixture models parameter. Models are typically trained by using maximum likelihood estimation techniques, which seek to maximise the probability, or likelihood, of the observed data given the model parameters as shown in Fig. 4.13 below.

EM is an iterative algorithm and has the convenient property that the maximum likelihood of the data strictly increases with each subsequent iteration. This means it is guaranteed to achieve a local maximum.

The EM algorithm undertakes the following steps:

- **Step 1:** Initialise the model parameters based on values derived from the data
- **Step 2:** Iterate over the expectation and maximisation steps until the model parameters converge

The first step calculates the components cluster probability, the mean and variance parameters. The second step maximises the expectations calculated in step one. The

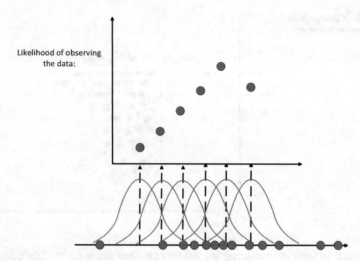

**Fig. 4.13** Likelihood of observing the data

entire iterative process repeats until the algorithm converges, giving a maximum likelihood estimate. Thus, by alternating between which values are assumed fixed, or known, maximum likelihood estimates, or the non-fixed values can be calculated efficiently as shown in Fig. 4.14.

Once the EM model has been run to completion, the fitted model can be used to perform various forms of inference. The two most common forms of inference done on GMMs are density estimation and clustering as can be seen in Fig. 4.14.

### 4.2.4  DBSCAN

Density-based spatial clustering of applications with noise (DBSCAN) is used to find clusters where they are arbitrary shaped or contain outliers [4]. The essential rule is that if a data point is close to many other datapoints then it belongs to that cluster. The two key parameters are eps which specifies the distance between two data points. If the distance is equal to or less than the eps datapoints are neighbours. The second parameter minPts is the minimum number of datapoints required to be considered a cluster. Based on the above results a data point can be one of the following:

- **Core point:** A point is considered a core point if the number of points surrounding it (including itself) is at least equal to minPts. Note that these points must also reside within a radius of eps.
- **Border point:** A point is considered a border point if it is reachable from a core point and the number of surrounding points is less than minPts.

**Fig. 4.14** EM algorithm convergence

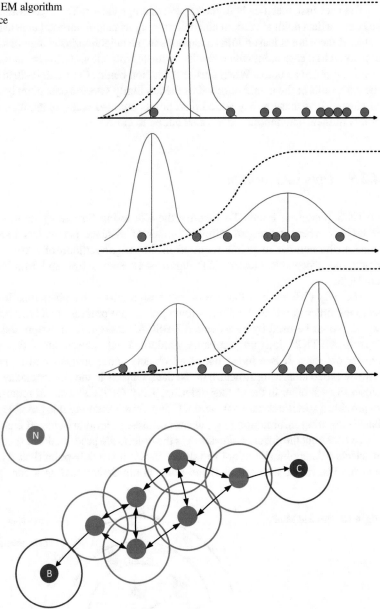

**Fig. 4.15** Core points and outliers

- **Outlier:** A point is an outlier if it is not a core point and not reachable from any core points.

Figure 4.15 shows the different types of points and outliers.

The user first specifies both the minPts and eps values. The algorithm begins by selecting a data point at random and determining its neighbourhood area using its eps value. If there are at least minPts datapoints in the neighbourhood then that datapoint is marked as a core point which results in cluster formation. If this is not the case the point is marked as noise. When cluster formation begins (let's call it cluster 1) all of the datapoints in the neighbourhood of the randomly selected data point become part of cluster 1. If these newly added data points are also core points, then all of the points in their neighbourhood are also added to cluster 1.

### 4.2.5 Optics Algorithm

OPTICS (Ordering Points To Identify the Clustering Structure) algorithm is like DBSCAN where it uses an infinite number of distance parameters like eps and minPts (the number of points required in the neighbourhood of a core object) to determine acceptable clusters [5]. Figure 4.16 shows Eps and MinPts used in OPTICS.

The only difference is that we do not assign cluster memberships. Instead, we store the order in which the objects (data points) are processed and the information which would be used by an extended DBSCAN algorithm to assign cluster membership. OPTICS does not explicitly produce a data cluster but rather outputs a cluster ordering. It is a linear list of all objects under analysis and represents the density-based clustering structure of the data. Objects in the denser cluster are listed closer to each other in the cluster ordering. Thus, OPTICS does not require the user to provide a specific density threshold. Using cluster ordering it is possible to extract basic clustering information (e.g., cluster centres, or arbitrary-shaped clusters).

To construct the different clustering's the objects are processed in a specific order. It selects a datapoint at random and determines if it is a core point (based on the eps and minPts values and rules). If the point is not determined as a core point this

**Fig. 4.16** Eps and MinPts

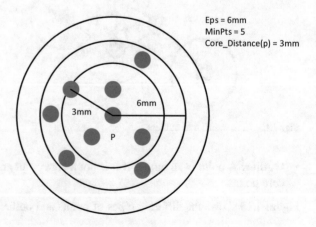

Eps = 6mm
MinPts = 5
Core_Distance(p) = 3mm

6mm

3mm

P

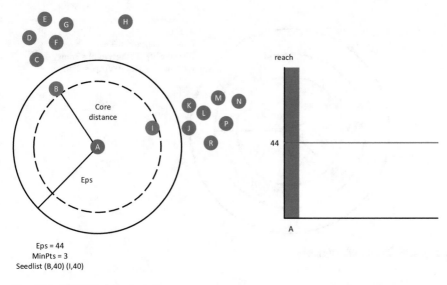

Eps = 44
MinPts = 3
Seedlist (B,40) (I,40)

**Fig. 4.17**  OPTICS eps and minPt

process is repeated until a core point is found. This order selects an object that is density-reachable concerning the lowest eps value so that clusters with a higher density (lower eps) will be finished first (this is based on core distances). When all points within eps have been processed then the next closest point to all the points that have already been processed is selected (based on the reachability distance). Figure 4.17 provides an example of the reachability distance and shows the seedlist being literately created.

Based on this idea two important pieces of additional information are required: Core distance (the distance between the core point and the points within the eps) and Reachability Distance (the ordered linear distances of all the points in the dataset) as shown in Fig. 4.18. The core distance takes precedence until all points in the core have been processed. When this happens the next closest value in the reachability table is selected.

It computes an ordering of all objects in a given database and it stores the core-distance and a suitable reachability-distance for each object in the database. OPTICS maintains a list called OrderSeeds to generate the output ordering. Objects in OrderSeeds are stored by the reachability-distance from their respective closest core objects, that is, by the smallest reachability-distance of each object as shown in Fig. 4.19. The algorithm iterates over the OrderSeeds and processes each object until OrderSeeds is empty.

Using the Seedlist values and the Reachability distance values it is possible to plot clusters and define the numbers of clusters required using epsilon value as shown in Fig. 4.20.

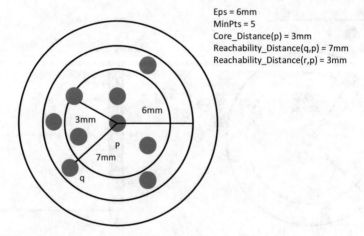

**Fig. 4.18** Reachability distance

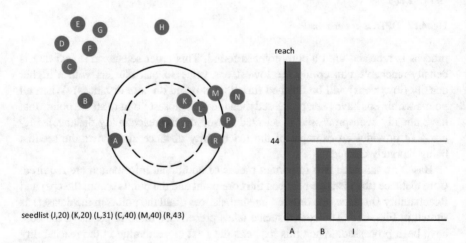

**Fig. 4.19** Seedlist

## 4.3 Principal Component Analysis

Principle Component Analysis (PCA) is a technique for reducing the dimensionality of data [6]. As we have already discussed high dimensional data can be problematic for some learning algorithms particularly where the number of features outnumbers the number of observations. PCA tries to extract features by projecting a high dimensional space into a lower-dimensional subspace. PCA aims to try and retain the part of the data which provides the most amount of variance while trying to remove features with lower variance. As previously discussed, dimensions are simply features within your dataset. At an abstract level, you take a dataset having

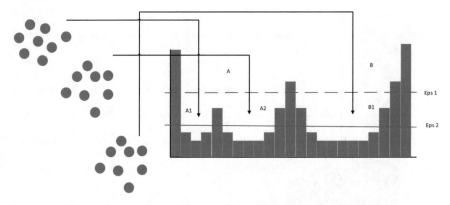

**Fig. 4.20**  Using Seedlist, reachability distance and cutoffs to define clusters

many features, and you simplify that dataset by transforming them into a lower number of Principal Components.

The most important aspect of PCA is the principal components that represent the most important aspects of your data. When the data is projected into a lower dimension from a higher-dimensional space the emerging principal components hold the most variance (information) in your data.

It uses an orthogonal transformation that converts a set of observations (which may have correlated variables) into a set of uncorrelated linear variables called principles components. The steps involved in PCA include:

- Standardise the dataset (normalisation). In a previous chapter, we have already discussed how a dataset can be standardised using a number of normalisation techniques.
- Calculate the covariance matrix for the features in the dataset. The covariance matrix accounts for variability in the dataset which is a way of summarising how much information we have in the data. The diagonal elements in the covariance matrix represent the variability of each variable in the dataset. While the off-diagonal elements describe how variables are correlated with each other. The challenge is to transform our original variables so that they contain as much information (account for as much variability) as possible. PCA performs such orthogonal transformations to convert the data into a set of new uncorrelated variables called principal components.
- Calculate the eigenvalues and eigenvectors for the covariance matrix. Eigenvectors and eigenvalues are the linear algebra concepts that we need to compute from the covariance matrix to determine the principal components of the data.
- Sort eigenvalues and their corresponding eigenvectors. The first principal component has the largest possible variance which means that the first component accounts for the most variability in the data. Each succeeding component has the highest variance possible under the condition that it is orthogonal to the preceding components.

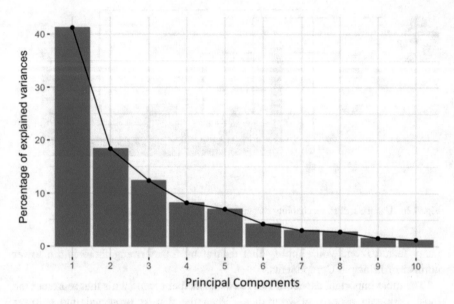

**Fig. 4.21** Ordered eigenvalues

- Pick k eigenvalues and form a matrix of eigenvectors. The general rule of thumb is to select the number of principal components that capture roughly 80% of the variance.
- Transform the original matrix. This transformation now becomes your new dataset.

Figure 4.21 shows ordered eigenvalues and their corresponding eigenvectors (principal components). As you can see the first principal component captures most of the variance in the data with subsequent components capturing the rest.

To account for 100% of the variability, you will usually need the same number of components as the original number of variables. But usually with a much smaller number of new components, we can explain almost 80% of the variability which is generally regarded as sufficient for most tasks. Thus, PCA helps us to reduce our focus from a possibly larger number of variables to a relatively small number of new components, while preserving most of the information from the data.

## 4.4   Association Rule Mining

Association Rule Mining is another example of an unsupervised learning technique that aims to uncover rules from observations and features within a dataset [7]. An association rule learning problem is where you want to discover rules that describe large portions of your data, such as people that buy X also tend to buy Y. Association rules are implemented to reveal relevant associations between features (for example

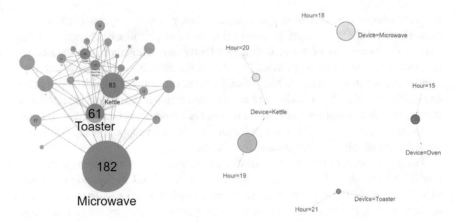

**Fig. 4.22** Association rules for device usage

**Table 4.1** Appliances

| Transaction ID | Appliances used |
|---|---|
| 1 | Kettle, toaster, microwave |
| 2 | Kettle, toaster |
| 3 | Kettle, oven, washing machine |
| 4 | Kettle, toaster, microwave |
| 5 | Kettle, toaster |

a set of features to describe an observation). If features frequently appear together, there is an underlying relationship between them as shown in Fig. 4.22. In this figure, we can use association rules to determine the correlation between appliances and the hour of the day.

Exploring the intrinsic relationships in the data is performed using Frequent Pattern Mining (FPM). This technique extracts all frequent itemsets from a dataset, which are then used to generate association rules. Using association rule mining, frequently occurring features are identified as items (itemsets) in different individual transactions as shown in Table 4.1. In other words, observations are transactions, features are items, and feature combinations are itemsets. Single features tend to have small effect sizes on observations. Therefore, by looking at the joint effect of multiple features, explanatory power can be increased. Typically, ARM assumes a common strategy for decomposing mining problems into two principal subtasks: (1) Frequent itemset generation and, (2) rule generation. Itemsets are sets of k-items where k starts with 1 to infinity. Unnecessary itemset candidates are produced if at least one of its subsets is infrequent. Hence, the frequent itemset generation is equipped with pruning steps to eliminate k itemset candidates based on a minimum support threshold. Support is the number of transactions that contain a particular itemset. Frequent itemsets are independent sets of features (itemsets) whose support is greater than or equal to a given minimum support threshold. Itemsets whose support count is lower than the minimum are removed. This strategy, based on support measures, is termed support-based pruning. Once frequent itemsets have been obtained the generation of association rules is performed. Association rule mining discovers sets of features that frequently occur together in a dataset and creates a relationship between those features in the form $X \rightarrow Y$. This relationship implies that when X occurs it is likely that Y also occurs. Such a relationship is called an association rule. The confidence of an association rule is the ratio of the number of transactions that contain A and B to the number of transactions that contain A. Given a set of transactions T, ARM searches for all the rules with support $\geq$ and confidence $\geq$ minimum support and confidence thresholds.

The significance of the association rules is measured in terms of their support and confidence although other interest measures such as lift, or Chi-Square can be used to validate rules. The support of a rule is the probability that a sample in a dataset contains both X and Y. Rules with very low support may occur by chance, therefore, support is an important measure that can be used to eliminate unimportant rules. Confidence of a rule, on the other hand, is the probability that a case contains Y given that it contains X. The generation of association rules is conducted using the Apriori algorithm [7]. The Apriori algorithm performs a breadth-first search (BFS), enumerating every single frequent itemset by iteratively generating candidate itemsets. Candidate itemsets of length k are generated from k-1 itemsets. The support of every candidate itemset is calculated iteratively where itemsets with support values under a defined threshold are disregarded. To manage the very large number of discovered association rules, the patterns are filtered, grouped and organised. This is a crucial step that highlights the most interesting association rules. Nearly all search algorithms rely on support-based pruning. It is also possible to add additional objective interest measures to each rule.

## 4.5  Summary

In this chapter, we introduced the basics of unsupervised learning and its application within the ML paradigm. We discussed how unsupervised learning does not rely on the presence of a class (dependant variable) to learn. Unsupervised learning allows us to use a variety of different algorithms to identify data structure and relationships while facilitating the reduction of dimensionality. In this chapter, we also discussed clustering which can be categorised as either hierarchical or density-based algorithms. These are sometimes used as an exploratory technique before the commencement of a supervised learning approach to identify unknown classes in your data.

This chapter introduced a variety of algorithms which included hierarchical clustering, K-Means, Mixture models, DBSCAN and OPTICS. The chapter also focused on Principal Component Analysis and its use in dimensionality reduction. Finally, the chapter was concluded with a discussion on association rule mining which is an unsupervised learning technique to analyse patterns and discover rules in data.

# References

1. S. C. Johnson, "Hierarchical clustering schemes," *Psychometrika*, vol. 32, no. 3, pp. 241–254, 1967.
2. E. W. Forgy, "Cluster analysis of multivariate data: efficiency versus interpretability of classifications," *Biometrics*, vol. 21, pp. 768–769, 1965.
3. D. A. Reynolds, "Gaussian mixture models.," *Encycl. biometrics*, vol. 741, pp. 659–663, 2009.
4. M. Ester, H.-P. Kriegel, J. Sander, X. Xu, and others, "A density-based algorithm for discovering clusters in large spatial databases with noise.," in *kdd*, 1996, vol. 96, no. 34, pp. 226–231.
5. H.-P. Kriegel, P. Kröger, J. Sander, and A. Zimek, "Density-based clustering," *Wiley Interdiscip. Rev. Data Min. Knowl. Discov.*, vol. 1, no. 3, pp. 231–240, 2011.
6. K. Pearson, "LIII. On lines and planes of closest fit to systems of points in space," *London, Edinburgh, Dublin Philos. Mag. J. Sci.*, vol. 2, no. 11, pp. 559–572, 1901.
7. R. Agrawal, T. Imieliński, and A. Swami, "Mining association rules between sets of items in large databases," in *Proceedings of the 1993 ACM SIGMOD international conference on Management of data*, 1993, pp. 207–216.

# Chapter 5
# Performance Evaluation Metrics

In the previous chapters, we introduced the concept of training a model either through a supervised or unsupervised learning approach. Evaluating a model's performance is a fundamental stage in the ML pipeline. It provides us with the opportunity to determine the optimal hyperparameters for the model and an indication of how the trained model will perform in production using unseen data. There are a variety of different evaluation techniques which can be used depending on the method and the type of problem you are trying to solve. These evaluation metrics will be split into distinct categories, one for supervised learning and one for unsupervised learning.

## 5.1 Introduction to Model Evaluation

Model evaluation is an essential part of training an ML model. Based on the data you have it is important to establish how well your model fits that data. Therefore, a fundamental skill that you will need to develop is how to use effective evaluation techniques to determine how well your models perform. There are many different tools and techniques to perform model evaluation however using them incorrectly can give you a false impression of how well your model is performing [1]. This is a common mistake that is often seen in both academic and industrial literature. It is important to report the performance of the model using all necessary evaluation metrics. Your customers will often use the results from a trained model to make important business decisions. Incorrectly evaluating the performance of a model will therefore have a detrimental effect on you and all stakeholders that utilise it.

© Springer Nature Switzerland AG 2022
P. Fergus, C. Chalmers, *Applied Deep Learning*, Computational Intelligence
Methods and Applications, https://doi.org/10.1007/978-3-031-04420-5_5

### 5.1.1  Evaluation Challenges

There are an increasing number of different algorithms and frameworks which can be confusing to the practitioner when determining the best strategy. In the case of more established algorithms, we could argue that there is a set of standard evaluation metrics. However, these algorithms are often adapted, and other evaluation metrics are proposed to improve on existing techniques. This is primarily where a lot of the confusion arises. The general rule of thumb is to develop evaluation strategies around algorithms that are well established. This is a good starting point. Depending on the problem domain and the acquired results alternative and more experimental approaches may be required. Yet it is important to note, ML evaluation must be easily reproducible. Choosing an appropriate metric (or set of metrics) is challenging when using imbalanced data.

Although not related to this section, a less obvious factor in evaluating model performance, is the hardware that underpins it. Different hardware configurations will lead to different sets of results. For example, software libraries utilise certain hardware features and different data sizes which can be utilised in a training cycle. This topic will be discussed in more detail in a later chapter.

### 5.1.2  Taxonomy of Classifier Evaluation Metrics

Depending on the model that you are developing there will be a set of common evaluation metrics used to evaluate its performance as shown in Fig. 5.1. These are typically split into supervised and un-supervised categories. However, other variations do exist for specialised forms of learning which are centred around cutting-edge research. We will visit some of these later in the book when we introduce and discuss DL. The methods shown in Fig. 5.1 act as a useful reference point when deciding what methods to use. Each of these methods will be discussed in detail throughout this chapter.

## 5.2  Classification Accuracy

Accuracy is a performance metric for evaluating classification models and is the fraction of predictions the model got right. Accuracy is defined as:

$$\text{Accuracy} = \frac{\text{Number of correct predictions}}{\text{Total number of predictions}}$$

Accuracy is often used to measure the performance of an ML algorithm and is one of the most common metrics that you will encounter. However, while accuracy is easy

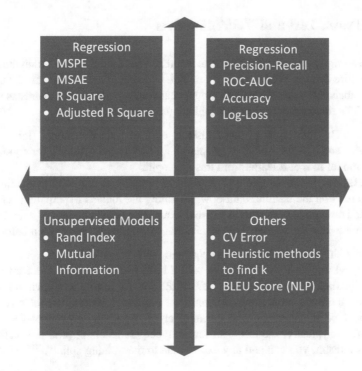

**Fig. 5.1** Evaluation techniques

to understand it does have drawbacks especially when you have an imbalanced dataset. In this instance, the ML algorithm will be biased towards the majority class given that there are more observations to learn from. Suppose only 3% of a population has a disease with the disease being 1 for positive and not having the disease being 0 for negative. We could create a model that always predicts 0 and it would be 97% accurate—would you consider this to be a good model? No, the model accuracy is linked to the number of observations in the majority class and not the performance of the model itself. For example, a model that always predicted 1 would be only 3% accurate. Again, this is because accuracy is linked to the number of correct observations and not necessarily the performance of the model. This is something to watch out for where people report a model's performance based on only the accuracy alone (unless you know that the dataset is balanced). You should always report a model's performance using additional metrics to gain a clear and better understanding of how your model will perform in different test conditions. Some will argue that is a sufficient metric if the dataset is balanced. While this is an acceptable approach is it good practive to include other metrics to verify the model's performance [2]. These additional metrics will be discussed below.

## 5.3  Train, Test and Validation Sets

The most important thing you can do to evaluate your model is to not train the model on the entire dataset. When training a model, you should not use the test data. If the test-set labels influence the learned model in any way, performance estimates will be biased. The three primary data sets include the following:

- **Train:** The train split of the dataset is used to train the model (for example weights and bias for ANNS, hyperplanes for SVMs and residuals for regression). The model sees and learns from this data split.
- **Validation:** is the sample of data used to provide an unbiased evaluation of a models fit on the training dataset while tuning the models hyperparameters.
- **Test:** The sample of data used to provide an unbiased evaluation of a final model fit on the training dataset. This is data that the model has never seen before.

Figure 5.2 shows the different data splits and the segregated test set.

A typical train/test/validation split would be to use 60% of the data for training, 20% of the data for validation, and 20% of the data for testing as shown in Fig. 5.3. However, there are other configurations you can use depending on the size of the data, the type of algorithm and the number of hyperparameters that need to be configured. Typically, models with fewer hyperparameters require less validation data. As a result, you can add any excess data to the training split.

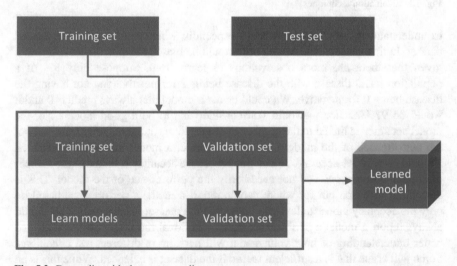

**Fig. 5.2**  Data splits with the corresponding test set

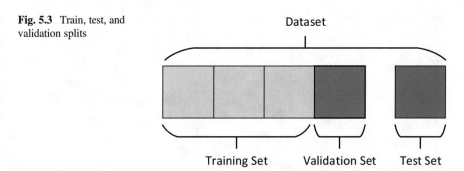

**Fig. 5.3** Train, test, and validation splits

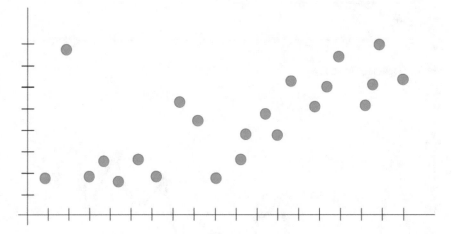

**Fig. 5.4** Sample dataset

## 5.4    Underfitting and Overfitting

ML has one fundamental goal and that is to generalise well to unseen data. This is the model's ability to produce sensible outputs given a set of inputs it has never seen before. The performance of the model and the service it will provide in production will rely on good generalisation of the model.

The performance of a model can be significantly impacted when it is either overfitted or underfitted during the training process. This means that knowing how well your model generalises will depend on how close the model is to overfitting or underfitting. The goal is to produce models that neither underfit nor overfit [3].

If we consider the following data in Fig. 5.4:

Using Linear Regression, we want our model to fit a line similar to the one shown in Fig. 5.5:

The line above is fitted to the data well and could provide good predictions for new unseen inputs. During the training process, several iterations are run using the

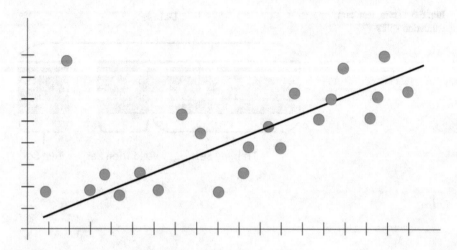

**Fig. 5.5** Optimally fitted line

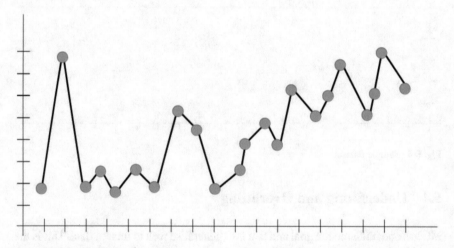

**Fig. 5.6** Overfitted line

dataset to minimise the error. Increasing the iterations will produce a minimal overall cost. However, training the model significantly longer than needed will fit the line into all the points (including noise), catching secondary patterns that may not be needed for the generalisability of the model. Considering our example again, an overfitted model would look something like the plot shown in Fig. 5.6.

An algorithm like Linear Regression aims to capture the dominant trend and fit our line within that trend. In the figure above, the algorithm captured all trends—but not the dominant one. If we want to test the model on inputs that are beyond the line limits we have (i.e., generalise), what would that line look like? There is no way to tell. Therefore, the outputs are not reliable. The more we leave the model training the

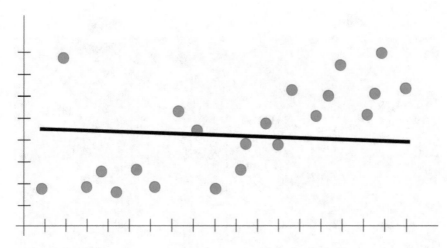

**Fig. 5.7**  Underfitted line

higher the chance of overfitting occurring. We always want to find the trend, not fit the line to all the data points. Overfitting leads to more bad than good. What use is a model that has learned very well from the training data but still cannot make reliable predictions for new inputs?

We want the model to learn from the training data, but we do not want it to learn too much (i.e., too many patterns). One solution could be to stop the training earlier. However, this could lead the model to not learn enough patterns from the training data, and not capture the dominant trend. This is called underfitting as shown in Fig. 5.7.

Underfitting is when the model has "not learned enough" from the training data, resulting in low generalisation and unreliable predictions. As you expected, underfitting (i.e., high bias) is just as bad for the generalisation of the model as overfitting. In high bias, the model might not have enough flexibility in terms of line fitting, resulting in a simplistic line that does not generalise well.

## 5.5   Supervised Learning Evaluation Metrics

When performing classification predictions, there are four types of outcomes that can occur:

- **True positives** are when you predict that an observation belongs to a class and it does belong to that class.
- **True negatives** are when you predict that an observation does not belong to a class and it does not belong to that class.
- **False positives** occur when you predict that an observation belongs to a class when it does not.

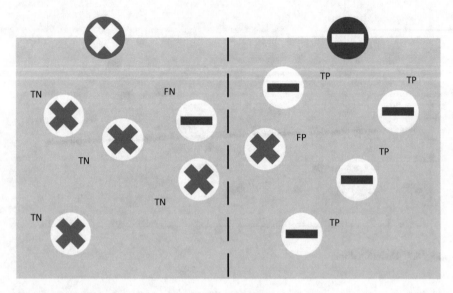

**Fig. 5.8**  TP, TN, FP, FN with the corresponding threshold

- **False negatives** occur when you predict that an observation does not belong to a class when in fact it does

Figure 5.8 shows the results for a given set of observations that have been run through our predictive model. The red x values represent one class while the green minus signs represent an alternative class. All the x values between 0 and 0.5 are true negatives while all the green minus values between 0.5 and 1 are true positives. You will notice that there are two misclassifications with one of the x values being misclassified as a positive when it is a negative (so a false positive) and one positive value being misclassified as a negative value when it is positive (false negative). You will notice that there is a threshold value of 0.5 which is configurable based on the application and your requirements.

### 5.5.1   Confusion Matrix

A confusion matrix works by plotting the predicted and actual values. The class labels are correlated with the number of classes in the dataset and the values in the grid represent the classification results over a set of experiments. A confusion matrix can be used for both binary and multiclass classification problems. The confusion matrix allows us to calculate the performance metrics for the classifier [4]. Figure 5.9 shows a typical confusion matrix for a binary classification problem. The predicted class labels are shown in the first column of the grid while the actual (expected values) are shown in the first row. The values in the white cells show the actual results obtained from our trained model using the test data. The diagonal set of

**Fig. 5.9** Confusion matrix

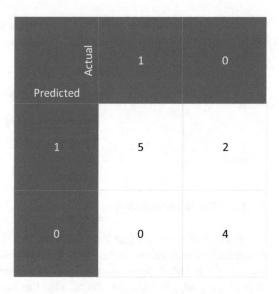

numbers represents expected correct classifications while numbers on either side of the diagonal represent either a false positive or a false negative. As you can see the model correctly predicted nine correct results however 2 were incorrectly classified as a 0 label instead of 1 label.

### 5.5.1.1  Accuracy

To calculate the accuracy from a confusion matrix you can use the following calculations:

$$\text{Accuracy} = (TP + TN)/(TP + FP + TN + FN)$$
$$\text{Accuracy} = (5 + 4)/(5 + 2 + 4 + 0)$$
$$\text{Accuracy} = (9)/(11)$$
$$\text{Accuracy} = 0.82$$

### 5.5.1.2  Precision

A more useful metric tells us the fraction of cases classified as positive that are positive. In the example, in Fig. 5.9 we were expecting the model to classify 7 observations as class 1 (the 1 and 0 class could represent anything I.e., male and female or cancer/not cancer). However, in this instance, the model incorrectly classified two observations as class 0. This means that the model is less effective at predicting positive cases. This is called Precision.

$$Precision = TP/(TP + FP)$$
$$Precision = 5/(5 + 2)$$
$$Precision = 5/(7)$$
$$Precision = 0.71$$

### 5.5.1.3  Recall (Sensitivity)

The fraction of examples that were predicted to belong to a class concerning all the examples that truly belong in the class. A model that produces no false negatives has a recall of 1.0. Following on from the previous example the model is 100% effective at predicting negative classes. Recall also has another name: True Positive Rate (TPR) or sensitivity.

$$Recall = TP/(TP + FN)$$
$$Recall = 5/(5 + 0)$$
$$Recall = 5/(5)$$
$$Recall = 1.00$$

### 5.5.1.4  Specificity

Specificity is the metric that evaluates a model's ability to predict the true negatives of each available category. These metrics apply to any categorical model.

$$Specificity = TN/(TN + FP)$$
$$Specificity = 4/(4 + 2)$$
$$Specificity = 0.66$$

### 5.5.1.5  False Positive Rate

The False Positive Rate (FPR) is the number of observations that are incorrectly classified as positive when they are negative.

$$(FPR) = FP/(FP + TN)$$
$$FPR = 2/(2 + 4)$$
$$FPR = 2/(6)$$
$$FPR = 0.33$$

#### 5.5.1.6  F1-Score

The F-Score, also called the F1-Score or F measure is a measure of a test's accuracy. The F-Score is defined as the weighted harmonic mean of the test's precision and recall.

$$F1 - Score = 2^* \, (precision^* \, recall)/(precision + recall)$$
$$F1 - Score = 2^* \, (0.71^* \, 1.0)/(0.71 + 1.0)$$
$$F1 - Score = 0.83$$

### 5.5.2  *Receiver Operating Characteristic*

A Receiver Operating Characteristic (ROC) curve allows us to plot the TPR and FPR for every threshold (the default is usually set at 0.5) [5]. An excellent model has an Area Under Curve (AUC) of one while a poor model has an AUC of 0. An AUC of

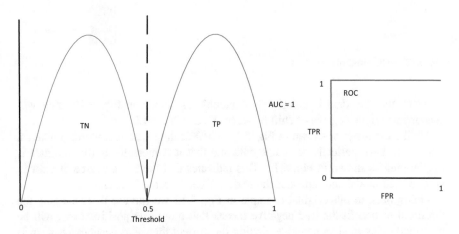

**Fig. 5.10**  AUC of 1

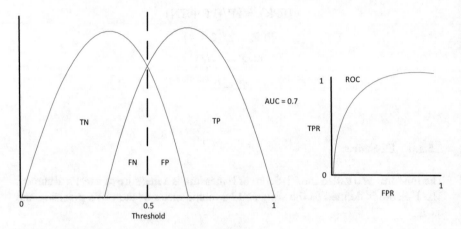

**Fig. 5.11** Overlapping data

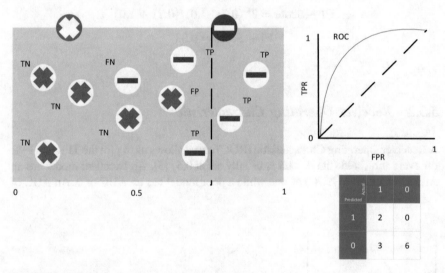

**Fig. 5.12** ROC threshold

1 means that the data is completely separable as shown in Fig. 5.10. You will encounter various degrees of shift between AUC values of 0 and 1.

Unlike the diagram shown in Fig. 5.10 when dealing with real-world problems, it's rare to have perfectly separable data and that it is more likely that the data is overlapping as shown in Fig. 5.11. This indicates that there is a degree of error in your trained model and indicates the trade-off between the TPR and FPR.

Going back to our original example in Fig. 5.12 we can see that changing the threshold to benefit the true negative means that more true positive cases will be incorrectly classified as negative. Setting the correct threshold depends on what is more important which is often guided by domain knowledge. The diagonal line on the ROC curve represents chance so if you see the curve hug the diagonal the model performance is low.

### 5.5.3 Regression Metrics

For regression, there are three main errors (metrics) used to evaluate the model's performance which includes Mean Squared Error (MSE), Mean Absolute Error (MAE) and R2 score. You can use these metrics to determine if a model's performance is accurate or misleading.

#### 5.5.3.1 Mean Square Error (MSE)

MSE is one of the most common metrics you will encounter when evaluating regression models [6]. During training, you would typically train a model over a different number of epochs. The fitting of the model continues as the error rate of the MSE decreases. The fitting process usually stops when a decrease in error has not been seen over a set number of epochs. The error estimate can be either positive (above the line) or negative below the line. Note that to ensure that negative and positive values don't cancel each other out each of the values are squared. The distance between the regression line and the data point is known as the residual as shown in Fig. 5.13.

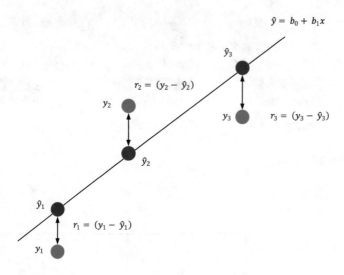

**Fig. 5.13** Residuals from the line

### 5.5.3.2   MAE

MAE works in a very similar fashion to MSE, but the values are not squared. Instead, the sign of the value $(+/-)$ is ignored and the mean value of the error is returned. Using MAE means that the error is less sensitive to outliers. As you can see in Fig. 5.14 the mean square can give the model an unfair weighting to any outliers.

### 5.5.3.3   R2 (Coefficient of Determination)

R2 is a way of measuring how well a linear line in a regression model fits the data. R2 tells us the percentage of the variance between two relationships. R2 works on a scale of 1 to 0 with 1 meaning that the two features represent 100% of the variance while a value 0 means that the two features capture 0 variance in the data.

The first step is to plot a horizontal line through all data points to determine the mean as shown in Fig. 5.15 and calculate the sum of the squares so that values do not cancel each other out as previously discussed.

| Evenly Distributed Errors | | | | Small Variance in Errors | | | | Large Error Outlier | | | |
| --- | --- | --- | --- | --- | --- | --- | --- | --- | --- | --- | --- |
| ID | Error | \|Error\| | Error^2 | ID | Error | \|Error\| | Error^2 | ID | Error | \|Error\| | Error^2 |
| 1 | 2 | 2 | 4 | 1 | 1 | 1 | 1 | 1 | 0 | 0 | 0 |
| 2 | 2 | 2 | 4 | 2 | 1 | 1 | 1 | 2 | 0 | 0 | 0 |
| 3 | 2 | 2 | 4 | 3 | 1 | 1 | 1 | 3 | 0 | 0 | 0 |
| 4 | 2 | 2 | 4 | 4 | 1 | 1 | 1 | 4 | 0 | 0 | 0 |
| 5 | 2 | 2 | 4 | 5 | 1 | 1 | 1 | 5 | 0 | 0 | 0 |
| 6 | 2 | 2 | 4 | 6 | 3 | 3 | 9 | 6 | 0 | 0 | 0 |
| 7 | 2 | 2 | 4 | 7 | 3 | 3 | 9 | 7 | 0 | 0 | 0 |
| 8 | 2 | 2 | 4 | 8 | 3 | 3 | 9 | 8 | 0 | 0 | 0 |
| 9 | 2 | 2 | 4 | 9 | 3 | 3 | 9 | 9 | 0 | 0 | 0 |
| 10 | 2 | 2 | 4 | 10 | 3 | 3 | 9 | 10 | 20 | 20 | 400 |

| MAE | RMSE | | MAE | RMSE | | MAE | RMSE |
| --- | --- | --- | --- | --- | --- | --- | --- |
| 2.000 | 2.000 | | 2.000 | 2.236 | | 2.000 | 6.325 |

**Fig. 5.14**   MSE vs MAE

**Fig. 5.15**   Fitting the mean

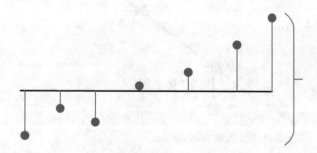

**Fig. 5.16** Calculating the
residuals

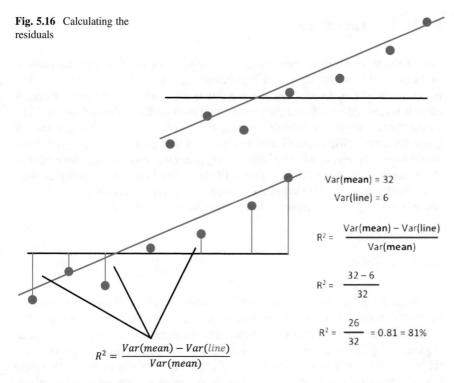

$$Var(mean) = 32$$

$$Var(line) = 6$$

$$R^2 = \frac{Var(mean) - Var(line)}{Var(mean)}$$

$$R^2 = \frac{32 - 6}{32}$$

$$R^2 = \frac{26}{32} = 0.81 = 81\%$$

$$R^2 = \frac{Var(mean) - Var(line)}{Var(mean)}$$

**Fig. 5.17** Calculating the R2 value

In the second step, we fit a corresponding regression line (least squared regression) to the same data and calculate the squared residuals as shown in Fig. 5.16.

We can use the two resulting values and the formula in Fig. 5.17 to calculate the R2.

In summary, R2 is a good metric for identifying the best combinations of features for your linear regression model.

## 5.6  Probability Scoring Methods

Probability scoring methods are used for predicting the probability as opposed to a class label. This allows more sophisticated methods to be used when evaluating predictive possibilities.

### 5.6.1  Log Loss Score

One of the most common measurements for evaluating predictive probabilities is Log Loss which is also known as logarithmic loss or cross-entropy [7]. Log loss works by comparing the predicated probability to the actual class of the prediction. A score is calculated to penalise the probability based on the distance from the class output value. The penalty is small for small differences while a much higher score is given for larger differences. Therefore, model's that produce perfect predictions would have a log loss of 0.0. Log Loss heavily penalises classifiers that are confident about an incorrect classification. Figure 5.18 shows that Log Loss gradually declines as the predicted probability improves the opposite is true as represented by the blue line whereby log loss decreases as the probability moves towards 0.

### 5.6.2  Brier Score

The Brier Score works by calculating the mean squared difference between the forecasted probabilities and the actual outcome [8]. With Brier score predictions that are further away from the expected probability are penalised, but less severely than log loss. Imagine that you are a weather forecaster and you are asked to predict what the probability of rain is for tomorrow. Looking at Fig. 5.19 you might say that there is a 70% chance of rain for tomorrow. Tomorrow comes and you were right it rained. To calculate the Brier Score (BS) as shown on the y axis we will plug in your probability of 0.70 and subtract it from the observation values (which is 1.0 as it did rain) this results in a value of 0.3. This value is now squared to obtain the final BS score which in this instance is 0.09. However, if we found that it did not rain, we could recalculate the BS score as your probability value of 0.7 minus the outcome (which is 0 as it didn't rain) which is 0.7. To obtain the final BS score we square the

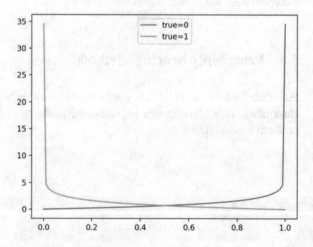

**Fig. 5.18**  Log loss vs probability

**Fig. 5.19** Brier score

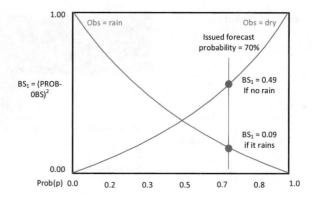

value of 0.7 which gives us a BS score of 0.49. Note that the closer the BS score is to 0 the better the outcome. So, in this instance, a BS value of 0.09 is a good score while a BS score of 0.49 is poor.

## 5.7  Cross-Validation

### 5.7.1  Challenge of Evaluating Classifiers

We may not have enough data to make sufficiently large training and test sets. Typically, a larger test set gives us a more reliable estimate of accuracy. A larger training set will be more representative of how much data we have for the learning process. Removing sections of your data to construct validation and test sets can be particularly problematic for smaller datasets [9].

### 5.7.2  K-Fold Cross-Validation

K-Fold cross-validation is a resampling technique that is used to evaluate machine learning models and is particularly useful for small datasets [10]. Instead of having to split our dataset up manually into train, validation and test sets like we discussed previously we can instead specificity a k number of partitions. The key difference is that the model is trained on the entire dataset, so we are not losing any observations during the training process. As with the other evaluation metrics described, cross-validation is primarily used to determine how well a machine learning model performs on unseen data. K-Fold Cross Validation performs the following steps as shown in Fig. 5.20.

1. The process begins by randomly shuffling the dataset.
2. We then split the dataset into a $k$ number of partitions (for example if $k = 5$ the number of partitions would be 5).

**Fig. 5.20** K-Fold cross-validation

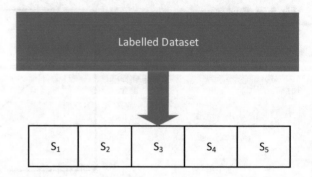

| Iteration | Train On | Test On |
|-----------|----------|---------|
| 1 | S2 S3 S4 S5 | S1 |
| 2 | S1 S3 S4 S5 | S2 |
| 3 | S1 S2 S4 S5 | S3 |
| 4 | S1 S2 S3 S5 | S4 |
| 5 | S1 S2 S3 S4 | S5 |

3. For each group we perform the following: Select one of your groups as a test data set and use the remaining groups for training (so if $k = 5$, one group would be for test and the remaining four groups would be used for training), once the model has been trained on the training data it is then evaluated on the test set, we the retaincollect the score and discard the model.
4. Summarise the results of the model using the stored evaluation scores.

## 5.8   Un-Supervised Learning Evaluation Metric

Just like supervised learning, it is important to correctly evaluate un-supervised models. Unlike supervised learning, there are no known answers or labels to guide the optimisation process or measure the model's performance against known data.

### 5.8.1   Elbow Method

As there are no dependent variables (class labels) it is hard to determine how many clusters there should be (for example defining the value for k in K-Means as previously discussed). However, for algorithms such as K-Means, there are tools that allow us to estimate how many clusters there are in our dataset. The most common approach is the elbow method which runs the algorithm multiple times to

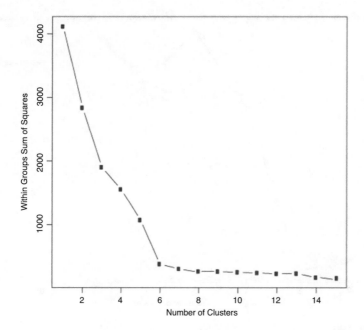

**Fig. 5.21** Elbow method to determine the number of clusters

increase the number of cluster choices [11]. The score (Sum of Squared Errors (SSE) which is the sum of the distances between each data point in the cluster and its centroid) of each cluster is plotted to determine the likely number of clusters in a dataset as shown in Fig. 5.21.

If you plot k against the SSE, you will see that the error decreases as $k$ gets larger; this is because when the number of clusters increases, they should be smaller, so distortion is also smaller. The idea of the elbow method is to choose the $k$ at which the SSE decreases abruptly. This produces an "elbow effect" in the graph as shown in Fig. 5.21.

## 5.8.2   Davies-Bouldin Index

As with the elbow method the Davies-Bouldin Index (DBI) is used to estimate the optimal number of clusters within a dataset. A lower DBI value means better separation between clusters while a high value indicates poorer separation between clusters [12]. Figure 5.22 shows a DBI for a given dataset. The number of clusters with the lowest DBI is typically chosen.

The DBI calculation works by calculating the average similarity measure of each cluster and clusters that are similar. Similarity is described as the ratio of within-cluster distances to the between cluster distances. Clusters that are further apart will

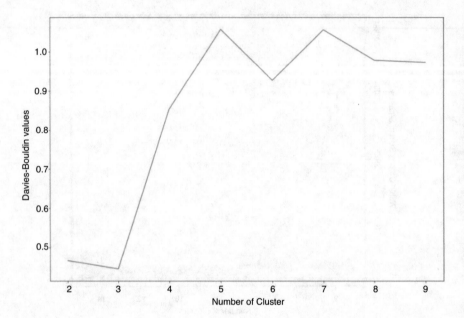

**Fig. 5.22** DBI

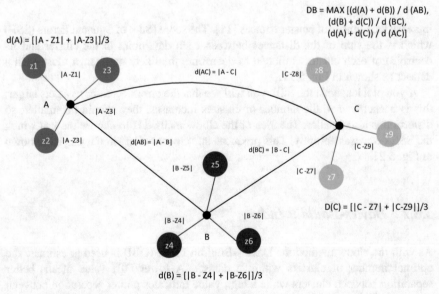

**Fig. 5.23** DBI process

have lower DBI scores. In other words, the lower the DBI value the better the clustering. For example, if we have three clusters consisting of three data points each the following steps can be performed to calculate the DBI score as shown in Fig. 5.23.

- Step 1: calculate the average intra-cluster distances for each of the three clusters.
- Step 2: calculate the distance between each pair of centroids.
- Step 3: for a pair of clusters, sum the intra-cluster distances and divide the value by the distance between those two centroids.

### 5.8.3   Dunn Index

The Dunn Index (DI) is used for determining the performance of a clustering algorithm. The Dunn Index assumes that better clustering means that clusters are compact and well-separated from other clusters [13]. These can be any distance metric, but the common one is Euclidean distance.

There are two primary ways of increasing the DI value. The first is to move the closest pair of clusters further apart, thus increasing the DI value. Conversely, if the same distance between cluster centroids is maintained, but the diameter of the clusters are shrunk (i.e., making the clusters denser), then the DI will also increase. Ideally, the optimal number of clusters will result in the largest DI. The largest DI is determined by two factors: firstly, the largest possible distance between all clusters and two, the smallest possible distance between the most outer points of each cluster as shown in Fig. 5.24.

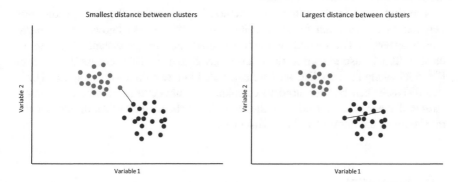

**Fig. 5.24**  Dunn index

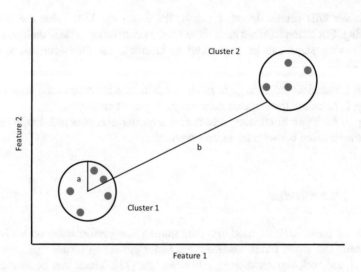

**Fig. 5.25**  Silhouette coefficient

### 5.8.4  Silhouette Coefficient

Silhouette analysis is used to determine the distance between different clusters [14]. The coefficient value ranges between −1 and 1. One means that the clusters are well separated from each other and are clearly distinguished. Zero means that the clusters are indifferent (the same) and the distance between clusters is small. A value of −1 means that the clusters are incorrectly assigned and suggests that there is a problem with the clustering procedure.

The first stage in the silhouetted method is to calculate the average distance between each data point in a particular cluster (this is also known as the intra-cluster distance). The second step is to calculate the average distance between all clusters (this is also known as the inter-cluster distance). This process is shown in Fig. 5.25 where the two distances are calculated in a two-dimensional space. These two distances can be then used to calculate the silhouette score where the inter-cluster distance is subtracted from the intra-cluster distance and then divided by the maximum of the intra/inter-cluster distances.

## 5.9  Summary

This chapter discussed the importance of model evaluation including the challenges faced by ML practitioners and under what circumstances each evaluation matric is used. The discussion outlined that not all evaluation metrics are equal and highlighted the importance of careful consideration when selecting which methods will provide sufficient metrics on how well your models will likely perform in the real world. Before diving into the metrics, a discussion was provided on how to split your data into train, validation and test sets and their specific roles within model training and evaluation.

The remainder of the chapter was split across the different evaluation metrics which support both supervised and unsupervised learning strategies. Under supervised ML an in-depth discussion around confusion matrix, accuracy, precision, recall, specificity, false-positive rate and the F1 score was presented. This was concluded with a discussion on tools that utilise these methods which included ROC and AUC. Under the supervised learning paradigm, we discussed how to evaluate regression-based models using the MSE, MAE and R2. The chapter introduced probability scoring methods where Log Loss and Brier score was discussed. The section on supervised evaluation was concluded with a discussion on Cross-validation.

The final part of the chapter focused on evaluation metrics for un-supervised ML. These included the elbow method, Davies-Bouldin Index, Dunn Index and the Silhouette Coefficient.

# References

1. M. Hossin and M. N. Sulaiman, "A review on evaluation metrics for data classification evaluations," *Int. J. data Min. \& Knowl. Manag. Process*, vol. 5, no. 2, p. 1, 2015.
2. S. M. McNee, J. Riedl, and J. A. Konstan, "Being accurate is not enough: how accuracy metrics have hurt recommender systems," in *CHI'06 extended abstracts on Human factors in computing systems*, 2006, pp. 1097–1101.
3. H. Jabbar and R. Z. Khan, "Methods to avoid over-fitting and under-fitting in supervised machine learning (comparative study)," *Comput. Sci. Commun. Instrum. Devices*, pp. 163–172, 2015.
4. F. Provost and R. Kohavi, "Glossary of terms," *J. Mach. Learn.*, vol. 30, no. 2–3, pp. 271–274, 1998.
5. J. Rothstein, "Probability and Information Theory, with Applications to Radar. PM Woodward. McGraw-Hill, New York; Pergamon Press, London, 1953. 128 pp. Illus. $4.50." American Association for the Advancement of Science, 1954.
6. L. JF, "A simulation study of ridge and other regression estimators," *Commun. Stat. Methods*, vol. 5, no. 4, pp. 307–323, 1976.
7. V. Vovk, "The fundamental nature of the log loss function," in *Fields of Logic and Computation II*, Springer, 2015, pp. 307–318.
8. G. W. Brier and others, "Verification of forecasts expressed in terms of probability," *Mon. Weather Rev.*, vol. 78, no. 1, pp. 1–3, 1950.
9. S. Arlot and A. Celisse, "A survey of cross-validation procedures for model selection," *Stat. Surv.*, vol. 4, pp. 40–79, 2010.
10. P. A. Lachenbruch and M. R. Mickey, "Estimation of error rates in discriminant analysis," *Technometrics*, vol. 10, no. 1, pp. 1–11, 1968.

11. R. L. Thorndike, "Who belongs in the family?," *Psychometrika*, vol. 18, no. 4, pp. 267–276, 1953.
12. D. L. Davies and D. W. Bouldin, "A cluster separation measure," *IEEE Trans. Pattern Anal. Mach. Intell.*, no. 2, pp. 224–227, 1979.
13. J. C. Dunn, "A fuzzy relative of the ISODATA process and its use in detecting compact well-separated clusters," 1973.
14. P. J. Rousseeuw, "Silhouettes: a graphical aid to the interpretation and validation of cluster analysis," *J. Comput. Appl. Math.*, vol. 20, pp. 53–65, 1987.

# Part III
# Deep Learning Concepts and Techniques

Part III
Deep Learning: Concepts and Techniques

# Chapter 6
# Introduction to Deep Learning

DL is a subset of AI which uses biologically inspired networks to solve a given problem. Neural networks are a key component in most DL architectures and are modelled on the human brain which allows computers to learn in a similar manner. Some of the common problems currently solved using DL include pattern recognition, time-series prediction, signal processing, anomaly detection, control and automation and computer vision [1]. Like traditional ML, as discussed in previous chapters, you will find that most of the common tools and techniques are also applicable in the DL domain. For example, you still need to undertake elements of the EDA process, pre-process and partition your data into train, validation and test sets and evaluate your model using some of the metrics previously discussed (in specific cases of DL we will introduce additional metrics where appropriate). However, many of the similarities end here as the fundamental architecture of DL models differ from their traditional ML counterparts.

Although feature engineering can be undertaken in the same manner as previously discussed, in this chapter you will see how this process can be automated whereby the network itself automatically extracts features. This is an important advancement in DL that has simplified the training pipeline, and can remove the need for domain knowledge as well as improve the quality of the features extracted. There has been a significant increase in the use of DL research and applications in both academia and industry in recent years sparking what is commonly known as the AI summer. DL is not new and can be traced back to the early '60s [2]. However, three fundamental components have helped to drive the widespread adoption of DL. These are advancements in deep neural network architectures, GPU's, and the availability of large and ever-growing high-quality datasets.

The combination of these technologies is driving significant advancements in innovative solutions such as driverless cars, smart cities and smart devices such as Alexa. Although you may not realise it DL is already playing a fundamental role in our daily lives to help, support and enhance the things we do. For example, in recommender systems, healthcare, safety, finance, entertainment and a multitude of services in many of the devices we own. In this and subsequent chapters, we will

© Springer Nature Switzerland AG 2022
P. Fergus, C. Chalmers, *Applied Deep Learning*, Computational Intelligence Methods and Applications, https://doi.org/10.1007/978-3-031-04420-5_6

provide an introduction to Artificial Neural Networks (ANNS) and explore the many aspects of DL architectures and the problems they are designed to solve.

## 6.1  So what's the Difference Between DL and ML?

ML and DL are very closely related in the sense that they allow machines to learn from prior data. The term ML is a catch-all for any machine that learns in this way. Whereas DL is a specific set of methods and techniques to enable a machine to learn and make decisions using very deep and complex networks. However, one of the most notable differences in DL is its ability to replace the human-driven feature extraction process and incorporate this stage within the networks itself to automatically decide which features best describe the data as shown in Fig. 6.1.

In certain applications, such as natural language processing and computer vision, it is difficult to apply algorithms like SVMs and Random Forests (RF) to understand and translate language or detect and classify objects within images. However, these are tasks that DL algorithms find relatively easy to do. Therefore, it is always important to understand what ML and DL algorithms can and cannot do before selecting an appropriate model to use. In cases where an ML algorithm, such as an

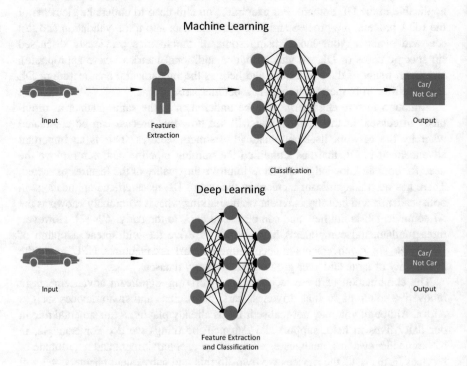

**Fig. 6.1** Automatic feature extraction

**Fig. 6.2** DGX1 and DGX2

SVM or RF, would suffice they should be selected for the following reasons a) they are computationally efficient, b) models can be interpreted, and c) they dont require as much data as DL.

Although DL models have proven to solve some of the most challenging problems, they can be data-hungry and computationally expensive. Careful consideration of the hardware requirements for training and hosting complex DL models is required before committing to a DL based solution. For example, building an application to detect 29 of the most common species found in Sub-Sahara Africa using HD camera trap images would take a single compute node with 4x NVidia Quadro M4000 GPU's (costing approximately £3000 collectively at the time of writing) roughly 4 days to train a model with 1000 images per species. Note that this is not a particularly complex model. In reality, you would need a vastly larger dataset and additional hardware to support this such as a DGX1 or DGX2 which at the time of writing rages between £100,000 and £300,000. Note that the DGX2 has 16x Tesla V100 GPU's. Both the DGX1 and DGX2 are shown in Fig. 6.2.

Once the model is trained, we then need to host the model to perform near real-time inference. Hardware such as the Tesla T4 and the RTX 8000 can range between £2100 and £8000 at the time of writing. There are several trade-offs when selecting the ML paradigm to adopt. This requires careful consideration as there may be time and cost considerations that impact both the budget and feasibility of the projects you undertake.

## 6.2   Introduction to Deep Learning

DL algorithms process data and develop abstractions. With DL, information is passed through each layer with the output of the previous layer providing inputs for the next layer. The first layer in a network is called an input layer while the last layer is called the output layer. All the layers between the two are referred to as hidden layers. The history of DL can be traced back to 1943 when the first computer model based on the neural networks of the human brain was created. Since then, DL has steadily evolved with only two significant breaks in its development both of which are known as AI winters.

One of the most significant breakthroughs in ANNs was the development of the back-propagation algorithm which was applied in 1985 [3] and fully implemented in 1989 at Bell Labs [4]. Backpropagation was combined with Convolutional Neural Networks (CNNs) in 1989 which were trained to recognise handwritten digits. In 1999 the integration of GPU technology and DL marked the next significant breakthrough which increased computational speeds 1000% over 10 years. In 2009 a database containing 14 million labelled images was released [5]. This was an important milestone for image processing research. By 2011 advancements in GPU's meant it was possible to train larger CNNs to solve complex problems [6]. Since then, the area of DL has expanded into many domains which focus on adjustments to neural network architectures, and tools and techniques to speed up and improve the accuracy of models. We will explore some of these advancements in the coming chapters.

DL has significantly advanced the area of AI, and the results produced have proved to be important as it can achieve meaningful and useful accuracy in many real-world applications. While ML has been used for classification on images and text for decades it has struggled to perform to a sufficient level required for business applications. DL has enabled us to surpass the threshold required to tackle real-world problems and deliver services that were not possible using traditional ML algorithms. Computer vision is a notable example of DL that is showing early signs of outperforming humans in many applications such as healthcare and manufacturing. A more well-known area of DL is in games like Chess and Go where it has become extremely difficult if not impossible to beat DL systems such AlphaGo. AlphaGo has even demonstrated creativity by producing moves not previously thought of by expert human players to give it a competitive edge. For example the famous match between Lee Sedol (who was the winner of 18 world titles) and AlphaGo where AlphaGo won 4–1 [7].

The explosion and adoption of DL has been attributed to the supporting frameworks provided by technology giants such as Google, Facebook and Microsoft. These companies are at the forefront of applied AI and its uptake within many business sectors. DL frameworks have simplified the training and hosting of models and are industry-led. As such their integration into existing business processes is becoming increasingly common within many software applications and services to solve real-world challenges. The most common DL frameworks in existence today include TensorFlow by Google, PyTorch by Facebook and CNTK by Microsoft.

## 6.3   Artificial Neural Networks

Neural networks are modelled on biological neural networks and attempt to enable computers to learn in an equivalent manner to humans. In the human brain, there are around 86 billion neurons with more than 100 trillion synapsis connections [8]. In contrast, the biggest ANN at the time of writing contained 16 million neurons (perceptron's) [9]. However more typically the number you encounter will be in the hundreds and thousands. Perceptrons, which are considered artificial neurons, can mimic certain parts of their biological counterparts. These parts include dendrites, cell bodies and axons as shown in Fig. 6.4. Signals are received from the dendrites and transmitted via the axon once enough of them have been received. This signal is then used as an input for other neurons and the process continually repeats. Some signals are more important than others which causes other connected neurons to fire more easily. Connections can become stronger or weaker while new connections can form or disappear completely (this is also known as plasticity) [10]. An ANN can mimic a significant part of this process by modelling a function using a set of weighted inputs which triggers an activation in the neuron (perceptron) if the nodes activation threshold is reached (i.e., the neuron fires). Once it fires some of the output is passed to the next neuron. As before this value is multiplied by the weight of the connection and propagated via connections to other neurons. As a result, the process continues causing activations throughout the network. Given a set number of neurons, an ANN can map a set of inputs to a corresponding set of outputs (known as universal approximation). Figure 6.3 shows the basic constructs of a human neuron and its associated connections with other neurons.

### *6.3.1   Perceptrons*

Perceptrons were inspired by how a biological neuron works. A perceptron consists of one or more inputs, a processor, and a single output. The inputs represent the input data you wish to model. For example, pixel intensities in an image, hot encodings describing words in a text, or signal information obtained from a speech recording or

**Fig. 6.3**  Biological neuron

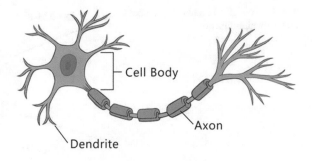

stream. The processor fires or activates if the sum of the inputs exceeds a given threshold which generates an associated output. Therefore, there are four main steps to the process: receive inputs, weight inputs, sum inputs and generate the output. Consider Fig. 6.4, where we have two inputs 12 and 4. Each input must be weighted (multiplied by a value) which is usually a number between −1 and 1 (initially weights are randomly assigned). In a comparable way to how we learn, this simple network will adjust these weights automatically through a feedback mechanism until a mapping between the inputs and the output(s) is found. The weights are used to describe how important that input is.

Once we have our randomly assigned weights, we multiply the inputs by the weights (input * weight). The results of the calculation are passed to an activation function (processor). In a simple binary output, the activation function determines if the perceptron (neuron) activates or not i.e., generates a 0 if the threshold is not reached and a 1 if it is. There are a wide variety of different activation functions such as Sigmoid and Hyperbolic Tangent which will be discussed later in this chapter. Figure 6.5 shows the relationship between the weighted inputs and the activation function.

The most basic activation function works as follows:

- If the sum is a positive number, the output will be 1.
- If the sum is a negative number, the output will be 0.

**Fig. 6.4** Perceptron with associated weights

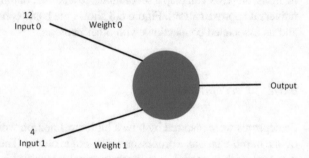

**Fig. 6.5** Weighted inputs and activation function

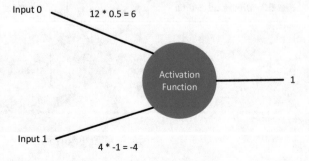

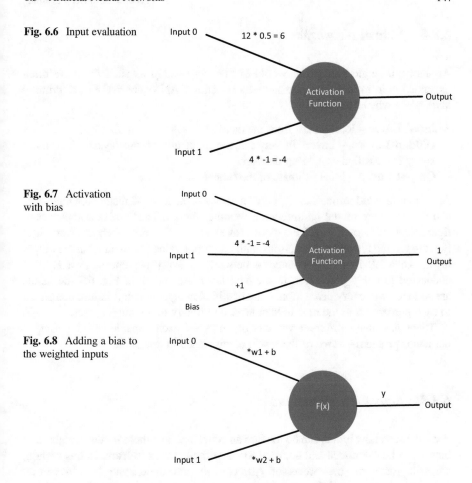

**Fig. 6.6** Input evaluation

**Fig. 6.7** Activation with bias

**Fig. 6.8** Adding a bias to the weighted inputs

So, in our example $6 + -4 = 2$ so our activation function would return 1 as shown in Fig. 6.6.

There is an issue with this. What if the initial inputs were both 0? The activation function would never activate. To solve this, we add a bias term to each input as shown in Fig. 6.7. It is important to note that the weight will not have an effect until it has surpassed the bias value. In this sense, the bias can act as a suppressant when the weighting is low. When the weighting surpasses the bias its effect on the network is correlated with the size of the weight itself (the smaller the weight the smaller the effect, the larger the weight the larger the effect).

Add the bias to each input as shown in Fig. 6.8.

### 6.3.2   Neural Networks

Arguably, a single perceptron would not be very useful as such these are often expanded to form more complex network structures. ANNs consist of three primary layer types which include:

- **Input Layer** – Real values from the data
- **Hidden Layers** – Layers in between the input and output layers—3 or more layers is classified as a "deep network"
- **Output Layer** – Final estimate of the output

As you go forward through the layers of a network, the level of abstraction increases, and this is where model interpretation becomes harder. These more complex configurations are known as MLP networks as shown in Fig. 6.9. Each layer provides input to the next layer of perceptrons until an output value is generated at the output layer. An MLP is a fully connected network as every perceptron in a layer is connected to every perceptron in the next layer. As shown in Fig. 6.9 the inputs are connected to every perceptron in the first hidden layer which is in turn connected to each perceptron in the next hidden layer and finally to the output layer.

There are many different variants of an ANN each capable of addressing a particular problem—some of these will be discussed in this book.

### 6.3.3   Activation Functions

We have seen how inputs can be fed into an ANN and how these inputs, weights and biases can be calculated and adjusted to allow the network to learn. In this section, we will focus on the processor (perceptron) and understand how a neuron (perceptron) is activated. This is achieved using activation functions and a significant

**Fig. 6.9** MLP

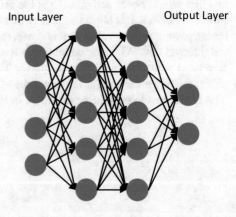

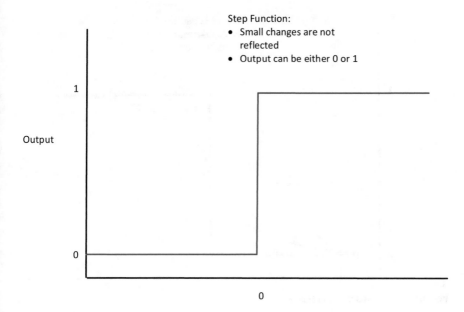

**Fig. 6.10** Step function

amount of research has been undertaken to understand their effectiveness. The input, weight and bias values are summed and passed to the activation function. Depending on the value the activation function will either fire or not.

Figure 6.10 shows the simplest activation function which is known as the step function [11]. If the summed value for our inputs, weights and bias produces a negative value the output is 0. A value of 0 and above will return an output value of 1. The problem with this function is that it is often too drastic and does not consider small changes.

An alternate activation function known as the sigmoid function is shown in Fig. 6.11 [12]. This function takes in the summed inputs, weights, and the bias value and like before it returns a value of either 0 or 1. With a sigmoid activation, it allows us to be more granular with the cut off whereby smaller alterations can change the output of the activation function (so rather than activation being dependent on a negative/non-negative value, the activation occurs between 0 and 1 with a threshold of 0.5). Therefore, the sigmoid activation function is more granular and sensitive to slight changes (i.e., where an input is equal to 0.5 it would result in an output of 1 and where an input of 0.4 would generate a 0 output.

Unlike the sigmoid activation function, the Hyperbolic Tangent (Tanh) activation function shown in Fig. 6.12 can be either 1 or −1. Having a range between 1 and −1 allows for larger updates to the weights and bias, therefore, speeding up the training time (this overcomes the main limitation with sigmoid activation functions) [13]. This will be discussed in more detail later.

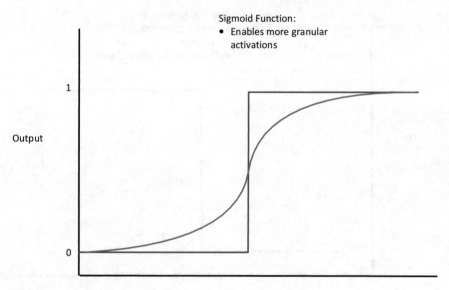

**Fig. 6.11**  Sigmoid activation function

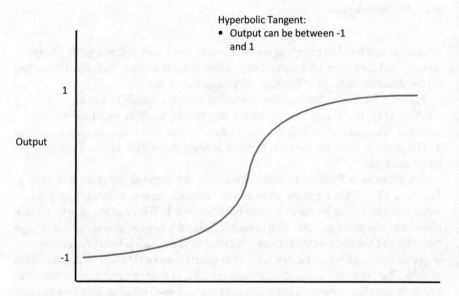

**Fig. 6.12**  Hyperbolic tangent

Finally, Fig. 6.13 shows the Rectified Linear Unit (ReLU) which is one of the most common activation functions in ANNs [14]. With ReLU the summed inputs, weights and bias are fed into the activation function. If the value is below zero, the activation function returns a value of 0. If an input of 0 or more is fed in the true value of the input is returned. The issue with both sigmoid and hyperbolic tangent

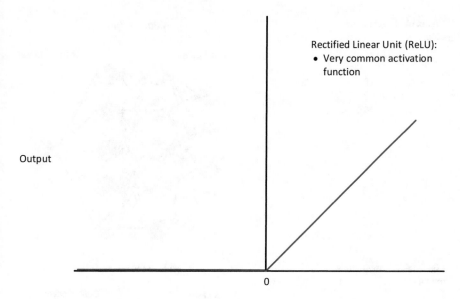

Rectified Linear Unit (ReLU):
• Very common activation
  function

Output

0

**Fig. 6.13** ReLU

they suffer from what is known as the vanishing gradient effect which will be discussed later in this chapter.

## 6.3.4  Multi-Class Classification Considerations

In the previous section, we notice that all these activation functions are used for a single output, continuous label or in binary classification (either a 0 or 1). However, none of these functions will work in a multiclass situation.

There are two main types of multi-class scenarios:

- **Non-exclusive classes**

  - A data point can have multiple classes/categories assigned to it. For example, a picture can contain multiple objects (e.g., sandcastle, person, kite, and a bird).

- **Mutually exclusive classes**

  - A data point can have one class/category assigned to it. It is when something cannot occur at the same time.

Previously we thought of the last output layer as a single node. This single node could output a continuous regression value or binary classification 0 or 1 as shown in Fig. 6.14.

**Fig. 6.14** Single node output

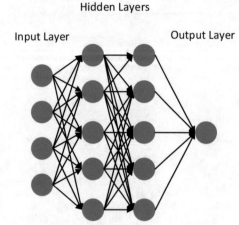

**Fig. 6.15** Multiple node outputs

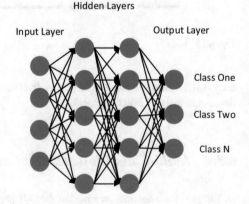

So, what happens if you require more than one output, i.e., 2, 3 or 4 outputs. In this instance, you would need to add additional nodes to the output layer as shown in Fig. 6.15. You would need one neuron per class.

As discussed earlier in the book you will remember that the output needs to be a number, i.e., you cannot use words such as "Red", "Cat" or "Dog". These will need to be a numerical value in a correctly ordered sequence (the column positions) as shown in Fig. 6.16. Therefore, you will need to perform a mapping between the text-based label and the corresponding numeric output value. This is commonly referred to as one-hot encoding. This technique is used for mutually exclusive classes where there can only ever be one value at a time.

For non-exclusive classes, this process changed to accommodate multiple outputs. For example, an image can have more than one object in it (i.e., a car and a bicycle). This is shown in Fig. 6.17.

Once we have encoded our data, we need to choose the correct architecture for our output layer and the appropriate activation function.

| Data Point 1 | RED |
|---|---|
| Data Point 2 | GREEN |
| Data Point 3 | BLUE |
| ... | ... |
| Data Point N | RED |

|  | RED | GREEN | BLUE |
|---|---|---|---|
| Data Point 1 | 1 | 0 | 0 |
| Data Point 2 | 0 | 1 | 0 |
| Data Point 3 | 0 | 0 | 1 |
| ... | ... | ... | ... |
| Data Point N | 1 | 0 | 0 |

**Fig. 6.16**  One-hot encoding

| Data Point 1 | A,B |
|---|---|
| Data Point 2 | A |
| Data Point 3 | C,B |
| ... | ... |
| Data Point N | B |

|  | A | B | C |
|---|---|---|---|
| Data Point 1 | 1 | 1 | 0 |
| Data Point 2 | 1 | 0 | 0 |
| Data Point 3 | 0 | 1 | 1 |
| ... | ... | ... | ... |
| Data Point N | 0 | 1 | 0 |

**Fig. 6.17**  Non-exclusive outputs

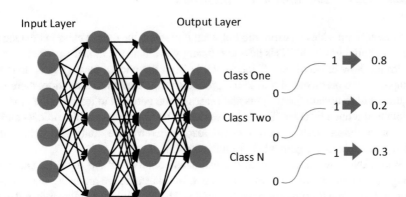

**Fig. 6.18**  Sigmoid activation

- **Non-exclusive**

  - Sigmoid activation—each neuron will output a value between 0 and 1, indicating the probability of that class assigned to it as shown in Fig. 6.18.

- **Mutually exclusive classes**

  - It allows each neuron to output a value independently of other classes
  - This means that it allows a single datapoint to be input to the network and allow multiple outputs to be generated

**Fig. 6.19**   SoftMax output

[Red , Green , Blue]
[ 0.1 ,    0.6  , 0.3 ]

But what do we do when each data point can only have a single class assigned to it? We can address this issue using the SoftMax function. The SoftMax function calculates the probability distribution over k-different events. As a result, this function will calculate the probabilities of each target class overall target classes. The class with the highest probability will be the correct class. Note that the range of probabilities across all outputs will be between 0 and 1 and the sum of all probabilities will be equal to one. The model returns the probability of each class and the class with the highest probability value is chosen. So, the main thing to keep in mind is that if you use the SoftMax activation for multiple classes you will get an output like the one below in Fig. 6.19. In this instance, the green class is selected as the correct class given that it has the highest probability value.

### 6.3.5   Cost Functions and Optimisers

The network provides an estimation of what it predicts the output class to be. One of the key challenges in ANNs is how to efficiently evaluate the model's prediction and determine how close or far off the model is from the correct class (this is done by comparing the predicted output to the ground truth). After this evaluation, there is a requirement to update the weights and biases of the network to improve the model's output and reduce its error. This is known as the learning phase of the process and is done in a similar way to how humans learn whereby; we study and update our internal models as we gain a better understanding.

With ANNs we need to take the estimated outputs of the network and then compare them to the real values of the label. In this stage, we are using the training dataset during the fitting/training of the model. The cost function (often referred to as the loss function must be averaged so it can output a single value). We need to keep track of our loss during the training phase to monitor network performance.

Cost functions enable us to evaluate the performance of a perceptron by telling us how far off we are from the target value. There are different cost functions, but the most popular is Cross Entropy. The benefits of Cross-Entropy is that it enables faster training. Typically, the larger the difference, the faster the neuron can learn. The next step is to use our neurons and our measurement of error (cost function) to correct the network's prediction (this is the learning part of the process). This is known as optimisation and is undertaken by optimisation algorithms. To explain this better imagine we are baking a loaf of bread and you need to weigh 380g of flower. You start by dumping an amount of flour into the scale and reading the digital display to see how much the flower weighs. As with most scenarios the amount of flower added will be either over or under your target value of 380g. To correct this, you gradually

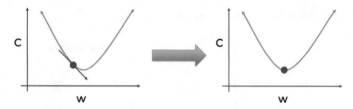

**Fig. 6.20**  Gradient descent

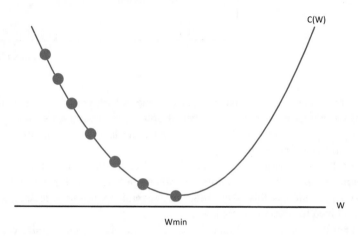

**Fig. 6.21**  Small step sizes to the minimum

add or remove spoons of flour until you reach the target of 380g (note that this might take several iterations (epochs) until you reach the desired target). This scenario is how optimisation and the cost function work in the training phase of an ANN.

To calculate and reduce the loss we use a set of algorithms known as optimisation algorithms. One of the most popular optimisation algorithms is Gradient Decent [15]. Gradient descent is an optimisation algorithm for finding the minimum of a function (in our case the cost function). For example, if you were to navigate down a foggy mountain the only information available to you would be the downwards direction. As you are moving downwards you can infer that you are descending the mountain. If suddenly you started to move upwards you would infer that you are climbing upwards again and therefore make appropriate adjustments to move back in a downwards direction. This is exactly what gradient descent is doing. In gradient descent, this process continues until the global minima has been found as shown in Fig. 6.20.

Gradient descent begins by calculating the slope at a given point and moves in the downwards direction of the slope. This is repeated until we converge on zero indicating the minimum. Smaller step sizes take longer to find the minimum as shown in Fig. 6.21. The step size is known as the learning rate. One of the key challenges in gradient descent is setting the optimal learning rate. If you set it too

**Fig. 6.22** Local and global minima

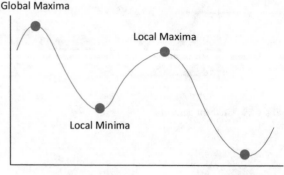

small, it may take a significant amount of time before your network converges (reaches the global minimum). However, if you set the learning too high you will create a ping pong effect in the bowl whereby the learner overshoots the global minima and never reaches it.

One of the issues with traditional gradient descent is that it can get stick in a local minimum instead of the global minima as shown in Fig. 6.22. It is possible to alter the learning to address this issue, however, several optimisation techniques have been developed to overcome this issue.

The learning rate shown in Fig. 6.22 was constant where each step size was equal. We can use other optimisers which can cleverly adapt our learning rate (step size) automatically. We could start with larger steps and then reduce them as the gradient begins to level off (this is known as adaptive gradient descent). The Adam optimiser is much more efficient when compared to gradient decent when searching for the global minima [16]. The Adam optimiser has also proven effective in overcoming the local minima problem and as a result, is one of the most popular optimisation algorithms. Many other optimisers try to minimise the error, but the general principles remain the same.

### 6.3.6   Backpropagation

Backpropagation allows us to update the optimal parameters for the entire network. It works by calculating the output error and then it traverses back through the network layers making the required adjustments (we want to know how the cost function results in changes in relation it these adjustments).

As discussed earlier in the chapter each input will receive a weight and bias as shown in Fig. 6.23. We have already seen how this process propagates forward but the next stage is to see how the error is backpropagated.

The idea is that we can use the gradient to go back through the network and adjust our weights and biases to minimise the output of the error vector on the last output

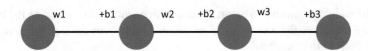

**Fig. 6.23** Forward propagation

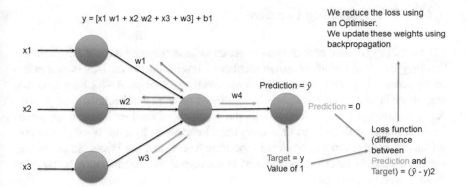

**Fig. 6.24** Backpropagation

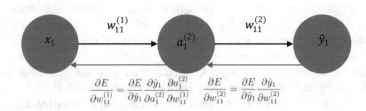

**Fig. 6.25** Chain rule for backpropagation

layer. Imagine that a driving instructor is teaching his student to reverse into a parking bay. Using the information from the mirrors (optimiser) he can tell the student to adjust the steering wheel (weights and bias) if it looks like the car is going to go over the parking lines. As the car reverses the instructor constantly provides feedback to the learner and tells the person how to adjust the wheel accordingly. This stops when the driver successfully parks the car. This process is shown in Fig. 6.24.

Backpropagation is an entire chapter in itself due to the complex mathematical constructs and theoretical principles required to understand it. The takeaway from this section that you need to understand is that information is fed forward through the network which results in a predicted output. This output is compared to the ground truth outputs and used to derive an error (loss) value which is propagated backwards using an optimisation algorithm to update the weights that connect each of the neurons in the network. All weights are updated using what is known as a chain rule. One cycle of information flowing forward, and the error derivatives propagated backwards are known as a single epoch. Figure 6.25 shows a simple chain rule where X is your input feature, y is your predicted output and a is your activation function.

W is the weight assigned to a particular connection while the equation on the bottom is used to calculate the loss which is propagated backwards through the network to update each of the weights.

### 6.3.7  The Vanishing Gradient

The vanishing gradient problem was never an issue in the early days of ANNs given that they were quite shallow (small number of layers) due to the lack of computational power [17]. This issue has become more apparent as ANNs have become deeper and hardware improvements have allowed network architectures to be grown. As more layers are added to the ANN the gradients of the loss function approach 0 which makes it difficult to train deep neural networks. In other words, there are substantial changes to the weights in the later layers than the layers closest to the input. This means that the layers closest to the output learn significantly better than those closest to the input.

Some activation functions, such as the sigmoid, transform the input values to an output value between 0 and 1. As shown in Fig. 6.26—the larger the input the smaller the derivative becomes. The derivative of a sigmoid activation ranges between 0 and 0.25. So, an input value of 0.9 would result in a derivative of 0.018.

As these derivatives for each perceptron are multiplied together from the output layer to the input layer the derivatives drastically decrease in value. In networks with many layers, these gradients begin to vanish leading to the vanishing gradient phenomena. To address this issue many DL networks, utilise ReLU. This activation function does not propagate small derivatives from the output to the input layer. The derivative for ReLU ranges between zero and one where any inputs above zero

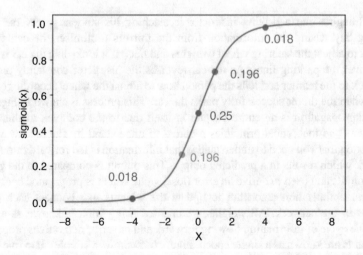

**Fig. 6.26**  Sigmoid activation with derivate

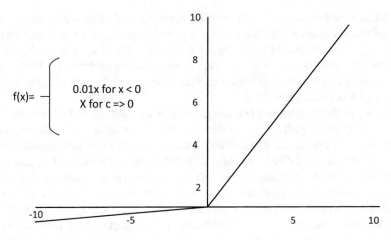

$$f(x)= \begin{cases} 0.01x \text{ for } x < 0 \\ X \text{ for } c => 0 \end{cases}$$

**Fig. 6.27** Leaky ReLU

return a derivative of one. Conversely, inputs below zero will be zero. The main limitation however is that having a zero value in the chain rule calculation can result in dead nodes and activations. This issue is resolved using Leaky ReLU which ensures that values below zero are increased by a small constant [18]. For example, as shown in Fig. 6.27, values that are less than zero are changed to a value of 0.01.

## 6.3.8   Weight Initialisation

The performance of a neural network can be largely dependent on how its tuneable parameters are initialised (weights) when training commences. Performing appropriate weight initialisation also has the benefit of preventing activation outputs from exploding or vanishing as previously discussed. There are several different methods for weight initialisation, which include constant values or Xavier weight initialisation. If weights are initialised randomly the results will not be reproducible. The careful initialisation of weights not only supports reproducible results but also aids in the training of ANNs. Weight initialisation typically follows three broad rules:

- Weights should not be initialised using small values
- Weights should not be initialised with the same values
- Weights should be initialised to provide good variance

At this point, it is worth noting that no single weight initialisation technique can be considered the best in all situations. Some will work better with specific datasets while others will work better with different activation functions.

Some of the techniques include:

- **Uniform distribution:** here the weights are initialised using values taken from a uniform distribution within a lower and upper range I.e., the lower range would be negative one divided by the square root of the sum of the number inputs to a particular neuron—the upper will be the same but the square root of the sum of the number of inputs divided by one. This approach works well with the sigmoid and tanh activation functions.
- **Xavier initialisation:** here two key techniques are used called Xavier normal and Xavier uniform [19]. With Xavier normal, the weights are initialised using the mean of the normal distribution set to zero and the standard deviation set to the square root of 2 divided by the sum of the number of inputs and outputs of the neuron. In Xavier uniform, the weights are initialised using a uniform distribution with a lower range calculated as the negative square root of six divided by the square root of the sum of the number of inputs and outputs and an upper limit calculated as the square root of six divided by the sum of the number of inputs and outputs. This approach also works well with the sigmoid and tanh activation functions.
- **He initialisation:** as with the previous example there are two approaches which are, He normal and He uniform [20]. In He normal, the weights are initialised using values taken from a normal distribution where the mean is zero and the sigma is equal to the square root of two divided by the total number of input features. In He normal, the weights are initialised using values from a uniform distribution with upper and lower limits. The lower limit is calculated as a negative square of six divided by the total number of input features. The upper limit is calculated using the square root of six divided by the total number of input features. This approach works well with the ReLU activation function.

### 6.3.9   Regularisation

One of the most important aspects of training an ANN model is the likelihood of overfitting as we discussed in Chap. 2. Avoiding overfitting can single-handedly improve our model's performance. Due to the complexity of ANNs (because of the number of tunable parameters) they are prone to overfitting. One of the most common techniques to combat overfitting is dropout [21]. At every iteration, the dropout randomly selects some nodes and removes them along with all their incoming and outgoing connections as shown in Fig. 6.28.

As each iteration has a different set of nodes this results in a different set of outputs. It can also be thought of as an ensemble technique in machine learning. Ensemble models usually perform better than a single model as they capture more randomness. Similarly, dropout also performs better than a normal neural network model.

There are a few different regularisation techniques such as L1 and L2 [22]. With these techniques they apply another term to the cost functions to control the weights—this encourages a smaller and more balanced model.

**Fig. 6.28** Drop out

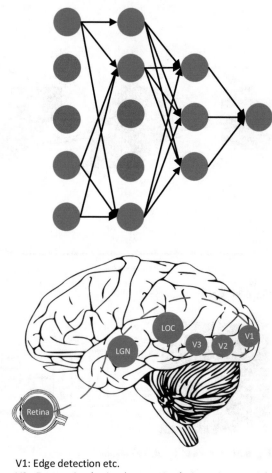

Input Image

Primitive Features

Object Parts

Object

V1: Edge detection etc.
V2 : Extract simple visual properties (orientation, spatial frequency. Colour, etc)
V3: Shape detection

**Fig. 6.29**   Primary visual cortex

## 6.4   Convolutional Neural Networks

When your inputs are images or videos, ANNs have limited use. Instead for this task, we can use a type of network known as a CNN [23]. CNNs are modelled on the primary visual cortex which is part of the cerebral cortex [24]. The primary visual cortex contains six layers which are responsible for extracting a variety of different features for example edges. The primary visual cortex is shown in Fig. 6.29.

CNNs are extremely computationally expensive and have a variety of different architectures which comprise filters, pooling and a final fully connected ANN. The

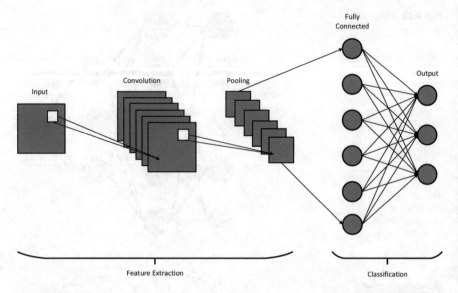

**Fig. 6.30** CNN

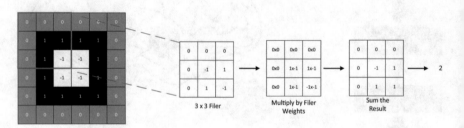

**Fig. 6.31** Filter and weight calculation

convolutional layers which are comprised of a number of filters along the pooling layers form the automatic feature extractor. The fully connected layers (dense layers) form the classification as shown in Fig. 6.30.

In the remainder of this chapter, we will discuss the key components of a CNN in more depth.

### 6.4.1 Image Filters and Kernels

Filters are also known as kernels and are a small matrix applied to an entire input space, such as an image. Kernels allow us to transform images. Figure 6.31 shows an example of a grayscale image where the values in the matrix reside between −1 and 1 where −1 represents white, 1 represents black, and zero represents grey. The size of the filter in this example is a 3 × 3 matrix which is applied to the input image staring at the top left. As the filter moves across the image (stride) the pixel values are multiplied by the filter weights (these weights will be initialised and tuned during the learning process). In the final stage of the process, the results are summed to return the final value.

The stride length can be adjusted depending on the task. By default, the stride length must at least be 1 but can be increased depending on the problem. There are a number of different image kernels which extract different features from a given image. For example, as shown below the Sobel operator is used in image processing and computer vision in edge detection algorithms where it creates an image representing edges. Figure 6.32 shows a Sobel filter applied to an image for edge detection [25].

In the context of a CNN, these features are referred to as convolutional kernels. The process of passing a kernel over an image is known as a convolution. Kernels can overshoot (go beyond the edge of an image) which results in a loss of information which is compensated by using a technique known as padding. Here the edges of the image are padded with zeros which allow the entire image to be processed by the filters as shown in Fig. 6.33.

## 6.4.2   Convolutional Layers

A convolutional layer describes a process by which we apply multiple filters to the input image [26]. A convolutional layer is trained to determine the best filter weight values for the input (learnable parameters). A CNN helps to reduce the number of parameters (which is an issue when processing images using a fully connected MLP due to a large number of trainable parameters and increased computational requirements) by using local connectivity. In a CNN not all neurons are fully connected. Instead, neurons are only connected to a subset of local neurons in the next layer, which is the filters. Figure 6.34 shows localised connections in a CNN to multiple filter layers on a one-dimensional space (1CNN).

When configuring a CNN, you can specify the number of filters that you require. There are common filters such as Sobel which are good for finding edges in an image whereby the weights are already known. However, if you are working with say facial recognition you will unlikely to be able to manually determine the weights required to pick out features such as an eyebrow or nose. Therefore, the CNN will determine a set of weights to extract the required features. The previous figure showed a 1DCNN however in basic images you would require a 2DCNN to process grayscale and preserve the 2D relational information in the convolutional layer. Figure 6.35 shows an example of a 2DCNN mapped to three filters which act as a two-by-two matrix that has a stride of two.

Colour images can be thought of as three-dimensional tensors (3D matrix) which consist of red, green and blue (RGB) colour channels. Alongside the height and width, the dimensions of an RGB image would be HxWx3 as shown in Fig. 6.36. For example, when an image is imported with a resolution of 1280 x 720, inspecting its

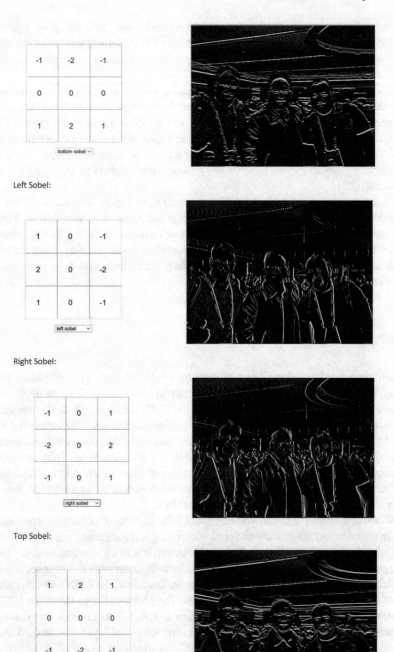

Left Sobel:

Right Sobel:

Top Sobel:

**Fig. 6.32** Sobel filter

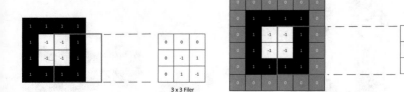

**Fig. 6.33** Padding

**Fig. 6.34** Localised
connections for multiple
filters

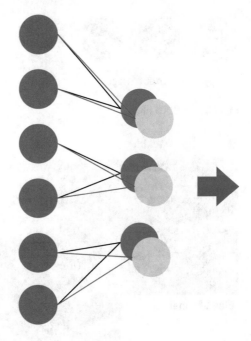

shape would result in a (1280,720,3) 3D matrix (tensor). Each of these values corresponds to 1280-pixel width, a 720-pixel height and 3 colour channels.

Unlike grayscale where a single channel of filters is used, in a 3DCNN we will require a set of features per channel (i.e., RGB). Fig. 6.37 shows the layers in our input image and the layers in the corresponding filters. Just like you would consider a colour image to be 3 dimensional you can think of your features as being 3 dimensional.

## 6.4.3 Pooling Layers

Even though CNN's use local connectivity, dealing with large images, RGB and a variety of different features can still result in many tunable parameters. We can use

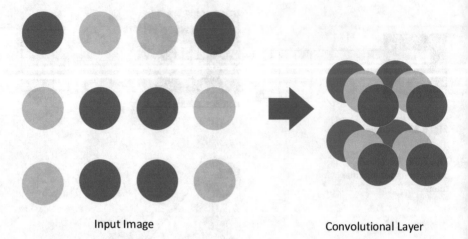

Input Image                                                    Convolutional Layer

**Fig. 6.35** 2DCNN filters

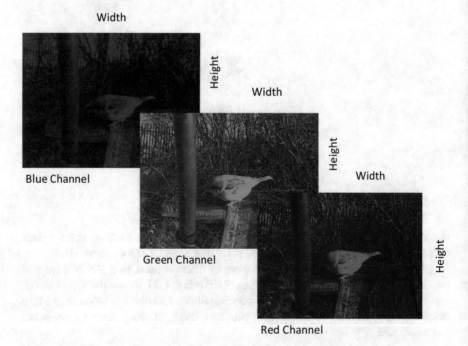

**Fig. 6.36** 3D matrix

pooling to reduce these parameters [27]. Pooling layers accept convolutional layers as input as shown in Fig. 6.38.

A convolution layer will consist of a number of filters, and we can use pooling to reduce the size of each filter. One common type of pooling is max pooling where the

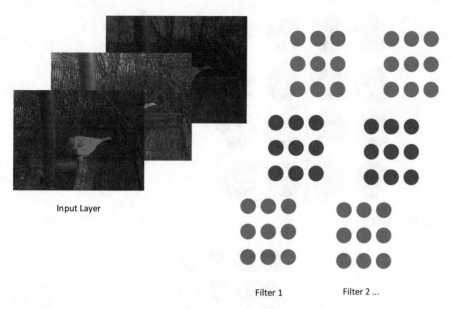

Input Layer

Filter 1          Filter 2 ...

**Fig. 6.37**   3D CNN filter

**Fig. 6.38**   Pooling layer

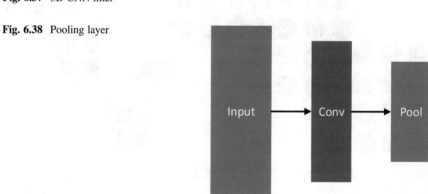

maximum value within a set stride for each filter in the convolutional layer is extracted. Figure 6.39 shows the max-pooling process.

While Fig. 6.40 shows one matrix resulting from one filter in the convolutional layer you will need to do this for each filter implemented in your solution as shown in Fig. 6.41. Note that pooling is performed on each filter in turn and not on a cross-section of the combined filters. Even a small pooling kernel of $2 \times 2$ with a stride of 2 will remove 75% of the input data.

Figure 6.41 shows a basic CNN called AlexNet which competed in the ImageNet large scale visual recognition challenge in 2012 and was widely considered to be the first CNN in the challenge [21]. Here the diagram shows the detailed interactions between the convolutional layers, max-pooling layers and the fully connected dense layers. The first convolutional layer contains a total of 96 filters followed by a

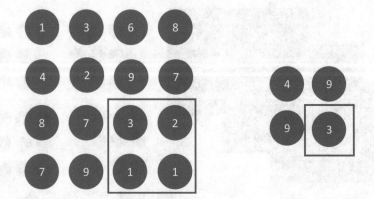

**Fig. 6.39** Max pooling

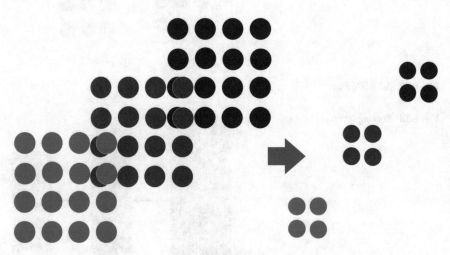

**Fig. 6.40** Pooling of each filter in the convolutional layer

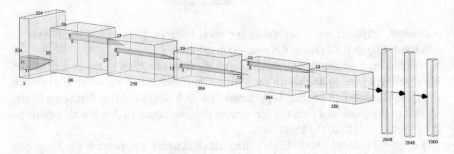

**Fig. 6.41** AlexNet

max-pooling layer. The filters in the first Conv 1 are tasked with finding edges and blobs, Conv 3 is tasked with analysing textures while Conv 5 finds object parts. The output from the final max-pooling layer is flattened before being classified in the dense layers.

### 6.4.4 Transfer Learning

Training CNNS from scratch which involves tuning the filters in the convolutional layers requires a significant number of images and computational resources. There are a variety of different datasets which have been used to train a CNN from scratch. The most common dataset is the COCO dataset which contains 200,000 images with 1.5 million object instances and 80 object categories [28]. Beyond your tech giants, very few people have the required infrastructure (and data) to successfully train a CNN from scratch. Luckily a number of the big tech organisations offer pre-trained models which you can use to make your predictions as long as the images of interest are contained in the original model. If you want a model to detect new objects which are not contained in the original model you would have to extend these models to include new objects of interest. This is achieved using a technique known as transfer learning [29].

For example, if you want to detect an object that is not in the original model such as a giraffe and rhino you could train a new CNN from scratch. However, to get results we would need to train the model on 10,000s of images. The other way is to use transfer learning to train a new model but with far fewer data. Transfer learning takes what a model has learned previously and applies it to a new domain [30]. The early layers of a CNN identify simple shapes. The later layers learn more complex shapes while the very last layer make the predictions. Most layers of a pre-trained model are useful in new applications because most visual problems involve similar low-level visual patterns. So, we can reuse most of the pre-trained model and replace the final layer to make the predictions we require as shown in Fig. 6.42.

Transfer learning is of particular interest in industry as it allows practitioners to build upon previously acquired knowledge without the need to start from scratch. As we begin to build these models over time much more advanced learning and capabilities will emerge. In effect, this mirrors human learning where we build upon concepts and knowledge acquired from other people. We will cover transfer learning and the specifics of each architecture in Chap. 7.

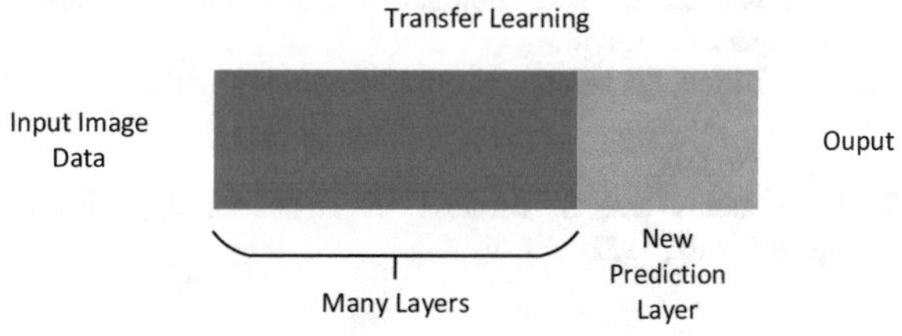

**Fig. 6.42** Transfer learning

## 6.5  Summary

This chapter provided an introduction to DL and how it differs from machine learning. It provided an in-depth discussion on ANNs which included information on perceptrons and different ANN architectures. The core principles in ANN architectures were introduced which included activation functions, binary and multiclass classification, cost functions and optimisers. It also focused on the learning aspects of neural networks and discussed the backpropagation algorithm and some of the issues surrounding the vanishing gradient. The chapter also discussed weight initialisation and the use of regularisation to combat overfitting.

Convolutional neural networks were introduced with a detailed discussion on image filters and kernels, convolutional layers and pooling layers. Transfer learning demonstrated how it is possible to capitalise on pre-trained CNNs to develop custom image processing applications to solve your own real-world problems.

# References

1. S. Pouyanfar et al., "A survey on deep learning: Algorithms, techniques, and applications," ACM Comput. Surv., vol. 51, no. 5, pp. 1–36, 2018.
2. A. Ivakhnenko, Cybernetics and forecasting techniques.
3. D. B. Parker, "Learning logic technical report tr-47," Cent. Comput. Res. Econ. Manag. Sci. Massachusetts Inst. Technol. Cambridge, MA, 1985.
4. Y. LeCun, D. Touresky, G. Hinton, and T. Sejnowski, "A theoretical framework for back-propagation," in Proceedings of the 1988 connectionist models summer school, 1988, vol. 1, pp. 21–28.
5. J. Deng, W. Dong, R. Socher, L.-J. Li, K. Li, and L. Fei-Fei, "Imagenet: A large-scale hierarchical image database," in 2009 IEEE conference on computer vision and pattern recognition, 2009, pp. 248–255.
6. D. Cirecsan, U. Meier, J. Masci, and J. Schmidhuber, "A committee of neural networks for traffic sign classification," in The 2011 international joint conference on neural networks, 2011, pp. 1918–1921.
7. D. Silver, A. Huang, C. J. Maddison, A. Guez, L. Sifre, and E. Al., "Mastering the game of Go with Deep Neural Networks and Tree Search," Nature, vol. 529, no. 7587, pp. 484–489, 2016.
8. S. DeWeerdt, "How to map the brain," Nature, vol. 571, no. 7766, pp. S6--S6, 2019.
9. T. B. Brown et al., "Language models are few-shot learners," arXiv Prepr. arXiv2005.14165, 2020.
10. J. Chakrabarty and W. J. Drugan, "Theory of plasticity," 1988.
11. H. Poritsky, "Heaviside's Operational Calculus—Its Applications and Foundations," Am. Math. Mon., vol. 43, no. 6, pp. 331–344, 1936.
12. D. E. Rumelhart, G. E. Hinton, and R. J. Williams, "Learning internal representations by error propagation," 1985.
13. D. L. Elliott, "A better activation function for artificial neural networks," 1993.
14. A. F. Agarap, "Deep learning using rectified linear units (relu)," arXiv Prepr. arXiv1803.08375, 2018.
15. H. Robbins and S. Monro, "A stochastic approximation method," Ann. Math. Stat., pp. 400–407, 1951.

16. D. P. Kingma and J. Ba, "Adam: A method for stochastic optimization," *arXiv Prepr. arXiv1412.6980*, 2014.
17. S. Hochreiter, "The vanishing gradient problem during learning recurrent neural nets and problem solutions," *Int. J. Uncertainty, Fuzziness Knowledge-Based Syst.*, vol. 6, no. 02, pp. 107–116, 1998.
18. A. L. Maas, A. Y. Hannun, A. Y. Ng, and others, "Rectifier nonlinearities improve neural network acoustic models," in *Proc. icml*, 2013, vol. 30, no. 1, p. 3.
19. X. Glorot and Y. Bengio, "Understanding the difficulty of training deep feedforward neural networks," in *Proceedings of the thirteenth international conference on artificial intelligence and statistics*, 2010, pp. 249–256.
20. K. He, X. Zhang, S. Ren, and J. Sun, "Delving deep into rectifiers: Surpassing human-level performance on imagenet classification," in *Proceedings of the IEEE international conference on computer vision*, 2015, pp. 1026–1034.
21. A. Krizhevsky, I. Sutskever, and G. E. Hinton, "Imagenet classification with deep convolutional neural networks," *Adv. Neural Inf. Process. Syst.*, vol. 25, pp. 1097–1105, 2012.
22. C. Cortes, M. Mohri, and A. Rostamizadeh, "L2 regularization for learning kernels," *arXiv Prepr. arXiv1205.2653*, 2012.
23. K. Fukushima and S. Miyake, "Neocognitron: A self-organizing neural network model for a mechanism of visual pattern recognition," in *Competition and cooperation in neural nets*, Springer, 1982, pp. 267–285.
24. K. Grill-Spector and R. Malach, "The human visual cortex," *Annu. Rev. Neurosci.*, vol. 27, pp. 649–677, 2004.
25. I. Sobel, R. Duda, P. Hart, and J. Wiley, "Sobel-Feldman Operator."
26. S. Albawi, T. A. Mohammed, and S. Al-Zawi, "Understanding of a convolutional neural network," in *2017 International Conference on Engineering and Technology (ICET)*, 2017, pp. 1–6.
27. D. C. Ciresan, U. Meier, J. Masci, L. M. Gambardella, and J. Schmidhuber, "Flexible, high performance convolutional neural networks for image classification," 2011.
28. T.-Y. Lin *et al.*, "Microsoft coco: Common objects in context," in *European conference on computer vision*, 2014, pp. 740–755.
29. S. Bozinovski and A. Fulgosi, "The influence of pattern similarity and transfer learning upon training of a base perceptron b2," in *Proceedings of Symposium Informatica*, 1976, pp. 3–121.
30. C. Tan, F. Sun, T. Kong, W. Zhang, C. Yang, and C. Liu, "A survey on deep transfer learning," in *International conference on artificial neural networks*, 2018, pp. 270–279.

# Chapter 7
# Image Classification and Object Detection

One of the most common applications for DL is image classification and object detection which aims to replicate one of the most important senses humans have. The influx of both data and compute capabilities have enabled the rapid growth and adoption of computer vision applications. This is one of the most significant technological revolutions which has demonstrated impact across multiple domains including manufacturing, healthcare, security, and autonomous vehicles. These vision systems are becoming increasingly integrated within the fabric of many vision applications currently deployed, such as CCTV, to understand and contextualise information for situational awareness.

Many aspects of computer vision have been research topics for many years. However, DL is regarded as a disruptive technology so much so that most computer vision applications now incorporate many aspects of DL. This is not to say that many of the traditional tools and techniques are redundant instead we would see them forming part of the application pipeline were DL and traditional computer vision tools work in conjunction. DL is good at extracting prominent features which allows them to detect and differentiate between different objects [1]. However, more complex computer vision tools are often required for detailed analysis. For example, packages such as OpenCV have a rich collection of non-DL algorithms to support the complex requirements for image analysis and processing [2].

In this chapter, we will introduce the main concepts associated with image classification and object detection which will include the hardware requirements, the different facets of object recognition, model architectures, supporting frameworks and the evaluation tools required to measure their performance.

© Springer Nature Switzerland AG 2022                                                      173
P. Fergus, C. Chalmers, *Applied Deep Learning*, Computational Intelligence
Methods and Applications, https://doi.org/10.1007/978-3-031-04420-5_7

## 7.1  Hardware Accelerated Deep Learning

Although you can train and inference (host) DL models using CPUs (which is supported in most frameworks) it is incredibly inefficient and slow. Simple model architectures can perform well however those which are comprised of hundreds of layers require alternative hardware such as GPU's. CPUs are designed to handle a wide range of tasks that can be processed very quickly. However, tasks can only be processed sequentially, and this means there is an inherent bottleneck in CPU computation when many calculations are required. GPU's address this limitation by running such calculations in parallel as shown in Table 7.1.

In the context of training a DL model both forward and backpropagation passes are undertaken. This process is the most computationally intensive part of the neural network which is made up of multiple matrix multiplications. Using a CPU to train large DL models would require considerable compute time. For example, in an object detection architecture, such as a ResNet50 with 23 million trainable parameters, it would take weeks if not months for the model to converge [3]. To deal with this level of complexity GPUs are often used to speed up the training and inferencing of DL models. A GPU allows us to perform all operations in parallel instead of doing them sequentially hence why they are used for training and hosting DL models.

There are a wide variety of different GPUs and selecting the right hardware is important when developing data-intensive applications such as object detection. The cost can range from £800 to over £10,000 per card and some heavy-duty models may require several cards to support both the memory and compute requirements.

For example, training a ResNet101-based model (using transfer learning) on a GeForce RTX 2080Ti using a batch size of 1, 1000 images with a resolution of $1024 \times 768$ takes around two hours to reach 25,000 epochs. This card costs £1125.00 at the time of writing.

Looking at a larger and more realistic example, training a ResNet101 model (again using transfer learning) on two Quadro RTX 8000 GPUs with a batch size of 16, 24,000 and images with a resolution of 1024 x 1024 would take around 7h to reach 20,000 epochs. These cards cost £5846.99 each at the time of writing.

**Table 7.1**  GPU vs CPU

| GPU | CPU |
| --- | --- |
| Hundreds of simpler cores | Few very complex cores |
| Thousands of concurrent hardware threads | Single-thread performance optimisation |
| Maximise floating-point throughput | Transistor space dedicated to complex integer linear programming |
| Most die surface for integer and floating-point units | Few die surface for integer and floating-point units |

## 7.1.1   Training and Associated Hardware

Whilst accelerated hardware is one of the most important components for DL the hardware requirements can vary significantly depending on whether you are developing, training, or inferencing a model. Each application has specific hardware requirements which need careful consideration.

### 7.1.1.1   Development Systems

DL workstations using GPU accelerators enable rapid performance for developing and debugging your DL and ML models. During this development stage, you can identify potential candidate models and prototype different architectures and alter hyperparameters before full-scale training is performed on a data centre solution. Some of the common GPU's available at the time of writing include:

- GeForce RTX 2080, 8GB RAM, 2944 CUDA cores
- GeForce RTX 2080 Ti, 11GB RAM, 4352 CUDA cores
- GeForce RTX 3090 Ti, 24GB RAM, 10496 CUDA cores, 328 Tensor Cores, 82 RT cores
- Quadro RTX 6000, 24GB RAM, 4608 CUDA Cores, 576 Tensor Cores, 72 RT Cores
- Quadro RTX 8000, 48GB RAM, 4608 CUDA Cores, 576 Tensor Cores, 72 RT Cores
- Quadro GV100, 32GB RAM, 5120 CUDA Cores, 640 Tensor Cores

### 7.1.1.2   Training Systems

Once initial model testing and selection has been undertaken full-scale training is performed on large scale training systems. Some of the most common GPU-based datacentre configurations at the time of writing include:

- NVIDIA DGX-1, 8 * Tesla V100s (each one has 5120 CUDA Cores, 640 Tensor Cores, and 32GB RAM)
- NVIDIA DGX-2, 16 * Tesla V100s (each one has 5120 CUDA Cores, 640 Tensor Cores, and 32GB RAM)
- NVIDIA DGX-A100, 8 * A100s (each one has 6912 CUDA Cores, 432 Tensor Cores, 40GB RAM)

### 7.1.1.3   Inferencing Systems

Once a model has been trained, the resulting neural network can be presented with new data to classify or make predictions - this is known as inferencing. Depending on the data the model was trained on it can either recognise and diagnose medical images, identify spoken words, or predict habits and routine behaviours. The first step when inferencing is to identify parts of the neural network that do not get activated after it is trained. These parts of the network are not needed, and it is beneficial to remove them in a process known as pruning. The second stage looks for ways to fuse multiple layers of the neural network into a single computational step. Other techniques will be discussed later in the book, but the aim is to compress and optimise the model for better runtime performance.

As the needs for inferencing are different from training, a dedicated set of hardware is recommended. Different hardware is required depending on where the inferencing is performed for example in the data centre or on the edge—such as remote cameras, drones, or autonomous vehicles. Some of the most common inferencing hardware at the time of writing include:

- Tesla T4, 2560 CUDA Cores, 320 Turing Tensor Cores, 16GB RAM.
- Jetson AGX Xavier, 512 Core Volta GPU, 16GB RAM

### 7.1.2   Tensor Processing Unit (TPU)

TPU's provide an alternative to GPUs for training DL models [4]. The first TPU's were manufactured by google and were available in 2016 – version 4 being the latest TPU release. Figure 7.1 shows the latest version of Google TPU.

TPU's offer a wide range of advantages which includes:

- Accelerated performance of linear algebra computation which is extensively used in ML.
- Minimises convergence when training large and complex neural network models.
- Minimise training time.
- Scale across multiple nodes.

A TPU is known as an application-specific integrated circuit (ASIC) and is specifically designed for DL/ML tasks. TPUs are 15 to 30 times faster than GPUs in inferencing and deliver between 30 and 80x improvement in TOPS/Watt usage [5]. In ML training, the Cloud TPU is more powerful in performance (180 vs. 120 TFLOPS) and four times larger in memory capacity (64 GB vs. 16 GB of memory) than Nvidia's best GPU Tesla V100.

The improved performance of TPU's is partially because parameters are loaded from memory into a matrix of multipliers and added together. As each multiplication is executed, the result is passed to the next multipliers while taking a summation at the same time. So, the output is the summation of all multiplication results between data and parameters. During the complete calculation process and data passing, no memory access is required.

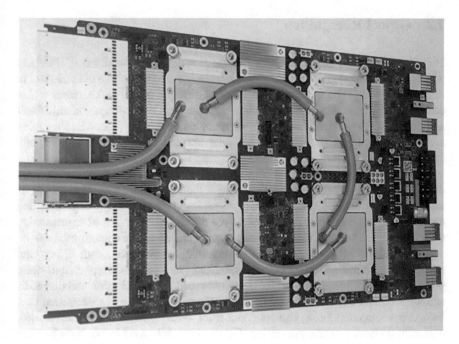

**Fig. 7.1**  Cloud TPU v3

## 7.1.3  Other Hardware Considerations

There are a few additional hardware considerations that are worth paying attention to. Firstly, GPU's can be power-hungry and require a Power Supply Unit (PSU) which meets the requirements of the GPU. Low voltage can cause training to fail or affect the performance of your GPU as it can be throttled by the driver. For example, you cannot simply put a NVidia RTX 8000 into a workstation without checking PSU, motherboard, and firmware compatibility. Certain types of hardware like the Tesla T4 are prone to thermal throttling if they are not cooled efficiently. You need to check with the manufacturer for both power and cooling requirements.

When installing a GPU, Random Access Memory (RAM) be equal to or greater than your highest GPU memory. If you are using large datasets you need to ensure that there is enough hard drive space with adequate throughput. One of the most common problems you are likely to encounter is GPU out of memory. In this instance, you can either replace your GPU with one that has a larger memory capacity or add additional GPU's if they are the same make and model and you have sufficient PSU capability.

## 7.2   Object Recognition

Object recognition is concerned with the detection and/or the localisation of objects within an image. Over the past few years, DL has matured to become the main tool in image processing. There are a wide variety of different model architectures which can be used depending on the problem and the application requirements. Most architectures have a balance between accuracy and compute time. More complex and deeper models will yield better results but can be expensive to train and inference.

Automated image analysis has been an active area of research since images were digitised and loaded onto computers. Between the 1970s and 1990s image analysis was performed using low-level pixel processing, typically using edge and line detector filters and region growing [6]. Some of the first examples of segmentation were edge-based segmentation approaches using snakes active contour models.

In the 1990s ML was first used in semantic segmentation, data fitting, and statistical classification using features extracted from images. Applications were primarily in the medical domain for computer-aided object detection and diagnosis and were completely designed by humans. DL changed this, and systems are now trained by computers using example data from which features are extracted automatically without human intervention. CNNs commonly used in DL have become the technique of choice in image processing.

Historical approaches have typically relied on classic image processing and traditional ML techniques. However, since AlexNet, DL has been utilised across many different domains [7]. However, as previously discussed training these models from scratch have proven to be problematic due to the substantial amounts of data and compute required. This has led to the introduction of transfer learning to train DL models. The use of computer vision has increased dramatically, due to advancements in DL, high-performance hardware and data availability. DL has facilitated developments in image processing, none more so than through the availability of frameworks like TensorFlow, Microsoft Cognitive Tool Kit (CNTK), PyTorch and Caffe 2. CNNs have become the gold standard for image processing tasks, in particular object detection and segmentation, which are now considered important techniques for analysing images.

There are four main ways to deal with visual recognition problems which include image classification, object detection, instance segmentation and semantic segmentation.

### 7.2.1   Image Classification

In image classification, the model is concerned with assigning the categorical class labels to the whole image (independent of how many classes are in the image) as

**Fig. 7.2** Image classification

shown in Fig. 7.2. This technique would be useful for automatically sorting images into distinct groups such as people, animals, and machinery.

### 7.2.2   Object Detection

In object detection, the model not only predicts the class labels but also localises each object instance using a bounding box as shown in Fig. 7.3. Bounding boxes are useful for counting objects and measuring the distance between them. It also becoming increasingly important in tracking applications for example in autonomous vehicles and adherence monitoring in construction sites and the use of protective equipment.

### 7.2.3   Semantic Segmentation

In semantic segmentation, the model tries to predict the categorical labels for each pixel without identifying different object instances as shown in Fig. 7.4. Semantic segmentation is used in autonomous driving, industrial inspection, classification of terrain and medical image analysis.

**Fig. 7.3** Object detection

**Fig. 7.4** Semantic segmentation

### 7.2.4   *Object Segmentation*

In object segmentation masks are used to identify different object instances within an image based on their pixel location as shown in Fig. 7.5. Examples of applications where object segmentation has been successfully used include medical imaging to measure volume in computed tomography and magnetic resonance imaging. These

**Fig. 7.5** Object segmentation

have been particularly useful for locating tumours, measuring tissue volumes, studying anatomical structure and intra-surgery navigation.

## 7.3 Model Architectures

Model architectures (different neural network configurations) and frameworks can be primarily divided into two categories which include one-stage detectors such as YOLO and two-stage detectors such as Region-based CNN (R-CNN). A one-stage detector makes predictions of objects located within an image whereas two-stage detectors use an intermediate component that suggests candidate proposals within the image which are then classified into distinct categories. One stage detectors are much faster in terms of compute time. While two-stage detectors often perform better in producing state of the art results.

Over the last decade there have been several different architectures trying to address the same problem but in different ways. Since AlexNet won the ILSVRC competition in 2012 there have been several additional complex architectures proposed which have decreased the error rate for detection year-on-year. The timeline of model architectures is shown in Fig. 7.6 starting with AlexNet and ending with EfficientNet (note there are many more but the most significant are shown).

The remainder of this section will introduce some of the more common architectures which are implemented in frameworks such as TensorFlow, CNTK and PyTorch.

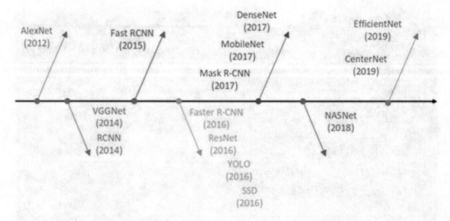

**Fig. 7.6**  Progression of model architectures

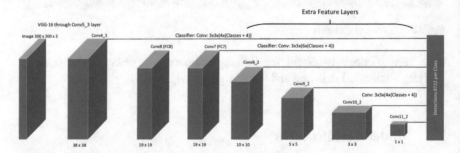

**Fig. 7.7**  SSD architecture

### 7.3.1  *Single Shot Detector (SSD)*

The SDD architecture was first proposed in 2016 [8]. The latest version at the time of writing is SSD 512. As the SSD is a single shot detector the inferencing time is much lower than other architectures such as the R-CNN. As such it can be used for real-time detection. Unlike other architectures, the image size cannot be increased during training and must remain fixed. Figure 7.7 shows the SSD architecture.

The SDD object detection network performs two tasks. Firstly, it extracts the feature maps and secondly, it applies convolution filters to detect objects. SSD uses the VGG16 backbone (although other base networks can be used, such as YOLO or MobileNet) to extract the feature maps which are then used to classify objects. As you can see in Fig. 7.8 the process is applied multiple times to accommodate for scale. This means that if there are two dogs in an image one in the foreground and one in the background both objects can still be detected. For each location it makes four predictions (our boxes) each box consists of a bounding box and the 21 classes one extra class for no object). Note that the 20 objects relate to the PASCAL VOC dataset which has 20 classes. The box with the highest scoring class is chosen.

**Fig. 7.8**  Object locations

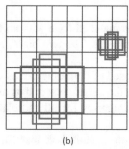
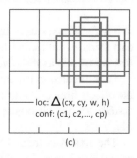

loc: $\Delta$(cx, cy, w, h)
conf: (c1, c2,..., cp)

(a)                          (b)                          (c)

**Fig. 7.9**  Default boxes based on filter size, (**a**) Image with GT boxes, (**b**) 8 x 8 Feature Map and (**c**) 4 x 4 Feature Map

Conv4_3 makes a total of $38 \times 38 \times 4$ predictions: four predictions per cell regardless of the depth of the feature maps as shown in Fig. 7.8. As expected, many predictions contain no object. SSD reserves a class "0" to indicate it has no object.

SSD uses different size filters to predict classes to accommodate for scale. SSD adds 6 additional convolution layers after the VGG16 to achieve this. Five of them will be added for object detection while the sixth is used for scaling [8]. In three of those layers, we make 6 predictions instead of 4. In total, SSD makes 8732 predictions using 6 layers (8732 default boxes distributed across the whole image). Multi-scale feature maps significantly improve accuracy. Each box at each location is evaluated using the feature maps associated with each aspect ratio (different convolutional layers in the SSD network).

During the training of an SSD, the default boxes are matched over aspect ratio, location and scale to the ground truth boxes. We select the boxes with the highest overlap with the ground truth bounding boxes. The Intersection Over Union (IOU) between predicted boxes and ground truth should be greater than 0.5. We select the predicted box with maximum overlap with the ground truth. Figure 7.9 shows that

loc: $\Delta$(cx, cy, w, h)
conf: (c1, c2,..., cp)

**Fig. 7.10** Default boxes based on filter size

two default boxes have been matched (one with an Common Eland and one with a car) using two different filter sizes. The two boxes are treated as positive while the rest are treated as negative.

Each prediction is composed of bounding boxes with a shape offset representing the offsets from the centre of the default box and its height and width. In addition, the confidence for all object categories for all the classes are included as shown in Fig. 7.10.

The model is trained using a multi-box loss function which contains both the confidence loss and localisation loss.

Higher-resolution feature maps are responsible for detecting small objects. The first layer for object detection conv4_3 has a spatial dimension of 38 × 38, resulting in a significant reduction from the input image. Hence SSD usually performs badly for small objects compared with other detection methods. In SSD, small objects can only be detected in higher resolution layers (leftmost layers). But those layers contain low-level features, like edges or colour patches, that are less informative for classification. Multi-scale feature maps improve the detection of objects at different scales. One of the key features of the SSD is its speed and low computational requirements. SSD models can therefore be easily deployed on edge and mobile devices. SSDs work well in controlled conditions where the input sizes are carefully managed and there are minimal environmental changes. An example where SSD can be used is in the detection of animals in close proximity using camera traps. They would however be less useful in applications such as autonomous vehicles (due to the need for more distance shots and the identification of smaller objects).

### 7.3.2  YOLO Family

YOLO is a state-of-the-art object detection model which has seen several iterations. The latest at the time of writing is YOLOv3 [9]. The complete architecture can be seen in Fig. 7.11.

YOLOv3 has 53 convolutional layers called Darknet-53 which it uses for its base network. No form of pooling is used. The convolutional layer has a stride value of 2 which is used to downsample feature maps as shown in Fig. 7.12.

YOLO is invariant to the size of the input image. However, in practice, it is better to stick to a fixed size. The network downsamples the image in relation to the stride of the network. For example, if the stride is 32 then an input image of size 416 x 416 will generate an output of 13 x 13. Generally, the stride of any network is equal to the factor by which the output of the layer is smaller than the input image to the network (downsampling).

The output for the detection kernel is $1 \times 1 \times (B \times (5 + C))$. B is the number of bounding boxes a cell on the feature map can predict, "5" is for the 4 bounding box attributes and one object confidence, and C is the number of classes. A YOLO v3 model trained with the COCO dataset would have, $B = 3$ and $C = 80$. Therefore, the kernel size would be $1 \times 1 \times 255$. The feature map produced by this kernel has the same height and width as the previous feature map and has detection attributes along with the depth as shown in Fig. 7.13.

YOLO v3 makes predictions at three scales which are given by downsampling the dimensions of the input image by 32, 16, and 8. Using a 32 x 32 stride will give you a $13 \times 13$ layer, which is sufficient for the detection of larger objects. For small objects, an $8 \times 8$ stride will give you a $52 \times 52$ layer which is good for detecting smaller objects. The predictions are made at layers 82, 94 and 106 as shown in Fig. 7.13.

The three different layers are designed to help detect objects at different scales which was a limitation of YOLO v1 and v2. The upsampled layers (by increasing the

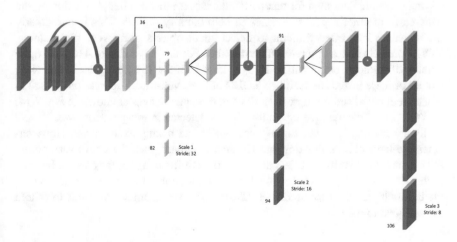

**Fig. 7.11** YOLOv3 architecture

**Fig. 7.12** CNN layers

| | Type | Filters | Size | Output |
|---|---|---|---|---|
| | Convolutional | 32 | 3 × 3 | 256 × 256 |
| | Convolutional | 64 | 3 × 3 / 2 | 128 × 128 |
| 1× | Convolutional | 32 | 1 × 1 | |
| | Convolutional | 64 | 3 × 3 | |
| | Residual | | | 128 × 128 |
| | Convolutional | 128 | 3 × 3 / 2 | 64 × 64 |
| 2× | Convolutional | 64 | 1 × 1 | |
| | Convolutional | 128 | 3 × 3 | |
| | Residual | | | 64 × 64 |
| | Convolutional | 256 | 3 × 3 / 2 | 32 × 32 |
| 8× | Convolutional | 128 | 1 × 1 | |
| | Convolutional | 256 | 3 × 3 | |
| | Residual | | | 32 × 32 |
| | Convolutional | 512 | 3 × 3 / 2 | 16 × 16 |
| 8× | Convolutional | 256 | 1 × 1 | |
| | Convolutional | 512 | 3 × 3 | |
| | Residual | | | 16 × 16 |
| | Convolutional | 1024 | 3 × 3 / 2 | 8 × 8 |
| 4× | Convolutional | 512 | 1 × 1 | |
| | Convolutional | 1024 | 3 × 3 | |
| | Residual | | | 8 × 8 |
| | Avgpool | | Global | |
| | Connected | | 1000 | |
| | Softmax | | | |

stride we increase the number of cells in the grid) concatenate with previous layers and this helps to preserve the fine-grained features. In other words, you are not just relying on the feature map for that particular aspect ratio/size but also including the features from other aspect ratio/sizes to help identify objects. This is particularly useful where it is often difficult to detect small objects using very big features. YOLO predicts boxes at three different scales. For an image size of 416 × 416 the number of predicted boxes will be 10,647 ($13 \times 13 \times 3 + 26 \times 26 \times 3 + 52 \times 52 \times 3$). Not all of these boxes are useful so YOLO utilises Non-Max Suppression (NMS) to reduce redundant and multiple detections in the same images as shown in Fig. 7.14.

YOLO predicts multiple labels for objects detected in images. However, YOLO no longer uses Softmaxing as only one object can belong to one class. However, when we have classes like dog and German Sheppard, then the above assumption fails. This is the reason YOLOv3 no longer uses Softmaxing for the classes. Instead, each class score is predicted using logistic regression and a threshold is used to predict multiple labels for an object. Classes with scores higher than this threshold are assigned to the box.

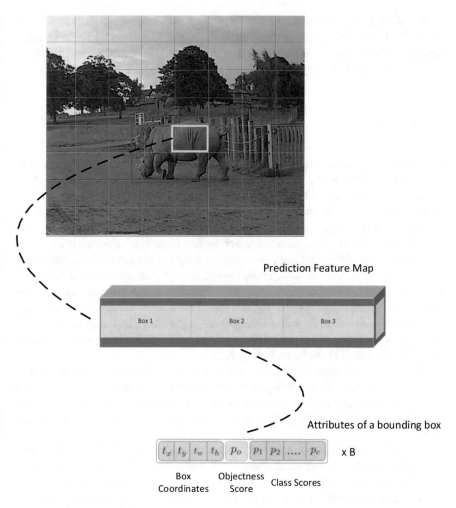

Prediction Feature Map

Attributes of a bounding box

$$t_x \quad t_y \quad t_w \quad t_h \quad p_o \quad p_1 \quad p_2 \quad .... \quad p_c \quad \text{x B}$$

Box          Objectness
Coordinates    Score      Class Scores

**Fig. 7.13**  Prediction feature map

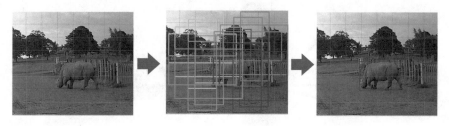

**Fig. 7.14**  NMS

YOLOv3 is fast, efficient and can be as accurate as two-stage detectors (when using 0.5 IOU). One of the main limitations of the YOLO architecture is that it struggles with small objects within the image. For example, it might have difficulties in detecting a flock of birds. This is due to the spatial constraints of the architecture.

### 7.3.3   R-CNN

Like other architectures, Region-based CNNs (R-CNNs) try to locate objects in an image (object detection) [10]. R-CNN first uses a sliding window approach which scans the entire image with different sized rectangles while analysing the obtained images using a brute-force approach. The issue with this method is that it generates many proposals (Region proposals are just smaller parts of the original image, that we think contains the objects we are searching for) to analyse as shown in Fig. 7.15.

There are a set of pre-defined region proposal algorithms that can be directly used in object detection architectures. In the case of R-CNN, the selective search method is implemented to generate region proposals. Selective search is based on computing hierarchical grouping of similar regions based on colour, texture, size and shape compatibility. Selective Search starts by over-segmenting the image based on the intensity of the pixels using the graph-based segmentation method by Felzenszwalb and Huttenlocher [11] as shown in Fig. 7.16.

However, at this stage, most of the actual objects contain two or more segmented parts. Regions that are close together are combined to form a single segment. Distinct regions described by prominent segments are used to derive bounding box coordinates (region proposals). Note Region proposals cannot be used for occluded objects.

This will create a large number of regions we will have to look at. This sounds like a big number, but it's still very small compared to the brute-force sliding window approach. In the next stage, we take each region proposal and create a feature map representing the image in a much smaller dimension using a CNN. The

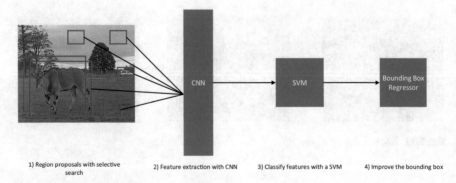

1) Region proposals with selective search          2) Feature extraction with CNN          3) Classify features with a SVM          4) Improve the bounding box

**Fig. 7.15**   R-CNN architecture

**Fig. 7.16**  Selective search

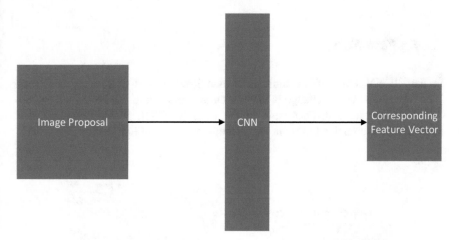

**Fig. 7.17**  AlexNet

R-CNN uses the AlexNet base network as a feature extractor. This means you cannot train the entire network at once instead AlexNet needs to be trained before the classification task. After AlexNet is trained the last SoftMax layer is removed and as shown in Fig. 7.17.

The input to AlexNet is always the same (227, 227, 3) however the image proposals will have different shapes. Many of them are smaller or larger than the required size therefore, each region proposal will need to be resized. Feature vectors are created from the image proposals which are later classified. The aim is to detect what class of object those feature vectors represent which is performed using an SVM classifier. There is one SVM for each object class. This means that for one feature vector we have $n$ outputs, where $n$ is the number of different objects we want to detect. The output is a confidence score which represents the confidence of the prediction.

The SVM is trained using the feature vectors created by the AlexNet backbone. This means, that the CNN must be fully trained before training the SVM can commence. The training is not parallelizable. The network can train the SVM using a supervised learning approach as each class is represented by a given feature vector.

The R-CNN architecture was a breakthrough in computer vision as it combined region proposals with a CNN. However, it has serious limitations:

- It is slow as the network must calculate a feature map (one CNN forward pass) for each region proposal.
- It is hard to train since the R-CNN architecture has 3 distinct parts (CNN, SVM, Bounding Box Regressor) that had to be trained separately.
- It has a large memory requirement since the architecture must save the feature map of each region proposal.

### 7.3.4   Fast–RCNN

In Fast-RCNN some of the limitations associated with R-CNN were addressed [12]. The most notable change is that the entire architecture can be trained end-to-end. Here the three distinct parts in the R-CNN (CNN, SVM, Bounding Box Regressor) are combined into one architecture as shown in Fig. 7.18.

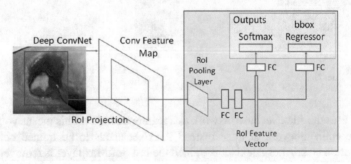

**Fig. 7.18** Fast-RCNN Architecture

Firstly, it processes the whole image using the CNN. This results in a feature map of the image. For each region proposal, the network extracts the corresponding part from the feature map. This is called the region proposal feature map. The region proposal feature map is resized into a fixed size using a pooling layer. The feature map is flattened into a fixed size one-dimensional feature vector which is inputted directly into the fully connected layers (MLP) which has two sets of outputs. The first is the softmax classification layer, which determines which class the object belongs to. The second is the Bounding Box Regressor, where the output is the bounding box coordinates for each object class.

The Fast-RCNN is considerably more efficient than an R-CNN given that you can train the complete network as a single unit. As such this also significantly improves the inference time. The training process itself can now also be conducted as a single unit using backpropagation.

## 7.3.5   Faster-RCNN

The Faster R-CNN architecture was developed by researchers at Microsoft [13]. It is based on the R-CNN architecture and uses a multi-phased approach to object detection. The Faster R-CNN has a Region Proposal Network (RPN) to generate a fixed set of regions. The RPN uses the convolutional features from the base network, to generate a set of region proposals. The RPN is implemented as a fully convolutional network that predicts object bounds and objectness scores at each position. The Faster-RCNN architecture is shown in Fig. 7.19.

RPN within the Faster R-CNN architecture identifies candidate regions using previously learnt features in the base network (ResNet/Inception). The RPN replaces the selective search method in early R-CNN networks where region proposals were input at the pixel level rather than the feature map level. The RPN tries to find bounding boxes in the image where each box has varied sizes and aspect ratios (nine in total) as shown in Fig. 7.20.

Anchors (fixed bounding boxes) are placed throughout the image. Each anchor is represented using 9 different size and aspect ratio bounding boxes. These are referenced by the RPN when first predicting object locations. The RPN is implemented as a CNN, using the convolutional feature map provided by the base network. Therefore, since we are working with a convolutional feature map of size conv_{width} * conv_{height} * conv_{depth}, we create a set of anchors for each of the points in conv_{width} * conv_{height}. Since we only have convolutional and pooling layers, the dimensions of the feature map will be proportional to those of the original image. Mathematically, if the image was w * h, the feature map will end up w/r * h/r where r is called subsampling ratio. If we define one anchor per spatial position of the feature map, the final image will end up with several anchors separated by r pixels.

For each anchor bounding box, the RPN generates two outputs a) a probability objectness score and b) a set of bounding box coordinates. The first output is a binary

**Fig. 7.19** Faster R-CNN

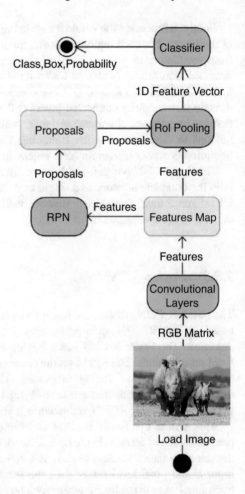

classification and the second is a bounding box regression adjustment. During the training process all the classified anchors are placed into one of two distinct categories a) those that overlap a ground-truth object with an Intersection over Union (IoU) bigger than 0.5, labelled as "foreground" and b) those that do not overlap any ground truth object or have less than 0.1 IoU with ground-truth objects, labelled as "background". Anchors are then randomly sampled to form a mini-batch of size 256 with a balanced ratio between foreground and background anchors. This mini-batch is used to calculate the classification loss using binary cross-entropy. The mini-batch anchors marked as foreground are used to calculate the regression loss and the correct change needed to transform the anchor into the object.

It is possible to end up with zero foreground anchors. In this case, the anchors with the biggest IoU to the ground truth boxes are used. This is far from ideal, but practical in the sense that we always have foreground samples and targets to learn from. Anchors usually overlap; therefore, proposals also end up overlapping over the

**Fig. 7.20**  RPN

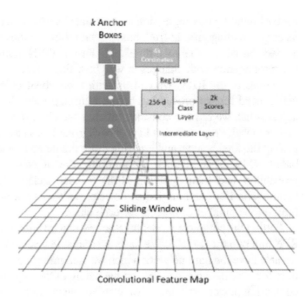

same object. To reduce the number of anchor boxes, NMS is performed, where the intersection anchor box will be deleted if it has a lower IoU value of the ground truth.

The RPN step concludes with a set of object proposals with no class assigned to them. These bounding boxes now need to be classified into the desired categories. A simple method, which is widely used by object detection implementations, including Faster R-CNN, is to crop the convolutional feature map using each proposal and resize each crop to a fixed-sized 14 * 14 * convdepth using interpolation. After cropping, max pooling with a 2x2 kernel is used to get a final 7 * 7 * 512 feature map for each proposal (via Region of interest Pooling). These dimensions are default parameters set by the Fast R-CNN.

The Fast R-CNN takes the feature map (7 * 7 * 512) for each proposal and flattens it into a one-dimensional vector that is connected to two fully-connected layers of size 4096 with ReLU activation. An additional fully-connected layer with N + 1 units where N is the total number of classes and an extra one for the background class is implemented to identify the object class. In parallel, a second fully-connected layer with 4N units is implemented for bounding box regression prediction. The 4 parameters correspond to the change centroid x, y values including the width and height of the box for each of the N possible classes.

Targets for Fast R-CNN are calculated in a similar way to RPN targets, but in this instance, the different possible classes are considered. The proposals and the ground-truth boxes are used to calculate the IoU between them. Proposals with an IoU greater than 0.5 with any ground truth box get assigned as foreground. Proposals with an IoU between 0.1 and 0.5 get labelled as background. Proposals without any intersection are ignored because at this stage we assume we only have good proposals and are more interested in solving the harder cases. These values are hyperparameters and can be tuned to better fit the objects of interest. The targets for the bounding box regression are calculated as the offset between the proposal and its corresponding ground-truth box, only for those proposals that have been assigned a class based on the IoU threshold. Fast R-CNN training is carried out using backpropagation with changes in weights using ADAM.

Similar to the RPN, we end up with a bunch of objects with classes assigned which need further processing before returning them. To apply the bounding box adjustments, we have to consider which is the class with the highest probability for that proposal. Proposals that have a background class assignment are ignored. After getting the final objects and ignoring those predicted as background, we apply class-based NMS. This is done by grouping the objects by class, sorting them by probability and then applying NMS to each independent group before joining them again. For our final list of objects, we also set a probability threshold and a limit on the number of objects for each class.

Putting the complete model together we end up with 4 different losses, two for the RPN and two for R-CNN. We have the trainable layers in the RPN and R-CNN, and we also have the base network which we can train (fine-tune) or not. The decision to train the base network depends on the nature of the objects we want to learn and the computing power available. If we want to detect objects that are similar to those that were in the original dataset on which the base network was trained on, then there is no need. On the other hand, training the base network can be expensive both in time and on the necessary hardware, to be able to fit the complete gradients. The four different losses are combined using a weighted sum. This is because we may want to give classification losses more weight relative to regression ones, or give R-CNN losses more power over the RPNs'.

One of the main advantages of a Faster-RCNN is its ability to detect smaller objects within a given image. It also has the added benefit of not requiring a fixed input resolution. However, one of the biggest issues with the Faster-RCNN architecture is speed. Real-time inferencing requires significant GPU hardware to achieve a reasonable frame rate. While other models such as the SSD are much faster, they cannot achieve the same level of performance as the Faster-CNN. The Faster-RCNN low-resolution feature maps for detection can dramatically hinder performance. Like will all models image resolution impacts performance significantly, whilst reducing the image size impacts accuracy it also reduces inferencing time.

### 7.3.6   EfficientNet

The EfficientNet Architecture works on the principle of model scaling [14]. Scaling is done to improve the model's accuracy on a certain task which is typically a tedious process. This requires the practitioner to manually trial and error different model scales until a sufficiently accurate model is produced and one that satisfies the resource constraints. This process is both time and resource-intensive and often yields models of suboptimal accuracy and efficiency.

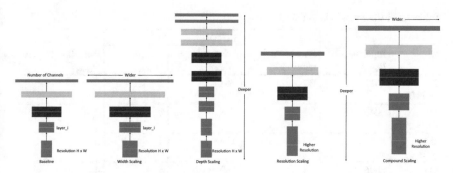

**Fig. 7.21** CNN scaling

There are three scaling dimensions of a CNN: depth, width, and resolution. Depth simply means how deep the network is which is equivalent to the number of layers in it. Width simply means how wide the network is. One measure of width, for example, is the number of channels in a Conv layer whereas resolution is simply the image resolution that is being passed to a CNN. Figure 7.21 shows the different scaling options.

It is critical to balance all dimensions of a network (width, depth, and resolution) during CNN's scaling for obtaining improved accuracy and efficiency. The EfficientNet architecture deploys a scaling technique that uses a compound coefficient to uniformly scale the networks width, depth, and resolution. Scaling does not change the layer operations; hence it is better to first have a good baseline network and then scale it along different dimensions using the proposed compound scaling. EfficientNet uses a Neural Architecture Search (NAS) that optimises for both accuracy and FLOPS to construct a base network.

The EfficientNet base network can be used with the EfficientDet architecture [15]. This architecture uses the Bi-directional Feature Pyramid Network (BiFPN), which is like the pyramid network used in YOLO v3 whereby features from different scales are aggregated at different resolutions. 3-7 input features which each represent an input feature at a given resolution. The FPN in this sense aggregates multi-scale features in a top-down manner. The FPN however is inherently limited by the flow of information, which is in one direction. The BiFPN extends this by adding a bottom-up path. The complete EfficientDet network architecture uses the EfficientNet backbone. The BiFPN in this network serves as a feature network that takes the features from levels 3-7 in the backbone and repeatedly applies the BiFPN. The fused features are input to a fully connected layer to predict the object class and bounding box. The EfficientDet compound scaling method for object detection was inspired by the compound scaling technique used in EfficientNet. This method uses a coefficient to jointly scale up all dimensions of the backbone network, BiFPN network, class/box network and resolution. The backbone network uses the same coefficients as defined in B0-B6 so that the ImageNet pre-trained weights can be reused. In the BiFPN the width is exponentially grown (channels) and the depth is linearly increased (layers). In the case of the Box/class prediction network, the width

**Table 7.2** EfficientDet-D0 to D6

| | Input size $R_{input}$ | Backbone network | BiFPN | | Box/class #layers $D_{class}$ |
|---|---|---|---|---|---|
| | | | #channels $W_{bifpn}$ | #layers $D_{bifpn}$ | |
| D0 (o = 0) | 512 | B0 | 64 | 2 | 3 |
| D1 (o = 0) | 640 | B1 | 88 | 3 | 3 |
| D2 (o = 0) | 768 | B2 | 112 | 4 | 3 |
| D3 (o = 0) | 896 | B3 | 160 | 5 | 4 |
| D4 (o = 0) | 1024 | B4 | 224 | 6 | 4 |
| D5 (o = 0) | 1280 | B5 | 288 | 7 | 4 |
| D6 (o = 0) | 1408 | B6 | 384 | 8 | 5 |
| D7 | 1536 | B6 | 384 | 8 | 5 |

is fixed to be the same as in the BiFPN but the depth is linearly increased. Finally, the input image resolution is also increased linearly since the resolution must be divisible by $2^7 = 128$. Using parameters, a family of networks have been created from EfficientDet-D0 to D6 as shown in Table 7.2.

The EfficientDet architecture has been shown to consistently achieve better accuracy and efficiency when compared to other architectures. EfficientDet achieves much better accuracy with fewer parameters and FLOPS. EfficientNet provides a compound scaling mechanism to manage the width, depth, and resolution. This allows for a baseline network to be constructed based on the underlying computational constraints while maintaining model efficiency. These EfficientNet models can be scaled up effectively to surpass the current state of the art performance with an order of magnitudes and reduce FLOPS using ImageNet and other transfer learning datasets.

## 7.3.7 Comparing Architectures

Many of these architectures have similarities in terms of techniques and structure but are designed to address different requirements which primarily is speed versus accuracy. This section is concluded with some key findings across all the models discussed and a summary of those that are most accurate and those that are fastest.

### 7.3.7.1 Key Findings

- SSD models are generally much faster than Faster R-CNN architectures with the SSD processing around 46 FPS and the Faster-RCNN processing 7 FPS. However, they are no match in terms of accuracy as offered by the Faster R-CNN.
- The use of low-resolution feature maps significantly impacts accuracy.
- Consideration needs to be given as to the image resolution. Reducing image resolution can adversely affect accuracy (a 50% reduction in height and widths can lower accuracy by 15%).
- The choice of the base network (feature extractor) can also affect detection accuracy for the Faster-RCNN but less so for the SSD.
- Not all computation is performed on the GPU for example NMS is run on the CPU. This can adversely affect the training times especially with large images and bigger datasets.
- By decreasing the stride in the base network, can improve the overall mAP. For example, decreasing the stride from 16 to 8 can improve the mAP by 5%. However, this will increase compute time by 63%.

### 7.3.7.2 Most Accurate

- The most accurate model at the time of writing is the Faster R-CNN using Inception ResNet with 300 proposals.
- EfficientDet is one of the most recent architectures that is showing good accuracy with less tuneable parameters while requiring a reduced number of FLOPS.

### 7.3.7.3 Fastest

- SSD with MobileNet provides the best accuracy when using fast detectors.
- SSD is fast but is particularly bad at detecting small objects when compared to other architectures.
- For large objects, the SSD can outperform both the Faster R-CNN and R-CNN in terms of accuracy with lighter and faster extractors.
- Faster R-CNN can match the speed of the SSD at 32mAP if we reduce the number of proposals to 50.

## 7.4 Evaluation Metrics

For object detection, there are a variety of different evaluation metrics which can be used to determine the performance of a model [16]. Most of these metrics stem from the various object detection competitions that exist such as the COCO object detection challenge. Most of these challenges use the same metrics although some additional metrics can be used. Building on the evaluation metrics discussed in the previous chapter (which can also be used to evaluate object detection models) more specific metrics are discussed below.

### 7.4.1   Confidence Score

The confidence score is the probability that an anchor box contains an object. It is usually predicted by a classifier. Both the confidence score and Intersection Over Union IoU (introduced later) are used as the criteria that determine whether a detection is a true positive or a false positive.

A detection is considered a true positive (TP) only if it satisfies three conditions: confidence score > threshold; the predicted class matches the class of a ground truth; the predicted bounding box has an IoU greater than a threshold (e.g., 0.5) with the ground-truth. Violation of either of the latter two conditions makes a false positive (FP). By setting the threshold for the confidence score at various levels, we get different pairs of precision and recall values.

### 7.4.2   Intersection over Union

To evaluate the performance of object detection models we need to use a different set of metrics. To measure how accurate the object identified in an image/frame we can make use of the metric IOU. There are two standards mAP @IOU.50 and mAP @IOU.75. As shown in Fig. 7.22 the closer the predicted box is to the object contained in the ground truth box the higher the mAP.

Obtaining a high IOU@.50 meaning that at least 50% of the object resides within the predicted bounding box is easy to achieve in contrast to .75 where at least 75% of the object resides within the predicted bounding box. An example training session is shown in Fig. 7.23 highlighting how the mAP improves throughout training.

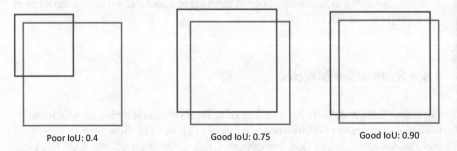

Poor IoU: 0.4                 Good IoU: 0.75              Good IoU: 0.90

**Fig. 7.22** Shows the different IOU

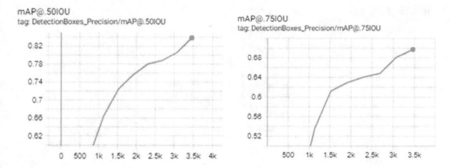

**Fig. 7.23**   IOU over training duration

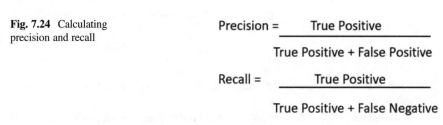

**Fig. 7.24**  Calculating
precision and recall

You can set a threshold value for the IoU to determine if the object detection is valid or not:

- If IoU $\geq 0.5$, classify the object detection as True Positive (TP)
- If IoU $< 0.5$, then it is a wrong detection and classify it as False Positive (FP)
- When a ground truth is present in the image and model fails to detect the object, classify it as False Negative (FN)
- True Negative (TN): TN is every part of the image where we did not predict an object. This metrics is not useful for object detection, hence we ignore TN
- Set the IoU threshold value to 0.5 or greater. It can be set to 0.5, 0.75. 0.9 or 0.95 etc.

### 7.4.3   Mean Average Precision (mAP)

You can see Precision and Recall as the metrics to evaluate the performance. Precision and Recall are calculated using true positives (TP), false positives (FP) and false negatives (FN) as shown in Fig. 7.24. Note it is important to calculate precision and recall for all objects present in the image.

It is important to consider the confidence score for each object detected by the model in the image. This is also true for all predicted bounding boxes with a confidence score above a certain threshold. Bounding boxes above the threshold value are considered positive boxes and all predicted bounding boxes below the

**Fig. 7.25** PR graph

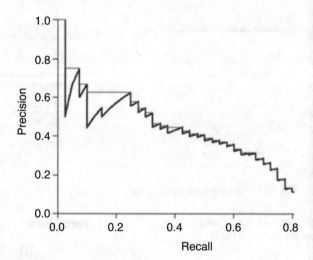

threshold value are considered negative. mAP is calculated using 11-point interpolation.

Precision and recall values are plotted using a Precision-Recall (PR) graph. A PR graph is monotonically decreasing, there is always a trade-off between precision and recall. Increasing one will decrease the other. Interpolated precision is average precision measured at 11 equally spaced recall levels of 0.0, 0.1, 0.2, 0.3 ....0.9, 1.0. Finally, the arithmetic mean of the interpolated precision is calculated at each recall level for information in the test collection. Figure 7.25 shows an example PR graph.

## 7.5   Summary

In this chapter, we introduced both image classification and object detection. This started with a discussion on hardware-accelerated DL including a discussion on CPU's, GPU's and TPU's. The specific details for training and inferencing hardware were presented with a detailed description of hardware considerations when implementing both pipelines. This was followed by a discussion on object recognition which included a description of image classification, object detection, semantic segmentation, and object segmentation. The main model architectures were introduced and these included, SSD-MobileNet, the YOLO family, R-CNN, Fast R-CNN, Faster R-CNN and EfficientNet. A summary of the benefits and limitations of each architecture where provided. The chapter was concluded with a discussion on the specific evaluation metrics for object detection.

# References

1. S. Albawi, T. A. Mohammed, and S. Al-Zawi, "Understanding of a convolutional neural network," in *2017 International Conference on Engineering and Technology (ICET)*, 2017, pp. 1–6.
2. G. Bradski and A. Kaehler, *Learning OpenCV: Computer vision with the OpenCV library*. " O'Reilly Media, Inc.," 2008.
3. K. He, X. Zhang, S. Ren, and J. Sun, "Deep residual learning for image recognition," in *Proceedings of the IEEE conference on computer vision and pattern recognition*, 2016, pp. 770–778.
4. N. P. Jouppi *et al.*, "In-datacenter performance analysis of a tensor processing unit," in *Proceedings of the 44th annual international symposium on computer architecture*, 2017, pp. 1–12.
5. Y. E. Wang, G.-Y. Wei, and D. Brooks, "Benchmarking tpu, gpu, and cpu platforms for deep learning," *arXiv Prepr. arXiv1907.10701*, 2019.
6. R. Maini and H. Aggarwal, "Study and comparison of various image edge detection techniques," *Int. J. image Process.*, vol. 3, no. 1, pp. 1–11, 2009.
7. A. Krizhevsky, I. Sutskever, and G. E. Hinton, "Imagenet classification with deep convolutional neural networks," *Adv. Neural Inf. Process. Syst.*, vol. 25, pp. 1097–1105, 2012.
8. W. Liu *et al.*, "Ssd: Single shot multibox detector," in *European conference on computer vision*, 2016, pp. 21–37.
9. J. Redmon, S. Divvala, R. Girshick, and A. Farhadi, "You only look once: Unified, real-time object detection," in *Proceedings of the IEEE conference on computer vision and pattern recognition*, 2016, pp. 779–788.
10. R. Girshick, J. Donahue, T. Darrell, and J. Malik, "Region-based convolutional networks for accurate object detection and segmentation," *IEEE Trans. Pattern Anal. Mach. Intell.*, vol. 38, no. 1, pp. 142–158, 2015.
11. P. F. Felzenszwalb and D. P. Huttenlocher, "Efficient graph-based image segmentation," *Int. J. Comput. Vis.*, vol. 59, no. 2, pp. 167–181, 2004.
12. R. Girshick, "Fast r-cnn," in *Proceedings of the IEEE international conference on computer vision*, 2015, pp. 1440–1448.
13. S. Ren, K. He, R. Girshick, and J. Sun, "Faster r-cnn: Towards real-time object detection with region proposal networks," in *Advances in neural information processing systems*, 2015, pp. 91–99.
14. M. Tan and Q. Le, "Efficientnet: Rethinking model scaling for convolutional neural networks," in *International Conference on Machine Learning*, 2019, pp. 6105–6114.
15. M. Tan, R. Pang, and Q. V Le, "Efficientdet: Scalable and efficient object detection," in *Proceedings of the IEEE/CVF conference on computer vision and pattern recognition*, 2020, pp. 10781–10790.
16. R. Padilla, S. L. Netto, and E. A. B. da Silva, "A survey on performance metrics for object-detection algorithms," in *2020 International Conference on Systems, Signals and Image Processing (IWSSIP)*, 2020, pp. 237–242.

# Chapter 8
# Deep Learning Techniques for Time Series Modelling

So far in this book, we have discussed traditional machine learning and deep learning concepts which have been primarily focused on tabular and image-based data. Time series data plays a significant part in our daily lives. From predicting stocks and shares in the stock market to monitoring the vital statistics of a patient and determining medical outcomes. There are many prediction problems and a common component between them all is time. Some of these include electronic patient records, activity recognition and cyber security. In recent years there has been a rapid increase in temporal data availability which directly benefits from the use of DNNs. Given the need to classify and predict time series data both industry and research leaders have proposed hundreds of different methods and developed a wide variety of frameworks and packages to solve this problem. Historically, techniques included algorithms such as nearest neighbour and distance functions to process temporal data structures. Other methods included the use of decision trees, random forest and support vector machines which outperformed some of the earlier traditional approaches. Following the successes of DNNs for computer vision the research for time series has now refocused and repurposed to solve complex temporal problems such as natural languages processing and machine translation.

In similar ways to computer vision and image processing whereby specialised algorithms are used to model image data for object detection and classification, the time-series domain also has a set of algorithms to model data for prediction. While many different algorithms have been proposed only a small number of them are DNNs. This is not surprising as DNNs have been used to solve many complex tasks and have obtained significant success in recent years. DL has revolutionised the field of computer vision using CNNs. However, sequential data such as text and audio can also be processed using DNNs and we starting to now see state-of-the-art performance in these areas. Some of algorithms being used include RNNs, LSTM networks Gated Recurrent Units (GRUs) [1] and 1D-CNNs. Each of these algorithms will be discussed in more detail in the remainder of this chapter. Just like CNNs revolutionised computer vision, we are now beginning to see similar advances in the use of DNNs in time series modelling.

© Springer Nature Switzerland AG 2022
P. Fergus, C. Chalmers, *Applied Deep Learning*, Computational Intelligence Methods and Applications, https://doi.org/10.1007/978-3-031-04420-5_8

## 8.1   Introduction to Time-Series Data

Among the many datasets you will encounter, sequence or time-series data are perhaps the most common. For example, you will be familiar with electrocardiography (ECG) data, timestamp sales data, stocks and shares, written language and weather forecast data. Figure 8.1 shows an example of time-series data.

Time series data has a natural temporal order or sequence. For example, when composing a text message, the software can pre-empt what you are typing and make relevant recommendations about what word should come next based on the words previously typed as shown in Fig. 8.2. Maintaining temporal structure is a key aspect of this data as changing the position of any feature will change the meaning of the complete sequence. This is in stark contrast to the previous datasets (excluding images data which also has a temporal structure) we have introduced whereby moving a column to a different position does not affect the overall meaning of the observation.

Another key aspect of time series data is the frequency which governs how often the data is recorded. To analyse time series effectively, all time periods must be equal and clearly defined. In other words, the same sample frequency must be used across all observations. Frequency is a measurement of time that can range from a few

**Fig. 8.1**   Heart rate trace

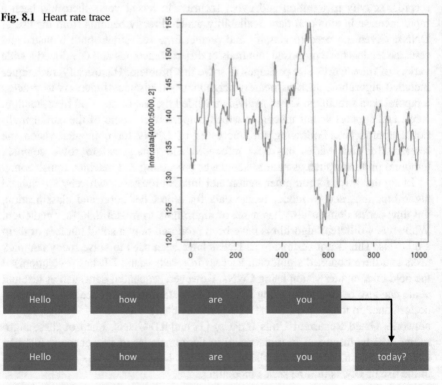

**Fig. 8.2**   Predictive text

milliseconds to hundreds of years. However, the most common frequencies you will encounter include daily, monthly, quarterly, and annually. Typically, we can expect the patterns that we observe in our time series data to reoccur at some point in the future. For example, the sun rose yesterday and is likely to rise tomorrow, the day after and even hundreds of years from now. Therefore, we try to predict the future by analysing the past. Unlike classification that we have previously discussed in this book whereby you are classifying something now based on something in the past, prediction is predicting something in the future based on previously collected data. In the remainder of this section, several types of DNNs that analyse time series data will be discussed.

## 8.2   Recurrent Neural Network

The first DNN for time series we are going to introduce is RNNs. The key aspect of RNN modelling is to make the perceptron aware of the previous history of outputs [2]. This is achieved by feeding the historical output back into the input aggregation and summation process as shown in Fig. 8.3. In other words, the neuron in Fig. 8.3 is the same neuron unrolled over time.

Neurons that are a function of inputs from previous time steps are also known as memory neurons. RNNs can be set using different input and output configurations for both sequences and single vector values. Just like the discussion on CNNs you can create multiple layers of recurrent neurons. In Fig. 8.3 we presented a single perceptron over time. However, we can add multiple neurons, take the collective output from the layer, and feed the result back into each neuron in the layer as shown in Fig. 8.4.

We can now unroll this process over time just like we did with the single perceptron as shown in Fig. 8.5.

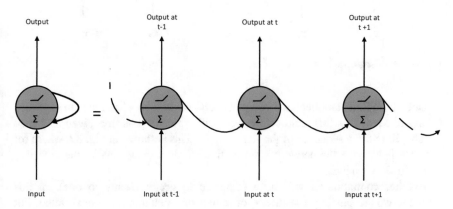

**Fig. 8.3**  RNN

**Fig. 8.4** RNNs and
multiple neurons

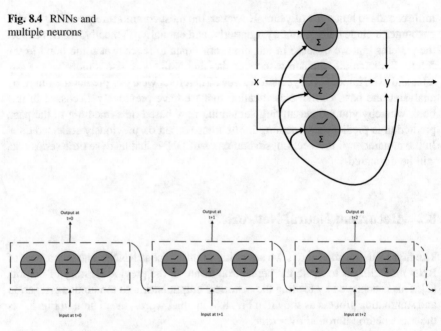

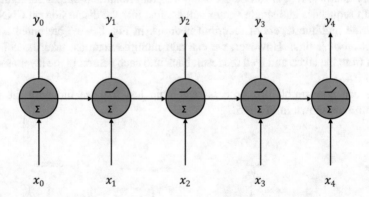

**Fig. 8.5** RNN multiple perceptron rollout

**Fig. 8.6** RNN sequence to sequence

One of the RNN architectures you will encounter will be a Sequence to sequence (Many to Many). In this architecture, you will typically pass in a given sequence which will return a sequence of the same length. This is shown in Fig. 8.6 where for example if we give the network a set of five words it could predict the next five words in the sequence.

Another configuration will be a sequence to vector (Many to one). In this instance, we are passing a sequence of values and predicting the next value. For

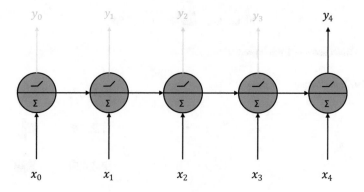

**Fig. 8.7** RNN many to one sequence

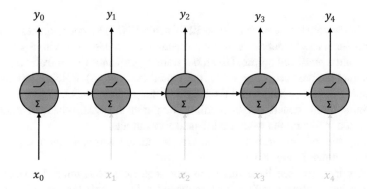

**Fig. 8.8** RNN one to many sequence

example, as in the case of using predictive text. Figure 8.7 shows the many to one configuration.

The final configuration is a vector to sequence (one to many). In this instance, you will give the network one word and it will predict the next five. For example, giving the network a single note from an audio file and it predicting the next five notes (Fig. 8.8).

RNNs have proven to be powerful neural networks for many prediction tasks. However, they have one clear disadvantage where historical knowledge is limited to one previous layer. This is known as short-term memory and there are many problems whereby a longer-term memory is required. We will address this problem later in the chapter when we discuss LSTMs.

[0,1,2,3,4]  ➡  [5,6,7,8,9]

**Fig. 8.9**  RNN sequence batch prediction

**Fig. 8.10**  Input/output
vectors

[0,1,2,3]  ➡  [4]

[1,2,3,4]  ➡  [5]

[2,3,4,5]  ➡  [6]

## 8.2.1   Developing RNNs for Time Series Forecasting

We will now consider how to train an RNN using RNN sequence batches. Like any previous supervised machine learning problem, the process starts with a set of input features and a predicted output. Given our training sequence (input features) the aim is to predict the next sequence value (the y predicted output). RNNs allow us to set the training sequence length and the length of the predicted label. Figure 8.9 shows the training set on the left and the predicted output on the right. What this is saying is that given our five inputs what are the next five outputs.

During the training process, we provide the model with batches of input/output vectors as shown in Fig. 8.10.

In this instance, we have three training sequences containing 4 values. Each sequence has a corresponding next sequence value (label) that we are trying to predict. The three training sequences along with their corresponding next sequence values comprise a single batch. Note that these are adjustable depending on the problem you are trying to solve. Therefore, if the model is given an input of [0,1,2,3] it would predict 4 and if it was given an input of [1,2,3,4] it would predict 5.

The training sequence and next sequence value configurations are the problems you are trying to model. However, sequences should be long enough to capture any useful trend information. For example, if you were to model seasonal data a sequence would have to contain a years' worth of data. Determining the length of the training sequence is often dependent on domain knowledge. A good starting point for the label is to use a single data point in the future and slowly increase it over time.

The primary goal of RNNs is to forecast the future based on the training sequences. This may be as simple as forecasting the next value but more likely than not you will want to forecast values much further into the future. This is achieved by incorporating the current prediction into the next sequence we use for the next prediction. Unlike the train-test splits used to train the model we are now interested in predicting something in the future (note this is not classification) that has never been seen before by our model. In other words, predicted values that are unknown and cannot be validated.

**Fig. 8.11**  Forecast

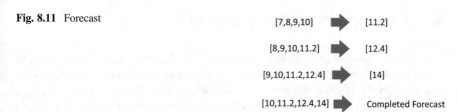

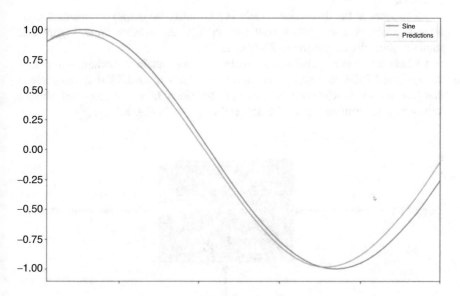

**Fig. 8.12**  Prediction vs ground truth divergence

The first step is to look at the very last sequence in our time series and use a batch that we have previously trained on. Given that this is the last of our training sequences, we are now asking the model to predict the output. As a result, we do not know for sure if the returned prediction is correct which is especially true if the data contains no clear pattern. For example, if the last sequence in our train-test dataset ends with [6,7,8,9], the model will generate a forecasted value which maybe 10. This is a relatively easy and predictable example. However, it may be more difficult to model and forecast values using more complex time series signals.

You will likely want to predict further into the future rather than a sequence. In this instance, you simply keep adding the predicted value to the end of your input sequence and drop the first value (what we already know). This process is repeated until the desired point in the future is reached as shown in Fig. 8.11.

The thing that you need to be aware of is that the further you forecast in the future the more error you will introduce into the application. For example, the time series shown in Fig. 8.12 shows that the predicted value starts to deviate from the ground truth. The divergence between the ground truth and predicted value will grow significantly as you look further into the future.

## 8.3  Long-Term Short-Term Memory

LSTM networks have been designed to address the shortcomings of RNN networks [3]. In RNNs the network begins to forget the first input as information is lost at each step through the RNN training process. LSTMs address this issue by providing a long-term memory cell (neuron) alongside the short-term memory cell found in RNNs.

As you saw in the discussion on RNNs previously the output is appended to the input sequence at $t + 1$ which continues through the training cycle. Figure 8.13 shows a given timestamp for an RNN cell.

LSTMs also have a chain-like structure to help retain important information through the LSTM sequence. The short-term aspect of an LSTM is the same as that provided by an RNN cell. However, an additional output is generated which is known as long-term memory. The new cell is shown in Fig. 8.14.

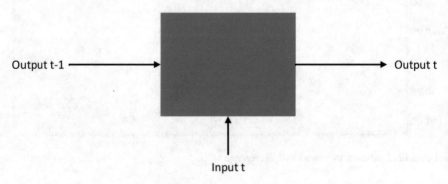

**Fig. 8.13**  Time stamp for RNN cell

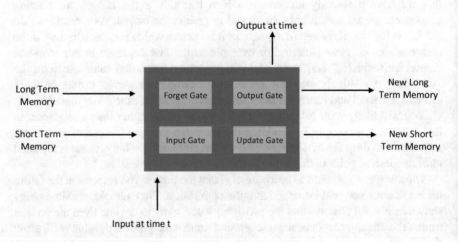

**Fig. 8.14**  LSTM cell

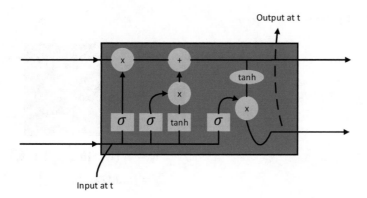

**Fig. 8.15** LSTM gate and activation functions

**Fig. 8.16** Forget gate

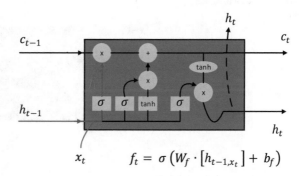

$$f_t = \sigma \left( W_f \cdot \left[ h_{t-1,x_t} \right] + b_f \right)$$

As shown in Fig. 8.14 the LSTM has four gates; forget gate, input gate, output gate and update gate. The forget gate will decide what should be forgotten from the previous memory units. The input gate will decide what to accept into the neuron. The update gate will update the memory and the output gate will output the new long-term memory. So, a gate lets some information through and acts the same as a sigmoid function. The values get compressed between 0 and 1. If it is a zero, the value is dropped or if it is a 1 the value is permitted.

The activation functions in the LSTM, as shown in Fig. 8.15, essentially act as a mechanism for determining both the importance of the input features and their influence on the state of the cell. Each gate and residing activation function has its own weights and biases which are tuneable through the optimisation and backpropagation algorithms.

The forget gate decides what information should be either discarded or kept. Information from the previous hidden state (ht-1) and information from the current input (feature i.e., the word "dog") is passed through the sigmoid function shown in red Fig. 8.16. A value between 0 and 1 is returned. If the value is closer to 0 it should be forgotten, while a value closer to 1 should be retained.

**Fig. 8.17** Input gate

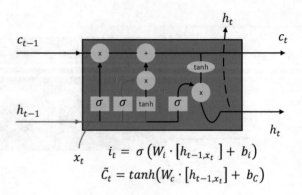

$$i_t = \sigma\left(W_i \cdot \left[h_{t-1,x_t}\right] + b_i\right)$$
$$\tilde{C}_t = tanh\left(W_c \cdot \left[h_{t-1,x_t}\right] + b_C\right)$$

**Fig. 8.18** Calculate cell state

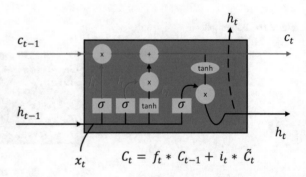

$$C_t = f_t * C_{t-1} + i_t * \tilde{C}_t$$

The input gate is used to update the cell state. First, we pass the previous hidden state and current input into a sigmoid function. This decides which values will be updated by transforming the values to be between 0 and 1 (0 means not important, and 1 means important). You also pass the hidden state and current input into the tanh function to squish values between $-1$ and 1 to help regulate the network. Then you multiply the tanh output with the sigmoid output. The sigmoid output will decide which information is important to keep from the tanh output (Fig. 8.17).

Now we should have enough information to calculate the cell state. First, the cell state gets pointwise multiplied by the forget vector. This has a possibility of dropping values in the cell state if it gets multiplied by values near 0. Then we take the output from the input gate and do a pointwise addition which updates the cell state to new values that the neural network finds relevant. That gives us our new cell state. The process is shown in Fig. 8.18.

Lastly, we have the output gate. The output gate decides what the next hidden state should be. Remember that the hidden state contains information on previous inputs. The hidden state is also used for predictions. First, we pass the previous hidden state and the current input into a sigmoid function. Then we pass the newly modified cell state to the tanh function. We multiply the tanh output with the sigmoid output to decide what information the hidden state should carry. The output is the

**Fig. 8.19** Output gate

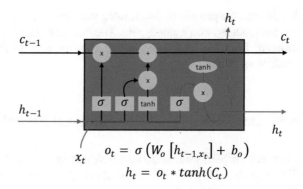

$$o_t = \sigma \left( W_o \left[ h_{t-1,x_t} \right] + b_o \right)$$
$$h_t = o_t * tanh(C_t)$$

hidden state. The new cell state and the new hidden is then carried over to the next time step (Fig. 8.19).

## 8.4  Gated Recurrent Unit

There are several differences between an LSTM and a Gated Recurrent Unit (GRU), but they are very similar [4]. Firstly, a GRU has one less gate than an LSTM. As we previously discussed an LSTM has an input gate, a forget gate, and an output gate. A GRU, on the other hand, has only two gates, a reset gate and an update gate. The reset gate determines how to combine new inputs with the previous memory, and the update gate defines how much of the previous memory remains (Fig. 8.20).

The key benefit of using a GRU is that it is faster to train due to the fact there are fewer parameters to tune. This said LSTMs are generally more accurate than a GRU model. The cell adopts the functionality of the hidden state from the LSTM design.

**Fig. 8.20** Gated recurrent unit

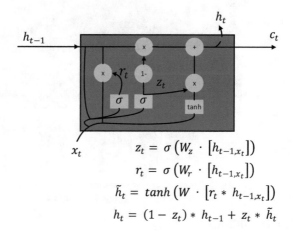

$$z_t = \sigma \left( W_z \cdot \left[ h_{t-1,x_t} \right] \right)$$
$$r_t = \sigma \left( W_r \cdot \left[ h_{t-1,x_t} \right] \right)$$
$$\tilde{h}_t = tanh \left( W \cdot \left[ r_t * h_{t-1,x_t} \right] \right)$$
$$h_t = (1 - z_t) * h_{t-1} + z_t * \tilde{h}_t$$

In addition, the process of determining what the cell forgets and what state is written are consolidated into a single gate. The final cell state is given as an output. This is different from the LSTM cell which chooses what to read from the cell state to produce an output.

## 8.5   One Dimensional Convolutional Neural Network

In the last chapter, we introduced CNNs) for image classification using both 2D and 3D image data. However, CNNs are also seeing extensive use in 1D time series data. The same process for image analysis can be applied to one-dimensional sequences of data. Just like before the model extracts features from sequence data and maps the internal features of the sequence. A 1D CNN is effective for deriving features from a fixed-length segment of the overall dataset, where it is not so important where the feature is in the segment. 1D-CNNS can be used for Realtime ECG monitoring, vibration base structural damage detection, condition monitoring in mechanical machinery and fault detection.

CNNs work the same way whether they have 1, 2, or 3 dimensions. The difference is the structure of the input data and how the filter, also known as a convolution kernel or feature detector, moves across the data. Figure 8.21 shows the

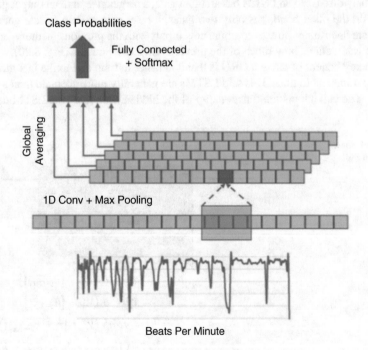

**Fig. 8.21**  1DCNN

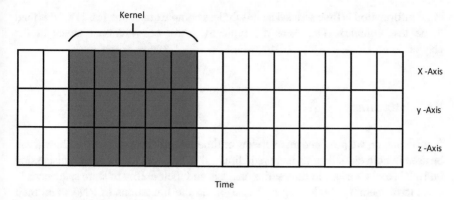

**Fig. 8.22** Kernel processing for 3 channels of data

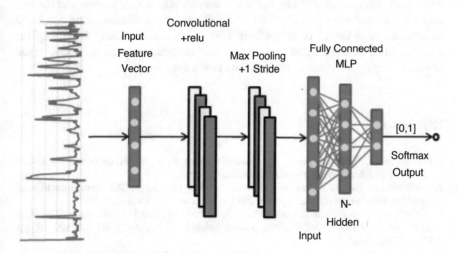

**Fig. 8.23** 1DCNN for CTG beats for minute feature extraction

filter movement across signal data. Each column represents a single time point while each square in the row represents a single value. Considering Fig. 8.21, the kernel is scanning three segments at a time.

In another example Fig. 8.22 shows a time-series signal from an accelerometer with three separate channels. Here each channel is processed in parallel using a kernel width of 5. When processing multiple channels an important aspect to note is that the sample frequency of each channel should be the same.

There will be instances whereby a single channel of data will be sufficient such as measuring a CTG as shown in Fig. 8.23. In this instance, the kernel will slide along the single channel to extract the relevant features. A single channel might not be sufficient to fully understand the context of the problem you are trying to model.

Beyond the initial input to 1DCNNs, the architectural constructs as utilised in 2D and 3D CNNs remain, the same (I.e., max pooling, feature maps). Given that the input information is time series data it is far less complex than images. 1DCNNs tend to be less complex (I.e., there are typically fewer convolutional layers in the network).

## 8.6  Summary

In this chapter, we provided an overview of time series data and discussed how it can be used in both classification and prediction tasks. This was followed by a discussion on RNNs and their use in time series analysis and their ability to store sequences in short term memory. Following a discussion on the limitations of RNNs and their inability to store information over longer periods, the LSTM architecture was introduced. This focused on cell states and the neurons' ability to store and retrieve data over longer time periods. This was followed by a discussion on the GRU architecture as a means of simplifying LSTMs and subsequently improving the compute time. A more recent architecture was introduced based on CNNs which contains a single dimension to model time series data.

## References

1. K. Cho *et al.*, "Learning phrase representations using RNN encoder-decoder for statistical machine translation," *arXiv Prepr. arXiv1406.1078*, 2014.
2. T. Mikolov, M. Karafiát, L. Burget, J. Cernock\`y, and S. Khudanpur, "Recurrent neural network based language model.," in *Interspeech*, 2010, vol. 2, no. 3, pp. 1045–1048.
3. K. Greff, R. K. Srivastava, J. Koutn\'\ik, B. R. Steunebrink, and J. Schmidhuber, "LSTM: A search space odyssey," *IEEE Trans. neural networks Learn. Syst.*, vol. 28, no. 10, pp. 2222–2232, 2016.
4. J. Chung, C. Gulcehre, K. Cho, and Y. Bengio, "Empirical evaluation of gated recurrent neural networks on sequence modeling," *arXiv Prepr. arXiv1412.3555*, 2014.

# Chapter 9
# Natural Language Processing

One of the most impressive feats a human can do is understand the verbal or written word. Many researchers and practitioners believe this feat to be a fundamental component of human intelligence. As with many aspects of AI such as image processing it is not surprising that a whole domain of research, tools and techniques have emerged which enable computers to do something similar. In the early days, a significant amount of research was undertaken using symbolic AI to construct and interpret language using syntax and semantic representations of language. Although these early attempts were impressive for the time, symbolic Natural Language Processing (NLP) failed to deliver anything near human-level abilities.

With the introduction of DL, however, we have seen significant advancements in NLP and its mainstream adoption into many consumer products such as Alexa, Siri, and Google Assistant [1]. Many of these advancements build upon the algorithms discussed in the previous chapter such as RNNs and LSTMs. There are many areas in NLP which include text classification, speech tagging, Semantics and Sentiment Analysis and Topic Modelling [2]. In this chapter, we will provide an overview of NLP within the context of DL and the various techniques and frameworks that are currently used.

## 9.1 Introduction to Natural Language Processing

NLP is a subset of computer science and AI which aims to build successful interactions between computers and human natural languages. The overarching aim is to program computers to process substantial amounts of natural language data whether this is either verbally spoken or textually inputted. This differs from conventional ML and data analysis where substantial portions of the data are represented numerically to allow for a numerical measurement. Computers are extremely efficient at handling direct numerical information and are not typically configured to handle textual data.

© Springer Nature Switzerland AG 2022
P. Fergus, C. Chalmers, *Applied Deep Learning*, Computational Intelligence Methods and Applications, https://doi.org/10.1007/978-3-031-04420-5_9

Humanity has instilled a plethora of information and knowledge inside written text which has been transferred from generation to generation. For a computer to gain access to this information specialised processing techniques are required for it to be able to understand raw text data and the information it contains. Typically, textual data is highly unstructured data and can often reside in multiple languages which further exacerbates the challenge. NLP attempts to use a variety of tools and techniques to create structure out of unstructured textual data. Examples include classifying emails as spam or non-spam, analysing the sentiment of movie reviews, analysing customer feedback, understanding text commands (i.e., hey Google play this song). NLP is an extension of the time-series and recurrent neural network topics we previously discussed.

NLP is continuously progressing and evolving and as we will see in this chapter, DL is driving many of the innovative solutions that you will encounter in the many devices that you already own.

### 9.1.1   Tokenisation

Tokenisation is the process of breaking up the original text into component pieces known as tokens [3]. The first step in the process will be to split a sentence on the white space as shown in Fig. 9.1. Next, we split on the prefix (the first speech mark). The exception stage splits the concatenation (i.e., 'We're' becomes 'We' and "re'). The suffix splits the last speech marks, and the final exception splits the exclamation point (i.e., '!'). This concludes the tokenisation stage.

The collection of generated tokens are just pieces of the original text. Tokens form the basic building blocks of a document. Everything which helps us to understand the meaning of the text is derived from tokens and their relationships between each other. Token types include:

- Prefix: character(s) at the beginning ($ ( ")
- Suffix: Character(s) at the end (km) , . !"
- Infix: Characters(s) in between (- --/ . . .)
- Exception: Special-case rule to split a string into several tokens or prevent a token from being split when punctuation rules are applied. (let's, U.S.)

### 9.1.2   Stemming

Stemming is a technique that returns similar words for a given word [4]. For example, searching the word car would return car, cars, car's, cars', where the car is the stem word. Stemming is a crude method for cataloguing related words. It works by chopping off the letters from the end until a stem is reached. Stemming

**Fig. 9.1** Tokenisation

**Table 9.1** Suffix mapping

| S1 | | S2 | word | | stem |
|---|---|---|---|---|---|
| SSES | -> | SS | caresses | -> | caress |
| IES | -> | I | Ponies | -> | Poni |
| | | | ties | -> | ti |
| SS | -> | SS | caress | -> | caress |
| S | -> | | cats | -> | cat |

works well in most cases but unfortunately, the English language has many exceptions and as such a more sophisticated approach is required.

There are two main types of stemmers which are the Porter and Snowball Stemmers [5]. The Porter algorithm is one of the most common and effective stemming tools which was developed by Martin Porter in 1980. The algorithm employs five phases of word reduction each with its own set of mapping rules. In the first phase, simple suffix mapping rules are defined such as the ones shown in Table 9.1.

From a given set of stemming rules, only one rule is applied based on the longest suffix S1. Thus, caresses reduces to caress but not cares. More sophisticated phases consider the length and complexity of the word before applying the rule as shown in Table 9.2.

The Snowball algorithm is a stemming language developed by Martin Porter and is more accurately called the English stemmer or the Porter2 stemmer [6]. It offers a

**Table 9.2** Considering length and complexity

| S1 | | S2 | word | | stem |
|---|---|---|---|---|---|
| (m>0) ATIONAL | -> | ATE | relational national | -> | relate national |
| (m>0) EED | -> | EE | agreed feed | -> -> | agree feed |

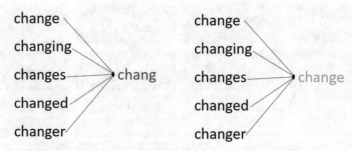

**Fig. 9.2**  Stemming and lemmatization

slight improvement over the original Porter stemmer both in logic and speed. One of the main advantages of Snowball is its ability to work across different languages, not just English as was the case with the Porter Stemmer.

### 9.1.3  Lemmatization

In contrast to stemming, Lemmatization looks beyond word reduction and considers a languages full vocabulary to apply a morphological analysis to the words [7]. For example, the lemma of the word 'was' is 'be' and the lemma of the word mice is mouse. Further, the lemma of 'meeting' might be 'meet' or 'meeting' depending on its use in the sentence. Lemmatization is regarded as a much more informative approach than simple stemming. Lemmatization analyses surrounding text to determine the role of a given word in the sentence. However, it does not categorise phrases. In short, lemmatisation is the process of grouping together the inflected forms of a word so they can be analysed as a single item, identified by the word's lemma, or dictionary form. Figure 9.2 shows the difference between stemming on the left and lemmatization on the right.

### 9.1.4  Stop Words

When processing natural language text there are a wide variety of words such as "a", "the", and "is" which appear frequently and do not provide any insights into the subject or context of the text. These are commonly known as stop words and can be

**Fig. 9.3**  Word cloud of stop words

```
pattern1 = [{'LOWER': 'unitedstates'}]
pattern2 = [{'LOWER': 'united'}, {'LOWER': 'states'}]
pattern3 = [{'LOWER': 'united'}, {'IS_PUNCT': True}, {'LOWER': 'states'}]

matcher.add('Unitedstates' , None, pattern1, pattern2, pattern3)
```

**Fig. 9.4**  Phrase matching

removed. For example, Fig. 9.3 shows a word cloud (for the paragraph you are reading) built on a histogram of stop words whereby the larger words show the common occurrence of words in the dataset. Common NLP libraries will have several functions containing a list of stop words that can be applied to text for removal.

## 9.1.5   Phrase Matching and Vocabulary

So far, we have seen how textual data can be divided into tokens and how individual tokens can be parsed and tagged with parts of speech, dependencies, and lemmas. The next stage is to identify and label specific phrases that match patterns we can define ourselves. We can think of this as a powerful version of regular expression where we consider parts of our speech for our pattern search. Figure 9.4 shows an example of a matcher based on a number key words that were interested in.

Using the phrase outlined in Fig. 9.5 below and the matcher above in Fig. 9.4.
This would result in Fig. 9.6.

```
pattern1 = [{'LOWER': 'unitedstates'}]
pattern2 = [{'LOWER': 'united'}, {'LOWER': 'states'}]
pattern3 = [{'LOWER': 'united'}, {'IS_PUNCT': True}, {'LOWER': 'states'}]

matcher.add('Unitedstates' , None, pattern1, pattern2, pattern3)
```

**Fig. 9.5**  Sentence matcher

```
15845173719804281779 UnitedStates 1 2 United States
15845173719804281779 UnitedStates 19 20 UnitedStates
15845173719804281779 UnitedStates 25 28 United-States
```

**Fig. 9.6**  Results from sentence matcher

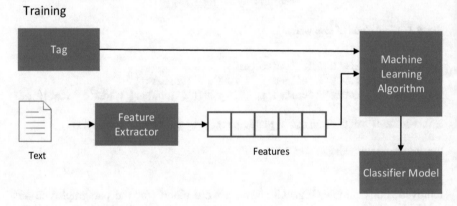

**Fig. 9.7**  Training pipeline for text classification

## 9.2   Text Classification

Now that we understand the basics of NLP and the required pre-processing needed to generate our machine learning models, we can focus on the tasks required for machine learning text classification. Text classification is the process of assigning tags or categories to text based on its context [8]. This stage is one of the fundamental aspects of NLP and has been used in a broad range of applications such as sentiment analysis, cognitive assistants such Alexa and Siri, and more recently in fake news detection.

Using machine learning in NLP has seen significant interest as it allows us to replace manually hand-crafted rules using a traditional software development process. Instead, text classification algorithms can model their own rules. Using pre-labelled training data, machine learning algorithms can learn different

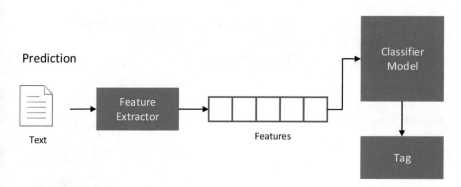

**Fig. 9.8**  Prediction pipeline

relationships between pieces of text while mapping these to different outputs. Figure 9.7 shows a typical training pipeline for text classification.

Figure 9.8 shows the prediction pipeline which takes in new text and maps extracted features to specific tags through machine learning modelling.

Historically, traditional machine learning algorithms such as SVMs and Naïve Bayes have been used in the text classification pipeline. However, more recent approaches use DL algorithms such as 1DCNNs, RCNNs and LSTMs. You will note that this is a similar transition to the image processing topics discussed earlier whereby DL replaced the more traditional machine learning approaches used to detect, segment, and classify objects in images. While DL algorithms outperform traditional machine learning algorithms in NLP tasks, they often require more data in the region of millions of tagged examples. Text classification is a key area as it is estimated 80% of all information is unstructured with text being one of the most common types of unstructured data. By using both machine learning and DL approaches, companies can develop new types of analytical pipelines to automatically deduce valuable information from legal documents, social media, surveys, emails, and chatbots.

## 9.2.1  Text Feature Extraction

The first step towards training a machine learning NLP classifier is feature extraction. This is a method used to transform the text into a numerical representation in the form of a vector. One of the most frequently used approaches is a bag of words, where a vector represents the frequency of a word in a predefined dictionary of words [9].

Most machine learning algorithms cannot process raw text. Instead, we use a feature extraction stage (like the extraction of features from other types of data such as images and time-series signals) so that we can transfer numerical features as inputs to machine learning algorithms. The main approaches include count vectorisation and term frequency, inverse document-frequency (TF-IDF) [10].

```
messages = ["Hey, lets go to the game today!",
            "Call your sister.",
            "Want to go walk your dogs?"]
```

**Fig. 9.9** Input message

**Fig. 9.10** Word feature
vector

```
['call',
 'dogs',
 'game',
 'go',
 'hey',
 'lets',
 'sister',
 'the',
 'to',
 'today',
 'walk',
 'want',
 'your']
```

**Table 9.3** Feature vectors

| Call | Dogs | Game | Go | Hey | Lets | Sister | The | To | Today | Walk | Want | Your |
|------|------|------|-----|-----|------|--------|-----|-----|-------|------|------|------|
| 0    | 0    | 1    | 1   | 1   | 1    | 0      | 1   | 1   | 1     | 0    | 0    | 0    |
| 1    | 0    | 0    | 0   | 0   | 0    | 1      | 0   | 0   | 0     | 0    | 0    | 1    |
| 0    | 1    | 0    | 1   | 0   | 0    | 0      | 0   | 1   | 0     | 1    | 1    | 1    |

Count vectorisation uses messages as input as shown in Fig. 9.9. Here we have three messages consisting of raw unstructured text. Using a count vectorisation algorithm, we can count the number of distinct works that exist across all messages.

The algorithm treats each unique word as a feature as shown in the vector in Fig. 9.10.

These features are used to count the occurrence of each unique feature in all documents. This is known as document term matrix (DTM). In other words, each message is represented in the DTM as a row of zeros and ones placed in the columns associated with each feature as shown in Table 9.3.

So, looking at Table 9.3 we can see that the word 'call' does not appear in the first or last messages only in the second one. The same is true for the word 'dogs' which only appears in the third message. We can see that this representation of messages is more conducive to machine learning-type modelling where we have rows for messages and columns for features. Most messages will not contain all of the words - as shown in Table 9.3 the representation contains sparse information (a matrix containing many 0's). Sparsity increases as documents become much larger.

An alternative approach to the count vectorizer is the TF-IDF vectorizer which also creates a document term matrix from the text. However, instead of completing the DTM with token counts, it calculates the term frequency-inverse document frequency value for each word. Term frequency $tf(t,d)$ is the raw count of a term in a document (the number of times that term $t$ occurs in document $d$). However, term frequency alone does not facilitate a comprehensive feature analysis of the text. This algorithm works by penalising common words such as "the", and "is" as they incur high counts which suggest they are important. However, they do not provide any real insights into the subject matter of the document. Less common words such as "dog" would normally be deemphasised due to their low count. The inverse document frequency aspect of TF-IDF is incorporated to diminish the weight of terms that occur very frequently in the document and increase the weight of terms that occur rarely. So, putting this all together a TF-IDF algorithm will calculate the term frequency weights and the inverse term frequency weights to form a word weighting matrix as shown in Fig. 9.14. TF-IDF, therefore, allows us to understand the context of words across an entire corpus of documents, instead of its relative importance in a single document. Note that the closer the value is to one for a particular word the more important that word is considered across the corpus (its frequency is less common). Alternatively, the closer the value is to zero the less important the word is (its frequency is common across the corpus of documents and as such provides little discriminative capacity) (Table 9.4).

## 9.3 Sentiment Analysis

Sentiment analysis is an important form of text analysis that uses unstructured data, such as social media, email, and customer service reports to understand opinions and emotions expressed within texts [11]. Sentiment analysis is concerned with the classification of positive, negative, and neutral emotions found in text using text analysis techniques. Sentiment analysis can be undertaken using traditional machine learning approaches but has recently seen widespread adoption within the DL domain.

The most common use of sentiment analysis is to classify text input as negative, neutral, or positive. The training data is typically mapped to specific domains of interest like social media, product reviews and customer feedback. As such, there exists a wide variety of pre-labelled data to represent different domains of interest. As with other text, analyses data needs to be pre-processed before an machine

| book | 0.15 | -0.27 | 0.04 |
| dads | 0.24 | 0.38 | -0.09 |
| dummies | 0.13 | -0.17 | 0.07 |
| estate | 0.18 | 0.19 | 0.45 |
| guide | 0.22 | 0.09 | -0.46 |
| investing | 0.74 | -0.21 | 0.21 |
| market | 0.18 | -0.3 | -0.28 |
| real | 0.18 | 0.19 | 0.45 |
| rich | 0.36 | 0.59 | -0.34 |
| stock | 0.25 | -0.42 | -0.28 |
| value | 0.12 | -0.14 | 0.23 |

| 3.91 | 0 | 0 |
| 0 | 2.61 | 0 |
| 0 | 0 | 2 |

| T1 | T2 | T3 | T4 | T5 | T6 | T7 | T8 | T9 |
|---|---|---|---|---|---|---|---|---|
| 0.35 | 0.22 | 0.34 | 0.26 | 0.33 | 0.49 | 0.28 | 0.29 | 0.44 |
| -0.32 | -0.15 | -0.46 | -0.24 | -0.14 | 0.55 | 0.07 | -0.31 | 0.44 |
| -0.41 | 0.14 | -0.16 | 0.25 | 0.22 | -0.51 | 0.55 | 0 | 0.34 |

**Fig. 9.14**   3-D SVD matrix

learning algorithm can be trained. In traditional machine learning common algorithms for sentiment analysis include SVM's, decision forests and Naïve Bayes.
There are a wide variety of pre-processing techniques however the main objective is
to reduce the dimensionality of features to improve classification performance.
Common techniques include removing numbers, stemming, speech tagging,
removal of punctuation, ensuring all text is lowercase and removing stop words.

## 9.4   Topic Modelling

Topic modelling allows us to analyse large volumes of data by clustering documents
into individual topics. A large amount of text is unlabelled meaning we cannot apply
supervised learning to create machine learning models of the data. The idea of topic
modelling is to cluster documents based on their common characteristics [12]. Just

**Table 9.4** TF-IDF word weighting matrix

| Call | Dogs | Game | Go | Hey | Lets | Sister | The | To | Today | Walk | Want | Your |
|---|---|---|---|---|---|---|---|---|---|---|---|---|
| 0.000 | 0.000 | 0.403 | 0.307 | 0.403 | 0.403 | 0.000 | 0.403 | 0.307 | 0.403 | 0.000 | 0.000 | 0.000 |
| 0.623 | 0.000 | 0.000 | 0.000 | 0.000 | 0.000 | 0.623 | 0.000 | 0.000 | 0.000 | 0.000 | 0.000 | 0.474 |
| 0.000 | 0.460 | 0.000 | 0.349 | 0.000 | 0.000 | 0.000 | 0.000 | 0.349 | 0.000 | 0.460 | 0.460 | 0.349 |

like unsupervised learning that we discussed earlier in the book, it is up to the end-user to identify what each of the clusters represent.

By detecting patterns such as word frequency and the distance between words, a topic model clusters documents that are similar, and words and expressions that appear most often. With this information, you can quickly deduce what each set of texts is talking about.

Topic Modelling refers to the process of dividing a corpus of documents into the following:

- A list of the topics covered by the documents in the corpus
- Several sets of documents from the corpus are grouped by the topics they cover.

There are two main algorithms for achieving this: Latent Semantic Analysis (LSA) [13] and Latent Dirichlet Allocation (LDA).

### 9.4.1  Latent Semantic Analysis (LSA)

LSA allows you to analyse documents to find the underlying meaning and or concepts contained in the documents [14]. However, this can be difficult in the English language where a single word can have multiple meanings such as a bank which refers to a financial institution or a place at the side of a river. In terms of NLP, it would be much easier if each word only meant one concept and each concept was described using one word only. In this sense, NLP algorithms would only have to map a single word to a single concept as shown in Fig. 9.11.

However, this is not the case. In English different words can often mean the same thing which is known as synonyms. This means concepts can become easily obscured making the task difficult for people to understand let alone NLP. This is highlighted in Fig. 9.12.

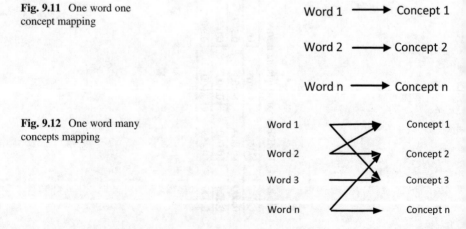

**Fig. 9.11**  One word one concept mapping

**Fig. 9.12**  One word many concepts mapping

**Table 9.5**  Count matrix

| Index words | Titles | | | | | | | | |
|---|---|---|---|---|---|---|---|---|---|
| | T1 | T2 | T3 | T4 | T5 | T6 | T7 | T8 | T9 |
| Book | | | 1 | 1 | | | | | |
| Dads | | | | | | 1 | | | 1 |
| Dummies | | 1 | | | | | | 1 | |
| Estate | | | | | | | 1 | | 1 |
| Guide | 1 | | | | | 1 | | | |
| Investing | 1 | 1 | 1 | 1 | 1 | 1 | 1 | 1 | 1 |
| Market | 1 | 1 | | | | | | | |
| Real | | | | | | | 1 | | 1 |
| Rich | | | | | | 2 | | | 1 |
| Stock | 1 | | 1 | | | | | 1 | |
| Value | | | | 1 | 1 | | | | |

In the context of NLP, the challenge is to understand the search terms (which can be typed or verbally spoken) and return relevant information such as documents, web pages and verbal responses. One way to address this challenge is to use LSA. Being able to compare meanings or concepts behind the words helps us to overcome the issue of synonyms. LSA solves this problem by mapping both words and documents into a concept space and making comparisons in this space. When people create documents, they have access to a wide variety of words. As discussed, the underlying concepts can be obscured due to the different word choices. LSA works by filtering out some of the noise (words) while performing a type of dimensionality reduction across all the documents. This is achieved by:

(A) Representing documents as a bag of words whereby the order of words in a document is not important but how many times a word appears in a document is (TF-IDF).
(B) Patterns of words are used to represent concepts for example scales, flour and spoon could appear in documents about baking.
(C) It assumes that a word has one meaning only to make the problem tractable.

LSA begins by creating a count matrix that shows which documents contain specific words and their frequency. This matrix is shown in Table 9.5.

In LSA the raw count matrix is modified so the rare words are weighted more heavily than frequently-used words. This is achieved using TF-IDF which replaces the count value with TF-IDF value which is known as a term matrix as shown in Fig. 9.5 (Table 9.6).

Once we have built our term matrix, we use Singular Value Decomposition (SVD) to analyse the matrix. SVD is used to find a reduced dimensional representation of our matrix (like PCA discussed previously in the book) [15]. This allows us to find or emphasise the strongest relationships while discounting any noise. The challenge however is to find how many dimensions or "concepts" to use when approximating the matrix. If a limited number of dimensions are used important

**Table 9.6** Term matrix

| | | | |
|---|---|---|---|
| Book | 0.15 | −0.27 | 0.04 |
| Dads | 0.24 | 0.38 | −0.09 |
| Dummies | 0.13 | −0.17 | 0.07 |
| Estate | 0.18 | 0.19 | 0.45 |
| Guide | 0.22 | 0.09 | −0.46 |
| Investing | 0.74 | −0.21 | 0.21 |
| Market | 0.18 | −0.3 | −0.28 |
| Real | 0.18 | 0.19 | 0.45 |
| Rich | 0.36 | 0.59 | −0.34 |
| Stock | 0.25 | −0.42 | −0.28 |
| Value | 0.12 | −0.14 | 0.23 |

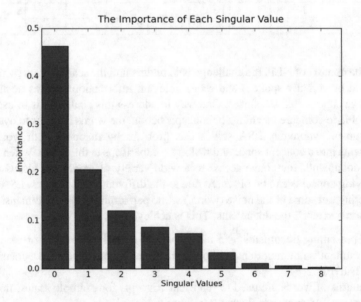

**Fig. 9.13** Histogram of the square of the singular values

patterns are left out, too many and important concepts become obscured and difficult to identify due to noise.

The SVD algorithm constructs three separate matrices. The $U$ matrix provides the coordinates for each word in our concept space. The $Vt$ matrix provides the coordinates of each document in the concept space while the $S$ matrix of singular values provides us valuable information as to how many dimensions (concepts) that need to be included. To achieve we can make a histogram of the square of the singular values which shows the importance and the contribution each singular value makes when approximating our matrix as shown in Fig. 9.13.

With a large collection of documents, the number of dimensions will increase to represent the broader range of concepts. The complete 3-dimensional SVD of our matrix is shown in Fig. 9.14. Each word has three numbers associated with it. The

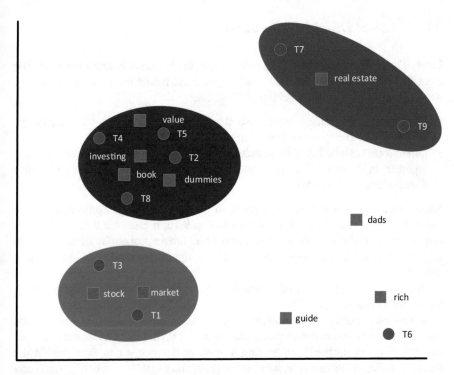

**Fig. 9.15**  Word, document and concept clusters

first number corresponds to the number of times that words appear in all titles and is not as informative as the second and third. In this case, there is one for each dimension. Similarly, each title also has three numbers associated with it, one for each dimension. Again, the first dimension is removed as it is not important given that it corresponds to the number of words in the title.

We can now use the second and third dimensions for our words and documents to plot and create clusters. The clusters capture the word, documents, and the concepts they belong to as shown in Fig. 9.15.

SVD allows us to plot both the words and document titles on the graph which allows us to identify clusters of titles. We can then use the words to label each of the clusters by looking at what words reside within a particular cluster. For example, Fig. 9.15 shows that the lower cluster has titles 1 and 3 which are both about stock market investing. While the middle cluster with titles 2, 4, 5, and 8 clusters around the words "value and "investing" which summarizes those titles.

## 9.4.2   Latent Dirichlet Allocation

Latent Dirichlet Allocation (LDA) works using the Dirichlet distribution [16]. The algorithm was developed in 2003 and is a graphical model for topic discovery. To use LDA there are two overarching assumptions:

- Documents with related topics use similar groups of words (documents are probability distributions of latent topics)
- Latent topics can be found by searching for groups of words that frequently occur together in documents across the corpus (topics themselves are probability distributions over words).

So, for example, any document is going to have a probability distribution over a given number of latent topics. As shown in Fig. 9.16, if there are five latent topics across various documents then any document will have a probability of belonging to each topic. In the figure, document one has the highest probability of belonging to topic two.

In another example, document two has the highest probability of belonging to topic 4 as shown in Fig. 9.17.

If we look at the topics themselves, they are modelled as probability distributions over words contained in the corpus as shown in Fig. 9.18. Here we can see that topic one has different probabilities relating to each of the words contained within the topic itself. So, in our example, it has a low probability that "he", "food", "read" and "home" have a low probability of belonging to that topic. Conversely, "cat" and "dog" have a much larger probability (chance) of belonging to topic 1.

When selecting words, you would define a threshold that only retains words above a specific probability value. So, in the example above if our thresholds only covered "cat" and "dog" we could infer that the topic is about animals or pets.

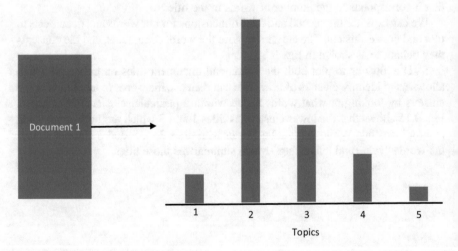

**Fig. 9.16**  Latent topic distribution

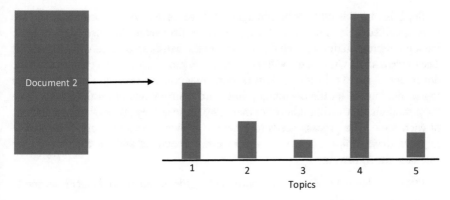

**Fig. 9.17** Latent topic distribution

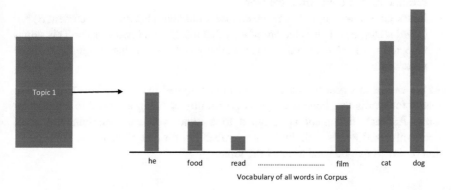

**Fig. 9.18** Word probability distributions

LDA represents documents as mixtures of topics that produce words with set probabilities. It assumes that documents are generated using the following steps.

- Step 1 specify the number of words ($N$) the document will have.
- Step 2 choose a topic mixture for the document (using the Dirichlet distribution over a fixed set of $k$ topics. For example, 60% business, 20% politics and 20% food).
- Step 3 generate each word in the document by

  - First select a topic according to the multinomial distribution that you sampled previously (I.e., 60% business, 20% politics, and 20%).
  - Second, using the topic to generate the word itself (according to the topics multimodal distribution). For example, if you select a food topic you might generate the word "apple" with 60% probability, "home" would be 30% probability and so on.Assuming this generative model for a collection of documents, LDA then tries to backtrack from the documents to find a set of topics that are likely to have generated the collection.

So, bringing this all together, imagine that we have a set of documents and we have specified a fixed number of $k$ topics to be discovered. We use LDA to learn the topic representation of each document and the words associated with each topic. The process starts with each document in turn and randomly assigns each word in the document to one of the $k$ topics. This random assignment already provides both topic representations of all the documents and word distributions of all the topics. Note these random topics will initially not make any sense as they are poor representations of each topic. The process needs to iterate over every word in every document to improve these topics. For every word in every document and for each topic $t$ we calculate the following:

- P(topic $t$ | document $d$) = the proportion of words in document $d$ that are currently assigned to topic $t$
- P(word $w$ | topic $t$) = the proportion of assignments to topic $t$ over all the documents that come from the word $w$.
- Reassign $w$ a new topic where we choose topic $t$ with P(topic $t$ | document $d$) * P (word $w$ | topic $t$). This is the probability that topic $t$ generated word $w$. This step is repeated until we eventually reach a steady state where the assignments make none or minor changes.

At the end of this process, each document is assigned to a topic. This allows us to search for words that have the highest probability of being assigned to a particular topic. As each document is assigned to a topic, you can determine the most frequently used words with the highest probability for that given topic. This collection of words can be used to label the topic.

### 9.4.3   Non-negative Matrix Factorization

Non-negative matrix factorization (NMF) is an unsupervised algorithm that simultaneously performs both dimensionality reduction and clustering [17]. It is typically used in conjunction with TF-IDF to model topics across documents. Unlike SVD which supports both negative and positive inputs, NMF only deals with positive values. Given a non-negative matrix A, find $k$-dimension approximations in terms of non-negative factors $W$ and $H$. The $A$ matrix is generated using TF-IDF. We state with vector (k). $K$ is the number of topics we choose, which is like LDA. We initialise $W$ and $H$ with random values (e.g., random matrices). Using an objective function, we can create a measure of the reconstruction error between $A$ and the approximation $WH$. This is achieved using expectation-maximisation optimisation to refine $W$ and $H$ to minimise the objective function. This is repeated until the model converges. The process NMF is shown in Fig. 9.19.

Bringing it all together we first construct a vector space model for documents (after removing stop words) which results in a term-document matrix ($A$). In the second step, we apply TF-IDF term weight normalisation to $A$. In step 3 we

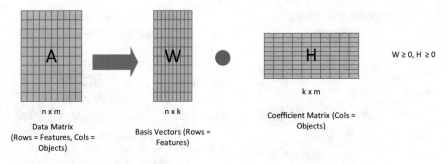

**Fig. 9.19** Non-negative matrix factorization

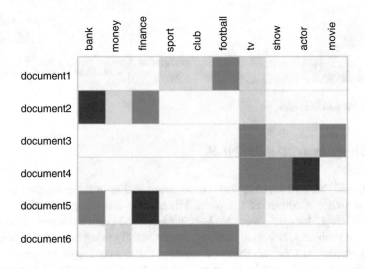

**Fig. 9.20** TF-IDF vectorisation

normalise TF-IDF vectors to unit length. This is followed by the initialisation of factors using NNDSVD on $A$. The last stage applies projected gradient NMF to $A$.

After doing these above steps we will have the basis vectors which are the topics (clusters) in the data. We also have a coefficient matrix that contains the membership weights for documents relative to each topic (cluster). So, A will look something like the image in Fig. 9.20 where this represents the TF-IDF vectorisation.

Further, the $W$ and $H$ matrices are shown in Fig. 9.21. Here words relate to specific topics and documents. Using $W$, we label our topics based on the word membership. So, Topic 1 could be TV shows, topic 2 sports and topic 3 financial. Using these labelled topics, we can now assign new documents to these topics. So, document 1 will be about sport, document 2 about finance, document 3 and 4 about TV shows, document 5 about finance and topic 6 about sports.

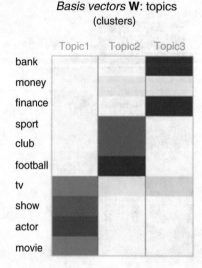
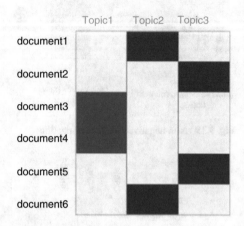

*Basis vectors* **W**: topics (clusters)

*Coefficients* **H**: memberships for documents

**Fig. 9.21**  W and H matrices

## 9.5   Deep Learning for NLP

Using the RNNS and LSTMS that we discussed earlier in the book we can create new text using a corpus of text data. Historically most methods used in NLP problems adopted shallow machine learning and hand-crafted features. This often-introduced problems such as high dimensional data. By using new techniques, such as word embeddings, (which are low dimensional distributed representations) ANNs can achieve improved results in various NLP tasks when compared to traditional machine learning approaches.

### 9.5.1   Word Embeddings

Word embeddings are one of the main breakthroughs in DL on NLP problems [18]. One of the main benefits is that it can create a low dimensional vector which improves the generalisation of the DL model. Word embeddings are a learned representation for text where words with similar meanings have similar representations. Each word is mapped to one vector and the vector values are learned using a neural network. Each word is represented using a real-valued vector which is often tens or hundreds of dimensions. This contrasts with thousands or millions of dimensions that are used in traditional approaches such as one-hot encoding. Figure 9.22 shows a vector for a simple one-hot encoding task. Here even a limited number of words can generate high dimensionality.

|          | 1 | 2 | 3 | 4 | 5 | 6 | 7 | 8 | 9 |
|----------|---|---|---|---|---|---|---|---|---|
| man      | 1 | 0 | 0 | 0 | 0 | 0 | 0 | 0 | 0 |
| woman    | 0 | 1 | 0 | 0 | 0 | 0 | 0 | 0 | 0 |
| boy      | 0 | 0 | 1 | 0 | 0 | 0 | 0 | 0 | 0 |
| girl     | 0 | 0 | 0 | 1 | 0 | 0 | 0 | 0 | 0 |
| prince   | 0 | 0 | 0 | 0 | 1 | 0 | 0 | 0 | 0 |
| princess | 0 | 0 | 0 | 0 | 0 | 1 | 0 | 0 | 0 |
| queen    | 0 | 0 | 0 | 0 | 0 | 0 | 1 | 0 | 0 |
| king     | 0 | 0 | 0 | 0 | 0 | 0 | 0 | 1 | 0 |
| monarch  | 0 | 0 | 0 | 0 | 0 | 0 | 0 | 0 | 1 |

Each word gets a 1x9 vector representation

**Fig. 9.22**  Word embeddings

**Fig. 9.23**  Reducing dimensional space using word embeddings

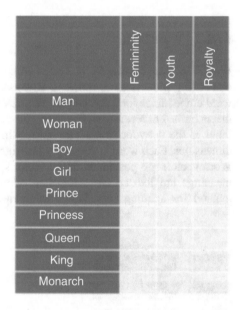

By using word embeddings, we can significantly reduce the dimensional space for the words we are trying to represent as shown in Fig. 9.23.

This approach allows words that are used in similar ways to have similar representations which capture their meaning. This is in stark contrast to the bag of words approach whereby different words have different representations regardless of how they are used.

## 9.5.2   *Word Embedding Algorithms*

There are a variety of word embedding algorithms that aim to place words into a vector space next to each other based on their similarity. The approaches are split into two overall categories which include probabilistic approaches (ANNs) and classical approaches outlined previously.

### 9.5.2.1   Embedding Layer

The embedding layer is learned during the training process by the neural network model on a specific NLP task such as language modelling or document classification. Like traditional methods, the text needs to be cleaned, pre-processed and one-hot encoded. The size of the vector space is specified as part of the model parameters such as (50 or 100 dimensions). The embedding layer forms the input to the ANN is shown in Fig. 9.24. The learning of the embedding layer requires a significant amount of training data.

### 9.5.2.2   Word2Vec

Word2Vec was developed by Tomas Mikolov [19]. Word2Vec aims to make the embedding process more efficient. It works by statistically generating standalone word embeddings for a text corpus. Word2Vec employs a two-layer neural network that is trained to reconstruct linguistic contexts of words. A large corpus of words is input to the network as a vector space which can be more than several hundred dimensions. Each word in the corpus is assigned a corresponding vector in the space. Word vectors are positioned in the vector space so that words that share common meanings are located close together. Word2Vec is a computationally efficient method for learning embeddings using raw text. Two methods can be used to

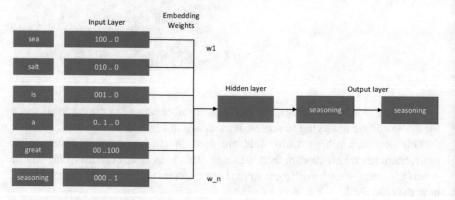

**Fig. 9.24** Embedding layer and ANN

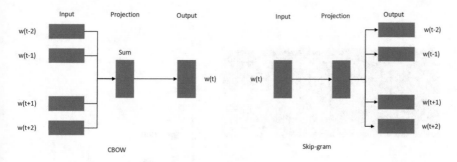

**Fig. 9.25** CBOW and Skip-Gram models

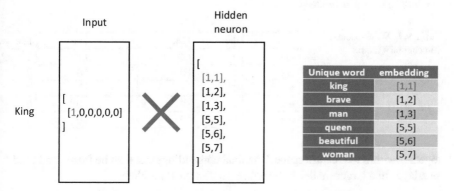

**Fig. 9.26** Input mappings to corresponding table of word embeddings

achieve this which includes Continuous Bag of Words (CBOW) and the Skip-Gram model. These approaches are similar and are shown in Fig. 9.25.

CBOW works by predicting target words such as mat from the surrounding context words "the cat sits on the . . . .". Skip-gram predicts the surrounding context words for the target words which is the inverse of CBOW. Typically, CBOW is used for smaller datasets while Skip-gram is used for larger datasets. Word2Vec is a simple neural network that uses a single hidden layer that has its own set of tuneable weights. Unlike normal MLP whereby the output is used as a mapping from our inputs, Word2Vec is only concerned with the hidden layer weights. These weights are used as our word embeddings. The architecture is like an autoencoder which is covered in a later chapter. Essentially is it a compression technique where you take a large input vector and compress is it down to a smaller dense vector? However, instead of decompressing it back to the original input vector. Once the corpus is encoded using one-hot encoding the generated vector is passed into our hidden layer which generates a set of weights to map the input vector to a corresponding table of word embeddings (the pattern of hidden layer weights is serialised as a vector which is then mapped to a word) as shown in Fig. 9.26.

By using word encoding the network can organise words with similar meanings into close vectors. This is shown in Fig. 9.27 where similar words are grouped close

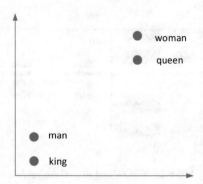

| Unique word | embedding | Word2vec embedding |
|---|---|---|
| king | [1,0,0,0,0,0] | [1,1] |
| man | [0,0,0,1,0,0] | [1,3] |
| queen | [0,0,0,1,0,0] | [5,5] |
| woman | [0,0,0,0,0,1] | [5,7] |

**Fig. 9.27** The final embeddings

**Table 9.7** Word-context co-occurance matrix

|  | the | cat | sat | on | mat |
|---|---|---|---|---|---|
| the | 0 | 1 | 0 | 1 | 1 |
| cat | 1 | 0 | 1 | 0 | 0 |
| sat | 0 | 1 | 0 | 1 | 0 |
| on | 1 | 0 | 1 | 0 | 0 |
| mat | 1 | 0 | 0 | 0 | 0 |

together within the feature space. The final embeddings can then be frozen and used as a layer in a larger model architecture used in NLP problems.

### 9.5.2.3   GloVe

Global Vector Word Representation (GloVe) is an extension to the previously discussed Word2Vec algorithm [20]. GloVe is designed to combine techniques such as LSA which uses global text statistics with local contest-based learning in Word2Vec. Instead of using a window to define local context, GloVe works by constructing a word-context matrix using statistics across the whole text corpus. This enables the construction of enhanced word embeddings which is reflective of the entire corpus.

The GloVe model generates a word-context co-occurrence matrix which consists of words and context pairs so that each element in the matrix reflects how often a word occurs within the context (sequence of words) as shown in Table 9.7. To build this matrix the entire corpus is analysed just once. After this step, p the generated co-occurrence matrix is used instead of the original corpus.

We can now construct the model using the generated co-occurrence matrix. The process works by determining vector values in a continuous space for each word observed in the corpus. This enables word vectors to be generated where they retain useful information on how every word pair occurs. This is a learned process whereby we minimise the objective function. When the function encounters extremely common pair words it will cut off its normal output and simply return 1. For all other

| | 1 | 2 | 3 | 4 | 5 | 6 | 7 | 8 | 9 | 10 | 11 |
|---|---|---|---|---|---|---|---|---|---|---|---|
| **so** | 0.60308 | -0.320240 | 0.088857 | -0.551760 | 0.531820 | 0.047069 | -0.36246 | 0.005702 | -0.37665 | 0.225340 | -0.13534 |
| **them** | 0.64642 | -0.556000 | 0.470380 | -0.820740 | 0.795120 | 0.287710 | -0.56426 | 0.146300 | -0.52421 | 0.021607 | -0.11266 |
| **what** | 0.45323 | 0.059811 | -0.105770 | -0.333000 | 0.723590 | -0.087170 | -0.61053 | -0.037695 | -0.30945 | 0.218050 | -0.43605 |
| **him** | 0.11964 | -0.045405 | 0.051100 | -0.828730 | 0.976650 | 0.111280 | -0.54588 | 1.156100 | -0.68081 | 0.060207 | -0.28765 |
| **united** | -0.39874 | 0.071993 | -0.069773 | 0.147060 | 0.118500 | 0.147700 | -0.84431 | 0.147600 | 0.64804 | -0.559260 | 0.50164 |
| **during** | 0.29784 | -0.018422 | -0.718910 | -0.465100 | -0.456610 | -0.004215 | -0.74598 | 0.346620 | -0.51781 | -0.587700 | 0.18398 |
| **before** | 0.30806 | -0.296650 | -0.257060 | -0.587100 | 0.095135 | -0.152110 | -0.91478 | 0.757270 | -0.30423 | -0.290580 | -0.13034 |
| **may** | 0.70480 | 0.222610 | 0.086997 | -0.212410 | -0.089356 | 0.437420 | -0.28170 | 0.133780 | -0.50859 | -0.182420 | 0.49506 |
| **since** | 0.15423 | -0.125520 | 0.022279 | -0.067561 | -0.359750 | 0.144090 | -1.09020 | -0.028693 | -0.43147 | -0.137810 | 0.37841 |
| **many** | 0.69790 | 0.082340 | 0.041526 | -0.507040 | -0.158010 | 0.360480 | -1.07450 | -0.239270 | -0.74704 | 0.160070 | -0.18420 |

**Fig. 9.28**  Word embeddings

word pairs, we return a weight in the range of 0,1 where the distribution of these weights is decided using an alpha term. An example of word embeddings is shown in Fig. 9.28. These embeddings are then used in the training pipeline as a pretrained layer.

### 9.5.2.4   Natural Language Understanding and Generation

Until now, most of this chapter has covered NLP which is focused on the conversion of text into structured and processable data. There are two additional components which include Natural Language Understanding (NLU) which is responsible for understanding the data based on grammar and the context [21]. Natural Language Generation (NLG) generates text based on structured data [22].

Traditionally, statistical language models were used for both NLU and NLG. Some example techniques include N-grams and Hidden Markov Models which learn the probability distributions of words. However, more recently neural language models have replaced these as they surpass the statistical language models in their effectiveness. You have already encountered the two main algorithms used in NLU and NLG in the previous chapter which are RNNs and LSTMs. These algorithms capture unbounded dependencies among the tokens of a sequence as shown in Fig. 9.29.

The NLU aspects are undertaken using networks such as RNNs and LSTMs while NLG is the predictive output generated by the RNNs and LSTMs.

## 9.6   Real-World Applications

### 9.6.1   Chat Bots

One of the major uses of DL for NLP is in chatbot applications. A chatbot is a conversational tool used to automate communications. They are typically programs

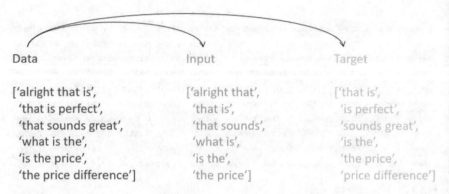

**Fig. 9.29** Capturing unbounded dependencies in sequences

that allow users to interact with a website or app using a chat interface. Traditionally, chatbots were developed using rule-based logic to complete scripted actions based on keywords. More recently, they are powered by AI which uses many of the techniques discussed in this chapter. This has allowed chatbots to converse more naturally. Rule-based chatbots are still popular in eCommerce for routine customer service requests as they are simple to implement and good at dealing with routine enquiries. However, as AI and machine learning advance, they are highly likely to increase in popularity [23].

Chatbots are used in two main dialogue systems: goal-oriented ones like Siri, and general conversation ones like Zoe. The former helps people to solve everyday problems using NLP while the latter attempts to converse with people more broadly. Business chatbots straddle both these two approaches as they are used to supply online customers with the same level of attention, they would get in a physical store, integrating them through the entire shopping experience via a live chat interface. The goal is to make the chatbot experience seamless to enhance the user experience. Machine learning chatbots can help the visitor find what they are looking for, answer FAQs and walk them through checkout.

### 9.6.2 Smart Speakers

The introduction of AI-enabled smart speakers demonstrates the significant advancements made in NLP. Smart speakers such as Echo and Google Nest use state-of-the-art NLP algorithms to power advanced cognitive assistants which can understand and react to the spoken word. These systems utilise NLG which provides the ability to generate natural-sounding writing and verbal responses based on the data inputted into the system. You can think of NLG as a writer that turns data into language that can be communicated. Voice-bases AI systems are appealing to many users as it facilitates communication that is natural to humans (no typing).

Cognitive assistants such as Alexa utilise many of the topics discussed in this and previous chapters. However, fully developed systems are complex. For Example, Alexa starts with signal processing to give Alexa as many chances as possible to understand the audio by cleaning the signal. This involves detecting a filtering ambient noise such as TVs and other background noise. To resolve this issue several microphones are used to identify where the signal is coming from so the device can focus on it. Acoustic echo cancellation can subtract that signal so that only the important signal remains. The next task is to perform wake-word detection such as Alexa to turn the device on to minimise false positives and false negatives. This is a complicated task as it needs to identify pronunciation differences that are done on a device with limited CPU power. If the wake-word is detected signals are sent to the speech recognition software in the cloud which converts the signal into text format. This is where a lot of the NLP elements discussed in this chapter come into play.

## 9.7 Summary

In this chapter we introduced NLP which covered key concepts such as tokenization, stemming, lemmatization, stop words, phrase matching and vocabulary. This was followed by a discussion on text classification which introduced text feature extraction. This chapter also provided a brief introduction to sentiment analysis before discussing topic modelling that described latent sentiment analysis and Latent Dirichlet Allocation. This section was followed by non-negative Matrix Factorisation before the chapter was concluded with a discussion on NLP which introduced word embeddings and algorithms such as Word2Vec and Glove. The section was finally concluded with a discussion on NLU and NLG and introduced some real-life examples of NLP which included chatbots and smart speakers.

## References

1. T. Young, D. Hazarika, S. Poria, and E. Cambria, "Recent trends in deep learning based natural language processing," *ieee Comput. Intell. Mag.*, vol. 13, no. 3, pp. 55–75, 2018.
2. P. M. Nadkarni, L. Ohno-Machado, and W. W. Chapman, "Natural language processing: an introduction," *J. Am. Med. Informatics Assoc.*, vol. 18, no. 5, pp. 544–551, 2011.
3. J. J. Webster and C. Kit, "Tokenization as the initial phase in NLP," 1992.
4. J. B. Lovins, "Development of a stemming algorithm.," *Mech. Transl. Comput. Linguist.*, vol. 11, no. 1–2, pp. 22–31, 1968.
5. M. F. Porter, "Snowball: A language for stemming algorithms." 2001.
6. M. F. Porter, R. Boulton, and A. Macfarlane, "The english (porter2) stemming algorithm," *Retrieved*, vol. 18, p. 2011, 2002.
7. J. Plisson, N. Lavrac, D. Mladenic, and others, "A rule based approach to word lemmatization," in *Proceedings of IS*, 2004, vol. 3, pp. 83–86.
8. C. C. Aggarwal and C. Zhai, "A survey of text classification algorithms," in *Mining text data*, Springer, 2012, pp. 163–222.

9. Y. Zhang, R. Jin, and Z.-H. Zhou, "Understanding bag-of-words model: a statistical framework," *Int. J. Mach. Learn. Cybern.*, vol. 1, no. 1–4, pp. 43–52, 2010.

10. J. Ramos and others, "Using tf-idf to determine word relevance in document queries," in *Proceedings of the first instructional conference on machine learning*, 2003, vol. 242, no. 1, pp. 29–48.

11. W. Medhat, A. Hassan, and H. Korashy, "Sentiment analysis algorithms and applications: A survey," *Ain Shams Eng. J.*, vol. 5, no. 4, pp. 1093–1113, 2014.

12. H. Zhao, D. Phung, V. Huynh, Y. Jin, L. Du, and W. Buntine, "Topic Modelling Meets Deep Neural Networks: A Survey," *arXiv Prepr. arXiv2103.00498*, 2021.

13. T. K. Landauer, P. W. Foltz, and D. Laham, "An introduction to latent semantic analysis," *Discourse Process.*, vol. 25, no. 2–3, pp. 259–284, 1998.

14. J. Boyd-Graber and P. Resnik, "Holistic sentiment analysis across languages: Multilingual supervised latent Dirichlet allocation," in *Proceedings of the 2010 Conference on Empirical Methods in Natural Language Processing*, 2010, pp. 45–55.

15. M. E. Wall, A. Rechtsteiner, and L. M. Rocha, "Singular value decomposition and principal component analysis," in *A practical approach to microarray data analysis*, Springer, 2003, pp. 91–109.

16. D. M. Blei, A. Y. Ng, and M. I. Jordan, "Latent dirichlet allocation," *J. Mach. Learn. Res.*, vol. 3, pp. 993–1022, 2003.

17. D. D. Lee and H. S. Seung, "Learning the parts of objects by non-negative matrix factorization," *Nature*, vol. 401, no. 6755, pp. 788–791, 1999.

18. M. Kusner, Y. Sun, N. Kolkin, and K. Weinberger, "From word embeddings to document distances," in *International conference on machine learning*, 2015, pp. 957–966.

19. T. Mikolov, I. Sutskever, K. Chen, G. S. Corrado, and J. Dean, "Distributed representations of words and phrases and their compositionality," in *Advances in neural information processing systems*, 2013, pp. 3111–3119.

20. F. Sakketou and N. Ampazis, "A constrained optimization algorithm for learning GloVe embeddings with semantic lexicons," *Knowledge-Based Syst.*, vol. 195, p. 105628, 2020.

21. J. Allen, *Natural language understanding*. Benjamin-Cummings Publishing Co., Inc., 1988.

22. E. Reiter and R. Dale, "Building applied natural language generation systems," *Nat. Lang. Eng.*, vol. 3, no. 1, pp. 57–87, 1997.

23. M. Adam, M. Wessel, and A. Benlian, "AI-based chatbots in customer service and their effects on user compliance," *Electron. Mark.*, vol. 31, no. 2, pp. 427–445, 2021.

# Chapter 10
# Deep Generative Models

In this chapter, we are going to introduce and discuss the concept of generative models which is an exciting and rapidly growing area of DL. Specifically, the chapter will introduce Autoencoders (AEs) which are primarily used for dimensionality and noise reduction and are a powerful tool in signal processing, image analysis and NLP. The chapter also discusses Generative Adversarial Networks (GANs) which facilitates the synthetic generation of complex data [1]. This area is seeing rapid development and practical application in image generation.

## 10.1 Autoencoders

AEs are a useful tool in the machine learning practitioner's toolbox for performing dimensionality reduction and noise removal. They can also be used in other types of tasks such as anomaly detection. They can be used with time series and image data. An autoencoder is considered to be an unsupervised learning ANN that learns how to efficiently compress and encode data then learns how to reconstruct the data back from the reduced encoded representation [2]. This mimics the original input as close as possible (approximation) as shown in Fig. 10.1.

### 10.1.1 Autoencoder Basics

An autoencoder is like the MLP you encountered in Chap. 6. The fundamental idea is to reproduce the input at the output layer using a reduced set of features. The key difference between an autoencoder and an MLP is that the number of input neurons is equal to the number of output neurons. In previous chapters on MLP, the output layer was equal in size to the number of classes we were trying to classify—in the

© Springer Nature Switzerland AG 2022
P. Fergus, C. Chalmers, *Applied Deep Learning*, Computational Intelligence Methods and Applications, https://doi.org/10.1007/978-3-031-04420-5_10

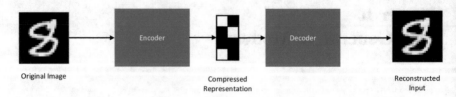

**Fig. 10.1** Encoder-decoder configuration

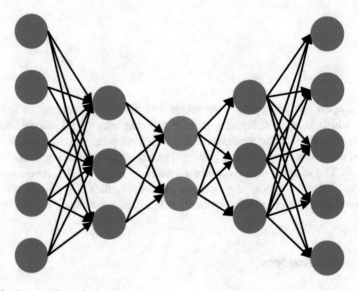

**Fig. 10.2** Autoencoder architecture

case of regression, a single perceptron is used to provide a single continuous value. An example autoencoder network would look like the one shown in Fig. 10.2.

In the example, we start with five input neurons and then we slowly reduce the number down to a specified number throughout the hidden layers. So, for example, we can go from five to three to two. This process captures the essential information in the data while removing the noise and data that are not important. This first stage is known as the encoding stage.

The layers to the right-hand side of the central two nodes are known as the decoding layers. These layers try to reproduce the inputs captured in the encoding layer and approximate them at the output layer via the decoder hidden layers. To evaluate the performance and determine how close the output data is to the input data a reconstruction loss is used to measure how well the decoder performs. The four main components used to construct an autoencoder are listed below.

1. Encoder: In which the model learns how to reduce the input dimensions and compress the input data into an encoded representation.

2. Bottleneck: which is the layer that contains the compressed representation of the input data. This is the lowest possible dimension of the input data.
3. Decoder: In which the model learns how to reconstruct the data from the encoded representation such that it is as close to the original input as possible.
4. Reconstruction Loss: This is the method that measures how well the decoder is performing and how close the output is to the original input.

An autoencoder learns to encode and decode using the same learning techniques to train an MLP which includes an optimiser and a loss function.

## *10.1.2   Autoencoder for Dimensionality Reduction*

The central idea behind an autoencoder is similar to PCA whereby we are trying to reduce the input into a smaller number of principal components. In the diagram above we are compressing five into two. It is important to note that the hidden layer is not simply sub-selecting only certain features. Instead, it works by calculating combinations of the original features represented in the original data in a reduced dimensional space. Figure 10.3 shows an example whereby a 3D representation is projected onto a 2D space. This is similar to what was presented in the discussion on LDA.

In the case of dimensionality reduction, you simply split the network in half and use the hidden layer (the input and output layer, including other peripheral hidden layers, are discarded). The central hidden layer now becomes your new input layer data. In this sense dimensionality reduction compresses the original data into a lower dimension. Once we have a lower-dimensional space, we can visualise data and reveal hidden relationships not seen in higher dimensions.

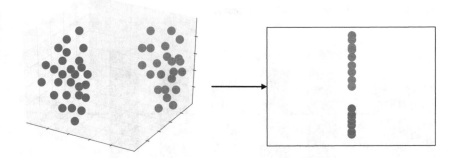

**Fig. 10.3**  3D projected representation into a 2D space

### 10.1.3   Autoencoder for Images

Autoencoders are particularly good at reducing the dimensionality of images. For example, an image with 28 × 28 pixels will result in 784 features or dimensions. In this sense, it might be useful to reduce this dimensionality as there will be redundant pixels and information. Bypassing the image into the autoencoder we can attempt to reconstruct the image by first passing it through a much smaller dimension (set of hidden layers). This allows the model to determine which pixels are important as its information is encoded in the hidden layers. These features will then be used to reconstruct the image into an approximation of the original input image. A sample autoencoder architecture to achieve this is shown in Fig. 10.4.

This would generate an autoencoder that understands which features of the original 784 pixels are important and which of those are not. For example, the image above it understands that pixels on the edge do not matter. We can use the same logic to train an autoencoder that removes noise since the autoencoder will know which pixels are important. By using an autoencoder we can feed in a noisy image as shown on the left-hand side of Fig. 10.5 and reproduce the new image on the right using the feature extraction process described.

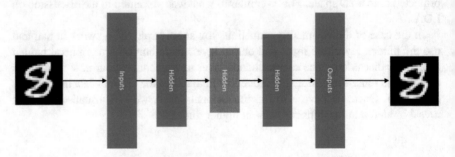

**Fig. 10.4**  Image compression using an autoencoder

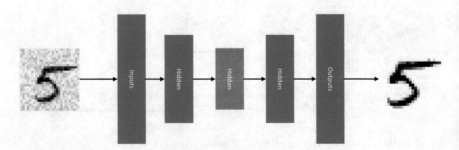

**Fig. 10.5**  Image denoising using an autoencoder

### 10.1.4 Stacked Autoencoders

Based on the previous definition of an AE, a Stacked Autoencoder (SAE) is used to learn relationships between data points and produce a significantly smaller input feature space [3]. This smaller input space can then be used to initialise the weights of an MLP classifier. As we previously saw an AE is a three-layered neural network that applies backpropagation to learn an output that is like the input data provided to the network. The AE learns any structure present in the data if it exists. By stacking a sequence of AEs layer by layer, an SAE can be constructed as shown in Fig. 10.6.

Once a single layer has been trained by an original AE, a second AE can use the hidden layer from the first AE as input as shown in the figure above. By repeating this procedure, it is possible to create SAEs of arbitrary depth. The first single layer AE maps inputs into the first hidden vector. Once the first layer AE is trained, its reconstruction layer is removed, and the hidden layer becomes the input layer of the next AE. In this way, AEs are stacked to enable greedy layer-wise learning where the hidden layer is used as input to the next subsequent AE. The results produced by the SAE are utilised to pre-train the weights for a proposed MLP, rather than randomly initialising the weights to small values to classify different outputs. Greedy layer-wise pre-training helps the model initialise the parameters near to a good local minimum and transform the problem space to a better form of optimisation. Adopting this approach, it is expected to achieve smoother convergence and higher overall performance in the classification tasks. The key thing to note is that as you increase the number of AEs you also decrease the number of inputs. If you do this too quickly (reduce the number of inputs drastically) you will produce poor results. The trick is to decrease the inputs slowly over a few AEs until the desired level of performance is reached.

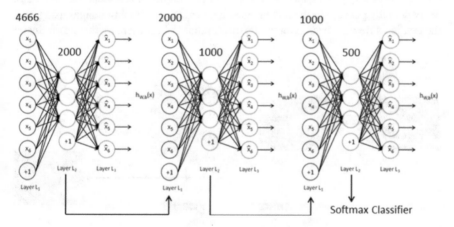

**Fig. 10.6** Stacked autoencoder architecture

### 10.1.5   Generative Adversarial Networks (GANS)

GANS were invented in 2014 and uses two networks competing against each other to generate data [4]. GANs are often described as a counterfeiter versus a detective. The network is split into two parts whereby the counterfeiter is the generator that receives random noise that is typically a Gaussian distribution. The counterfeiter outputs data which is often an image. The discriminator (detective) takes a dataset consisting of real images from the real dataset and fake images from the generator. It performs a binary classification to classify real and fake images.

As shown in Fig. 10.7 the process starts with noisy data which is fed into the generator as input. The generator's goal is to create images that fool the discriminator. So, in the first stages of training the generator will create noise. In addition, we also select images from our real-world dataset and use these two outputs to train the discriminator. The discriminator labels the fake generated images as zeros and the real images as one.

As the training process continues the generator improves the images it generates to fool the discriminator. This process continues until the generator can produce images that fool the discriminator as shown in Fig. 10.8. At this stage, the discriminator cannot distinguish between real and fake images.

The training includes two phases. Phase 1: train the discriminator and phase 2: train the generator. In phase 1 real images labelled as one are combined with fake images from the generator labelled zero. The discriminator trains to distinguish real from fake with backpropagation occurring only on the discriminator weights. In phase 2 the generator produces fake images which are only sent to the generator with all labels set to one. This causes the generator to attempt to produce images that the discriminator believes to be real. Because we feed in fake images all labelled one, we only perform backpropagation on the generator weights in this step. The generator never actually gets to see the real images. It generates convincing images using only the gradients flowing back through the discriminator. Furthermore, the discriminator

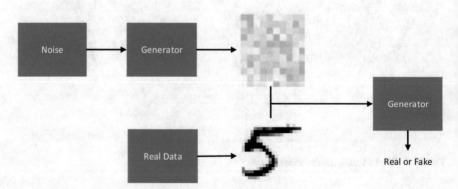

**Fig. 10.7**  Generative adversarial network

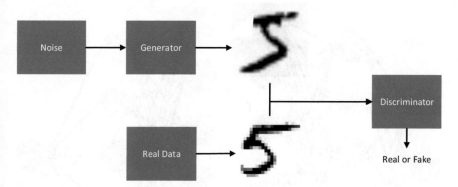

**Fig. 10.8** Generator fooling the discriminator

is also improving during the training phase meaning that the generated images will also need to get better to trick the discriminator.

There are a wide range of difficulties with GAN architectures. Firstly, they can be extremely computationally expensive to train. As GANs are often trained with images they require high-end GPUs with adequate memory. This is particularly problematic as you are training two separate networks at the same time. A further challenge is mode collapse which occurs when the generator figures out a few images or a single image that can fool the discriminator. This means that the generator eventually collapses to produce only that image. In theory, it would be preferable to have a variety of images that can fool the discriminator. However, GANs can still collapse to only produce a single number of faces, regardless of input noise. There are several ways to combat mode collapse such as using Deep convolutional GANS (DCGANs). In addition, researchers have also experimented with mini-batch discrimination, which punishes generated batches of images that are too similar.

A further challenge with GANs is instability as it can be difficult to ascertain the performance and appropriate training epochs since the generated images are always truly fake. Due to the design of a GAN, the generator and discriminator are constantly in conflict with each other leading to performance oscillation between the two. When using more complex images, you are required to experiment with the various hyperparameters such as number of layers, number of neurons, activation functions and learning rates, etc.

### 10.1.5.1   GANs Network Architectures

In a most basic GAN model, both the generator and discriminator are fully connected neural networks. The architecture of a GAN can be depicted as shown in Fig. 10.9.

GAN's come in two flavours. The first is based on an MLP architecture as shown above. The second is a DCGAN which is used for generating more complex images.

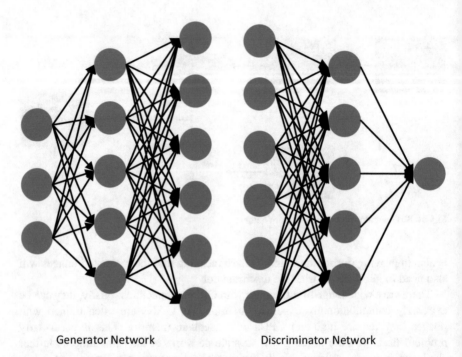

Generator Network          Discriminator Network

**Fig. 10.9** GANs neural network architecture

The key difference between the two architectures is that the latter includes a series of CNN layers as shown in Fig. 10.10.

Looking at the architecture in Fig. 10.10 the discriminator is simply a CNN as discussed in the book already. However, the generator is a deconvolutional neural network DCNN. The generator converts a class vector into a complete image whereas the CNN converts an image into a class vector. The generator using the DCNN is creating images from scratch. This means that these new network architectures can produce any kind of object such as chairs, cars, landscapes, and people. It also allows us to take a photo of an object and generate a new image from a new angle. It can generate faces of non-existent people and even change facial expressions, clothes, and body poses.

## 10.2  Summary

The chapter begins with a discussion on autoencoders and their use in dimensionality reduction and noise removal. This is followed by a discussion on how they can be stacked to extract more complex features. Generative Adversarial Networks were also introduced to show how images can be artificially generated. The discussion

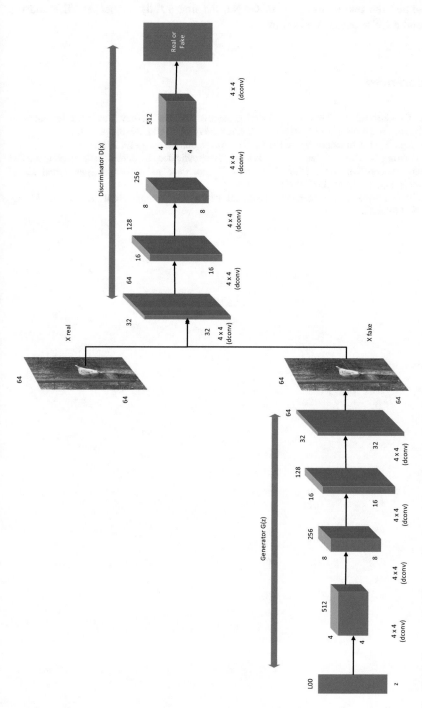

**Fig. 10.10** Deep convolutional generative adversarial network architecture

presented the two major types of GANs: the first a fully connected MLP and the second a CNN-based architecture.

# References

1. A. Oussidi and A. Elhassouny, "Deep generative models: Survey," in *2018 International Conference on Intelligent Systems and Computer Vision (ISCV)*, 2018, pp. 1–8.
2. A. Ng, "Sparse Autoencoder," *CS294A Lect. Notes*, no. 72, pp. 1–19, 2011.
3. J. Gehring, Y. Miao, F. Metze, and A. Waibel, "Extracting deep bottleneck features using stacked auto-encoders," in *2013 IEEE international conference on acoustics, speech and signal processing*, 2013, pp. 3377–3381.
4. I. Goodfellow *et al.*, "Generative adversarial networks," *Commun. ACM*, vol. 63, no. 11, pp. 139–144, 2020.

# Chapter 11
# Deep Reinforcement Learning

In this chapter, we will introduce and discuss the concept of deep reinforcement learning (DRL) which is an exciting and rapidly growing area of machine learning [1]. DRL is primarily used to learn from actions enacted in an environment. This is like how humans learn from experience. This area is seeing rapid development in a broad range of disciplines which include driverless cars, simulation, and gameplay.

## 11.1    What Is Reinforcement Learning?

Reinforcement Learning (RL) is a branch of machine learning where algorithms learn from their actions in the same way humans learn from experience [2]. In this machine learning paradigm, the concept of agents is used that are rewarded and penalised for the actions that they take [3]. Actions that move the agent to the desired target outcome are rewarded (reinforced) while those that do not are penalised. Figure 11.1 shows a simple example of an agent (for example this could be a dog) interacting with an environment (the dog owner) where the agent is rewarded (owner throws stick) when the agent performs an action in the environment (for example a dog fetches and drops a stick).

This process occurs through a series of trial-and-error actions within an environment that allows the DRL algorithm to learn. The learning entity (agent) is not told what actions to take, but instead must discover for itself which actions produce the greatest rewards and move it closer to its goal. These actions can affect not only the immediate reward but also the future ones, "delayed rewards" since the current actions will determine future situations (this happens in real life). These two characteristics, "trial and error" and "delayed reward," are two distinguishing characteristics of RL.

RL has been a research topic for several decades. However, it has only recently been combined with DL and is now beginning to solve several real-world problems. The "deep" part of DRL refers to the deep layers in an ANN. DL is one of the best

© Springer Nature Switzerland AG 2022
P. Fergus, C. Chalmers, *Applied Deep Learning*, Computational Intelligence
Methods and Applications, https://doi.org/10.1007/978-3-031-04420-5_11

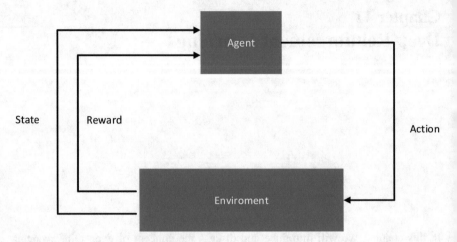

**Fig. 11.1** High-level reinforcement learning concept

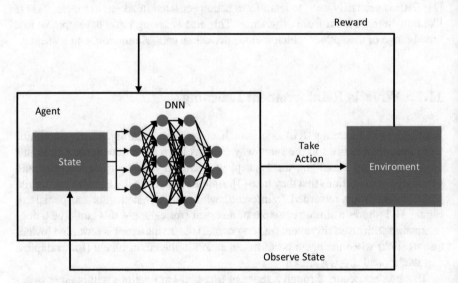

**Fig. 11.2** Deep reinforcement learning architecture

methods for handling unstructured environments; they can learn from large amounts of data and discover unique patterns [4]. But this is not decision-making; it is a recognition problem. RL provides the decision-making component. Combining the two approaches allows us to utilise both to learn and generalise over data and sequentially move forward in the environment through several carefully considered decision points. Figure 11.2 shows a sample architecture for deep reinforcement models. Here the DNN implemented on the agent uses the current state to predict an action that will lead to the highest reward and close to the overall goal.

DRL is being used to solve a wide range of problems with the most famous being DeepMind's AlphaGo that defeated the then Go grandmaster Lee Sadel in March 2016 in Seoul. However, as well as being able to play Go, DRL has already achieved human-level abilities in other games which include Chess and Poker and is now being used to solve other real-world problems in manufacturing, healthcare, and engineering. Progress has been slow given that realistic problem-based environments are required that do not cause real-world damage. This said, simulation technology has helped provide trial-and-error environments for DRL that is scalable and safe.

## 11.2 Reinforcement Learning Definitions

RL is presented using the concept of agents, environments, states, actions, and rewards.

- An **agent** receives actions. For example, a drone may be designed to take instructions to deliver a parcel or a Super Mario agent to navigate a particular video game. In these instances, the algorithm is the agent, in real-life, it would be you.
- An **action** is all the possible moves an agent can make. Actions are self-explanatory, but it should be noted that agents will choose from a list of discrete actions. In a video game, the list might include running, jumping, crouching, and standing. While in a stock market application the list might include buying, selling, or holding.
- A **discount factor** is multiplied by future rewards discovered by an agent to dampen the effect of rewards on the agent's choice of action. This is designed to make future rewards worth less than immediate rewards. This enforces a short-term high in the agent.
- Agents interact with an **environment** which is a world through which the agent moves, and which the environment responds to the agent. An environment takes as input an agent's current state and action and returns the agents reward and its next state. If you are the agent, the environment acts as the laws of physics and the rules of society that process your actions and determine the consequences of them.
- A **state** is a concrete and immediate situation in which the agent finds itself.
- A **reward** is the feedback by which we measure the success or failure of an agent's actions in each state.
- **Policies** are used by agents to devise strategies to determine the next action based on the current state. This allows the agent to map states to actions and identify the actions that promise the highest reward.
- Expected long-term returns of the current state under specific policies are described as a **value**.

- A **Q-value** or **action-value** is like value except that it takes an extra parameter, which is the current action. Q maps state-action pairs to rewards.
- The sequence of states and actions that influence those states are described as a **trajectory**. Note that rewards are immediate signals that are received in each state, while value is the sum of all rewards you might anticipate from that state. Value is a long-term expectation, while a reward is an immediate pleasure.

Environments are functions that transform an action taken in the current state into the next state and a reward. Conversely, agents are functions that transform the new state and reward into the next action. RL represents an agent's attempt to approximate the environment's function, such that we can send actions into a black box environment that maximises the rewards the environment outputs. The agent and the environment continuously interact so that the agent attempts to influence the environment through actions, and the environment reacts to the agent's actions. How the environment reacts to specific actions is defined by a model that may or may not be known by the agent, and this differentiates two circumstances:

- when the agent knows the model, we refer to this situation as a model-based RL. In this case, when we fully know the environment, we can find the optimal solution by dynamic programming.
- When the agent does not know the model, it needs to make decisions with incomplete information; (undertake model-free RL) or try to learn the model explicitly as part of the algorithm.

Unlike other forms of machine learning—such as supervised and unsupervised learning—RL can only be thought about sequentially in terms of state-action pairs that occur one after the other. The environment is represented by a set of variables related to the problem (dependent on the type of problem we want to solve). This set of variables and all the values that they can take is referred to as the state space. A state is an instantiation of the state space. The agent does not have access to the actual full state of the environment but only observes part of the state that the agent can observe. Much like in real-life in that you only see a window of the environment at a time as you move through it, not the complete environment all at once.

RL algorithms judge actions based on the results they produce. It is goal-oriented, and it aims to learn sequences of actions that will allow an agent to achieve its goal or maximise its objective function. In this sense, RL differs from both supervised and unsupervised learning by how it interprets inputs. For example, in unsupervised learning, the algorithm learns similarities while supervised learning algorithms learn the correlations between data instances and their labels. In RL, actions based on short and long-term rewards, such as the number of calories you ingest, or the length of time you survive, can be thought of as supervised learning in an environment of sparse feedback. The RL cycle used to enable this is shown in Fig. 11.3.

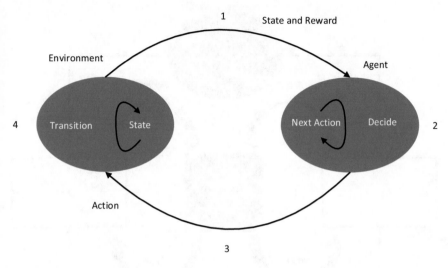

**Fig. 11.3**  Reinforcement learning cycle

## 11.3   Domain Selection for Reinforcement Learning

One way to think about an RL agent is to consider a blind person attempting to navigate the world with only their ears and a white cane. Agents have small windows that allow them to perceive their environment, and those windows may not even be the most appropriate way for them to perceive what is around them. Deciding what types of input and feedback your agent should pay attention to is a hard problem to solve. This is known as domain selection. Typically, RL algorithms that are designed to play games can ignore this problem as the environments are man-made and limited. Domain selection requires human decisions, usually based on knowledge or theories about the problem to be solved. For example, selecting the domain of input for an algorithm in a self-driving car might include choosing to have radar sensors in addition to cameras and GPS data.

## 11.4   State-Action Pairs and Complex Probability Distributions of Reward

The goal of RL is to pick the best-known action for any given state, which means the actions must be ranked, and assigned values relative to one another. Actions are state-dependent therefore we need to gauge the value of state-action pairs. For example, if an action is marrying someone, then marrying a 35-year-old when you are 18 means something different than marrying a 35-year-old when you are 90, and those two scenarios have different motivations and lead to different outcomes. In another example, if your action is yelling "Fire," then performing the action in a

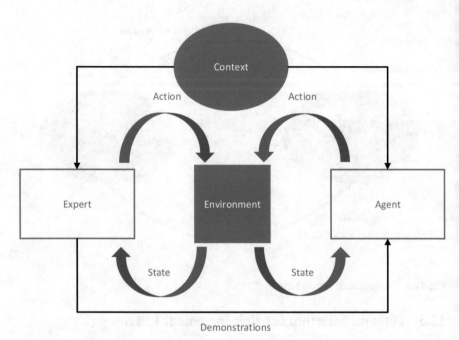

**Fig. 11.4**  Adding context to RL solutions

crowded theatre should mean something different from performing the action next to a squad of men with rifles. We cannot predict the outcome of an action without knowing the context. Figure 11.4 shows how context can be added to an RL solution.

We map state-action pairs to the values we expect them to produce with the $Q$ function. The $Q$ function takes as its input the agent's state and action and maps them to the probable rewards. RL is the process of running the agent through sequences of state-action pairs and observing the rewards that result and adapting the predictions of the $Q$ function to those rewards. This continues until it accurately predicts the best path for the agent to take. As described above, a prediction is known as a policy.

RL is an attempt to model a complex probability distribution of rewards in relation to many state-action pairs. This is one reason why historically RL has been paired with a Markov decision process to infer its properties. It closely resembles the problem that inspired Stan Ulam to invent the Monte Carlo method, which tries to infer the chances that a given hand of solitaire will turn out successful. In another example, as shown in Fig. 11.5 an autonomous car can be modelled to perform several outcomes when the car is driving slow or fast.

The Markov decision process is used to approximate the probability distribution of reward over state-action pairs. However, a reinforcement learning algorithm tends to repeat actions that lead to a reward and cease to test alternatives. This leads to a tension between the exploitation of known rewards and continued exploration to

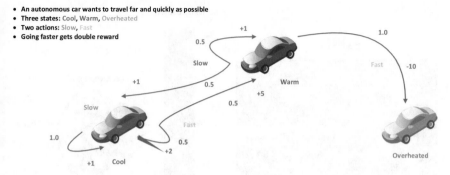

**Fig. 11.5** Autonomous car driving using reinforcement learning

discover new actions that also lead to victory. RL algorithms can be made to both exploit and explore to varying degrees, to ensure that they do not pass over rewarding actions at the expense of known winners.

Hopefully, you can now see that RL is an iterative process whereby algorithms do not begin by knowing which rewards state-action pairs will produce. It learns relationships by running through states repeatedly as athletes or musicians iterate through states to improve their performance.

Algorithms can quickly aggregate the lessons of time. RL algorithms have a different relationship to time than humans do. Algorithms can run through the same states repeatedly with different actions until they can infer which actions are best from which states. This means that RL algorithms have the potential to learn more, and better, than humans. An algorithm trained on the game of Go, such as AlphaGo, will have played many more games of Go than any human could hope to complete in 100 lifetimes.

## 11.5   Neural Networks and Reinforcement Learning

So where does DL fit into RL frameworks? ANNs are function approximators, which are particularly useful in RL when the state space or action space is too large to be completely known. ANNs can learn to map states to values, or states-action pairs to $Q$ values. Rather than using a lookup table to store, index and update all states and their values, which is a significant challenge with large problems. We can train an ANN on samples from the state or action space to learn to predict how valuable those are relative to our target in RL. In other words, DRL is a technology that combines RL and DL to create a sequential RL process, in which DL determines the action taken at every stage.

Like all ANNs, they use coefficients to approximate a function that relates inputs to outputs. Their learning consists of finding the right coefficients, or weights, by iteratively adjusting those weights along gradients that produce less error. RL is not

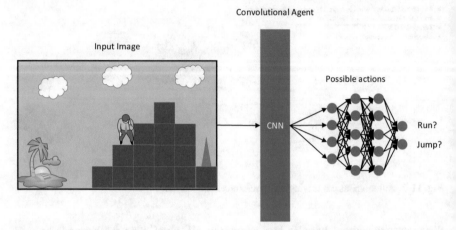

**Fig. 11.6**  Convolutional agents in DRL

limited to ANNs only, CNNs can be used to recognise an agent's state when the input is visual, e.g., the screen that Mario is on, or the terrain before a drone.

CNNs however, derive different interpretations from images in RL than in supervised learning. In supervised learning, the network applies a label to an image; that is, it matches names to pixels as previously discussed earlier in this book. In RL however, given an image that represents a state, a CNN can rank the actions possible to perform in that state; for example, it might predict that running right will return 5 points, jumping 7, and running left none (Fig. 11.6).

At the beginning of RL, the ANN coefficients may be initialised stochastically, or randomly as we have seen previously in this book. Using feedback from the environment, the neural network can use the difference between its expected reward and the ground-truth reward to adjust its weights and improve its interpretation of state-action pairs. This feedback loop is analogous to the backpropagation of error in supervised learning. However, supervised learning begins with knowledge of the ground-truth labels the ANN is trying to predict. Its goal is to create a model that maps different images to their respective names. RL relies on the environment to send it a scalar number in response to each new action. The rewards returned by the environment can be varied, delayed, or affected by unknown variables, introducing noise to the feedback loop.

This leads us to a more complete expression of the $Q$ function, which considers not only the immediate rewards produced by an action but also the delayed rewards that may be returned several time steps deeper into the sequence. Like human beings, the $Q$ function is recursive.

## 11.6 The Deep Reinforcement Learning Process

There are two learning methods in DRL which are the value-based method and the policy-based method.

- **Value-Based Method:** Algorithms such as Deep-Q-Network (DQN) use CNNs to help the agent select the best action. While the algorithms are complex, they typically follow these basic steps.

  - Take the image representing the state, convert it to grayscale, and crop unnecessary parts.
  - Run the image through a series of convolutions and pooling to extract the essential features that can help the agent make the decision.
  - Calculate the Q-Value of each action.
  - Perform back-propagation to find the most accurate Q-values.

- **Policy-Based Method**: In the real world, the number of actions can be extremely high or unknown. For example, a robot learning to walk on open terrain could have millions of actions within the space of a few minutes. In these environments, calculating Q-values for actions is not feasible. Policy-based methods learn the policy function directly, without calculating a value function for each action. An example of a policy-based algorithm is Policy Gradient. The process follows these basic steps.

  - Take in a state and get the probability of each action based on previous experience.
  - Select the most probable action.
  - Repeat until the end of the game and evaluate the total rewards
  - Update the parameters in the network, based on the rewards, using backpropagation.

## 11.7 Practical Applications of Deep Reinforcement Learning

Toolkits such as OpenAI Gym, DeepMind Lab and Psychlab provide training environments to catapult large-scale innovation for DRL and train DRL agents. As more organisations apply DRL to their unique business use cases, there will be a dramatic growth in practical applications.

- **Manufacturing**: robots that move and manipulate products utilise DRL to gain knowledge based on whether it succeeds or fails which it then uses to perform more efficiently in the future.
- **Automotive**: DRL is used in autonomous vehicles, but it is also helping to transform factories, vehicle maintenance and overall automation in the industry.

DRL with data from customers, dealers and warranties provides new ways to improve quality, save money and improve safety.

- **Finance**: DRL is being used to evaluate trading and improve strategies to increase returns on investment.
- **Healthcare**: The use of DRL in healthcare ranges from optimal treatment plans and diagnosis to clinical trials, new drug development and automatic treatment.
- **Bots**: Conversational user interfaces are now powered by DRL to allow bots to learn the nuances and semantics of language over many domains for automated speech and NLP.

There is a great deal of interest in DRL as it learns by interacting with its environment, so there is no limit to the number of possible applications.

## 11.8   Summary

In this chapter, we introduce the concept of RL as a suite of algorithms that learn from their actions in a comparable way to how humans learn from experience. The chapter discusses the limitations with RL when mapping large actions state pairs and how this has been overcome with DL. Rather than using an index table to store, index, update all states and their values DL is used to model and determine actions that need to be taken at each stage. The chapter is concluded with some examples of where DRL is used.

## References

1. K. Arulkumaran, M. P. Deisenroth, M. Brundage, and A. A. Bharath, "Deep reinforcement learning: A brief survey," *IEEE Signal Process. Mag.*, vol. 34, no. 6, pp. 26–38, 2017.
2. R. S. Sutton and A. G. Barto, *Reinforcement learning: An introduction*. MIT press, 2018.
3. L. P. Kaelbling, M. L. Littman, and A. W. Moore, "Reinforcement learning: A survey," *J. Artif. Intell. Res.*, vol. 4, pp. 237–285, 1996.
4. P. Henderson, R. Islam, P. Bachman, J. Pineau, D. Precup, and D. Meger, "Deep reinforcement learning that matters," in *Proceedings of the AAAI conference on artificial intelligence*, 2018, vol. 32, no. 1.

# Part IV
# Enterprise Machine Learning

# Chapter 12
# Accelerated Machine Learning

## 12.1 Introduction

Accelerated machine learning is an exciting new paradigm in the field of AI which aims to improve the efficiency of training machine learning models. This is achieved by providing users with the ability to execute end-to-end data science pipelines on GPU's or large-scale CPU based clusters. Although this is a widespread practice for DL applications, historically the training of traditional machine learning models such as SVM's and RF's have been restricted to CPU compute. Architectures based on single CPU's which are found in all types of computer hardware (Intel/AMD) have started to stall in terms of their performance due to restrictions on the manufacturing process and heat dissipation issues. The performance of CPUs has seen limited improvement in recent years which is in stark contrast to the early decades which saw CPU performance double every year (Moores Law) [1]. To combat some of these limitations' CPU vendors have switched to the development and manufacture of multi-core CPUs that enable multithreading tasks. These processors facilitate rapid performance and enable giga floating-point operations per second (GFLOPS). Traditionally applications were designed to run sequentially and therefore dramatically slowing down the execution of the running process.

Although multithread and multicore CPUs address some of these limitations as sequences of the application can be run and scheduled on the CPU in parallel, the effect on time execution is limited. Until recently high-performance parallel computing also known as (HPC) focused on adding additional CPUs into each compute node and joining multiple nodes through InfiniBand connections to allow large parallel processing tasks to be run at scale. HPC developers have been designing and implementing parallel programs for years that can run on large scale HPC infrastructures. In the domain of data processing and AI there resides some of the most computationally demanding applications which have led to significant interest in large parallel computing architectures.

© Springer Nature Switzerland AG 2022
P. Fergus, C. Chalmers, *Applied Deep Learning*, Computational Intelligence
Methods and Applications, https://doi.org/10.1007/978-3-031-04420-5_12

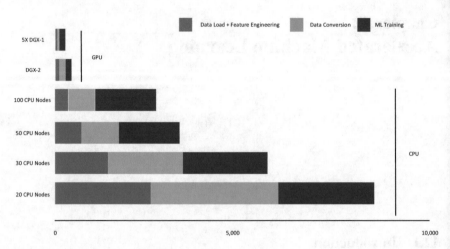

**Fig. 12.1** Comparison between GPU and CPU compute times

Over the last few years, hardware vendors have come to realise that bottlenecks in multicore and multithreaded CPUs are starting to limit the types of computational jobs we can undertake. This has led to an increase in the use of GPU's within HPC to try and remove processing bottlenecks and provide the compute needed in high-end applications such as data analytics and AI. GPUs are designed for high throughput parallel processing which can be 10X+ faster than CPUs for parallel code execution. As such new frameworks and libraries (discussed later in this chapter) have been developed to exploit the underlying architecture of GPUs and are a key component in many data processing pipelines.

With the ever-increasing volume of data, traditional approaches to the machine learning pipeline introduce significant bottles necks and delays from training to inference. With the introduction of GPU accelerated machine learning more data can be processed at scale which in turn delivers results significantly quicker.

Machine learning practice has traditionally resulted in extended periods of wasted time due to slow stages in the Extract Transform and Load Process (ETL). This has led to underutilisation in data science teams while delaying the time to extract intelligence from the data science pipeline and deliver new products and services. However, with the utilisation of GPUs and the associated frameworks and libraries to exploit them, we can now utilise GPUs for general purpose data analytics and machine learning tasks.

This approach provides a much more efficient workflow through GPU acceler-ated data processing, therefore, giving organisations a competitive edge. As shown in Fig. 12.1 the time needed to run the entire data processing pipeline is significantly quicker when run on GPUs. This also has the added benefit of a reduced infrastruc-ture footprint. For example, a single 3U DGX1 comprising of 8 Tesla V100 GPUs totalling 256GB of GPU memory costs less than $130,000. In comparison, the footprint for an on-premise server or cloud base provider would be more expensive overall.

From a datacentre management point of view, this means there are typically fewer nodes to manage (firmware/software patching) and facilitates a more scaleup approach instead of scaling out. In this chapter, we will introduce you to the concepts and techniques used in accelerated machine learning starting with CPU base hardware solutions and concluding with newer GPU offerings.

## 12.1.1   CPU/GPU Based Clusters

As previously discussed architecturally, the CPU is composed of just a few cores with lots of cache memory that can handle a few software threads at a time. In contrast, a GPU is composed of hundreds of cores that can handle thousands of threads simultaneously. According to Data Centre Dynamics, the CPU has been the main brain of computer systems since the 1950s. CPUs are completely dedicated to executing a linear stream of data. In contrast, GPUs were originally developed to enhance the graphics of computers for either gaming or engineering design applications. Now, due to its ability to perform multidimensional processing, GPUs are utilised in machine learning and AI. Although 64 cores are a lot for CPUs, the number pales in comparison to the number of cores in a GPU. While GPU cores are simpler and target more specific applications, general-purpose GPUs (GPGPUs) are becoming more flexible. Programming platforms like OpenCL have incorporated GPGPUs into the programming mainstream and they were the initial workhorses in the rise of AI/machine learning applications.

Accelerated computing can be achieved in several ways. Big data frameworks are designed to utilise specific hardware types based on infrastructure configurations. For example, HPC data centres in most organisations will have large CPU availability and this has led to the implementation of frameworks such as Spark. In contrast, some organisations have a blend of hardware containing both CPU's and GPU's. As a result, frameworks such as Apache Arrow and RAPIDS can be used to speed up data analytics by taking advantage of GPU hardware and the parallelisation it offers.

## 12.2   CPU Accelerated Computing

At the time of writing Intel remains the dominant player in the data centre with its Xeon family. To facilitate large data analytics tasks datacentres are comprised of many individual compute nodes that can be joined together to form a cluster. The combined compute capability of this cluster enables the processing of large data analytical tasks promptly. Frameworks such as Spark (discussed later) can exploit large computational clusters to perform complex ETL pipelines while undertaking data modelling tasks such as machine learning. In this section, we will investigate CPU based HPC and some of the most popular accelerated computing frameworks.

## 12.2.1  Distributed Accelerated Computing Frameworks

Accelerated computing frameworks are significantly different compared to existing data storage and processing technologies such as SQL Server. They are designed to process data independently of its format (structured, semi-structured or unstructured). The data processing aspects are handled differently. Processing tasks are distributed across multiple nodes as shown in Fig. 12.2.

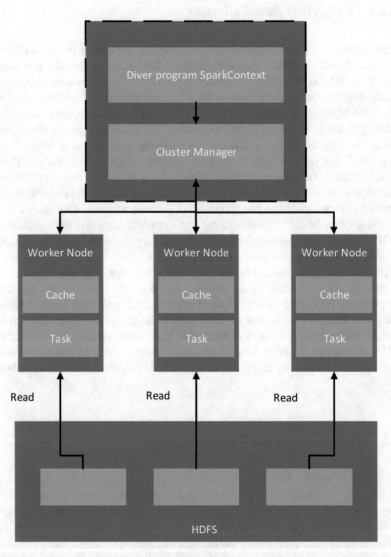

**Fig. 12.2** Processing tasks distributed across multiple nodes

Distributed data and analytics demand a comprehensive end-to-end architecture. Implementing accelerated compute solutions requires appropriate infrastructure to support scalability, distribution, and management of data from both a hardware and framework perspective. Solutions must incorporate a data management and analytics architecture that can support changing and varied data and analysis needs. It must accommodate not only traditional data analysis but also newer, advanced analytics techniques. When implementing these solutions, it needs to address two fundamental questions. Firstly, how much data do we need to manage currently and in the future, and how will we manage data in real-time or near real-time.

### 12.2.1.1   Local Vs Distributed

A local system is limited to the amount of Random-Access Memory (RAM) and Hard Disk Drive (HDD) space contained within a single node. A distributed system is comprised of multiple compute nodes. A master node is used to coordinate jobs within the cluster. Data and calculations are distributed across the nodes (workers) as shown in Fig. 12.3.

A distributed system allows us to rapidly scale our computational capabilities. This is significantly beneficial for computationally expensive tasks. Calculations and data can be distributed across multiple nodes. The more work nodes a cluster has means the more CPUs can be included for computation workflows. Figure 12.4 shows a scalable distribution of CPUs across multiple nodes.

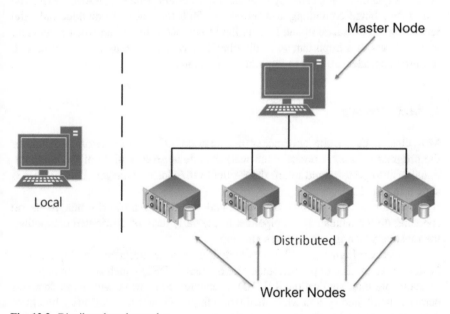

**Fig. 12.3** Distributed worker nodes

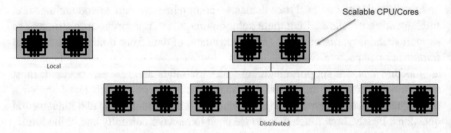

**Fig. 12.4** Distributed CPUs/cores

A local process will utilise the computational resources of a single node. A distributed process can access the computational resources of many nodes which are connected through a high-speed network (fibre). This is fundamentally different to scaling up (more powerful machines). Instead, distributed computing is all about scaling out (more machines). Once you hit a limit, it is easier to scale out your infrastructure using lower-powered compute nodes than try to scale up to a single node with a high specification (Fig. 12.5). A distributed compute cluster also has the advantage of easy scaling. Once you hit the computational limitations of the cluster you can simply add more nodes as shown in Fig. 12.5.

### 12.2.1.2   Benefits of Scaling Out

With a single node, you can only upgrade it to a certain point e.g., RAM, CPUs. The use of distributed computing also introduces fault tolerance. If one node fails, the remaining nodes can continue. Having fault tolerance is important when processing large datasets. It is important when distributing data across a cluster. With scale-out, resource upgrades are easy to implement and manage.

### 12.2.1.3   Hadoop

Most clusters have a cluster manager (master node) to launch executors and monitor the progress of worker nodes. Each worker node is given a piece of the computational task to perform and return the results to the cluster manager. This process is shown in Fig. 12.6.

There are a wide variety of accelerated computing fireworks that focus on speeding up the data analytics pipeline. In the early days of distributed computing, the most common framework was Hadoop.

The Hadoop framework allows us to distribute large files across multiple nodes. Hadoop uses the Hadoop Distributed File System (HDFS) which is commonly used in many big data applications [2]. HDFS enables us to work with large data sets across a distributed system while facilitating fault tolerance by duplicating blocks of data. Hadoop uses MapReduce which allows us to perform calculations on the data.

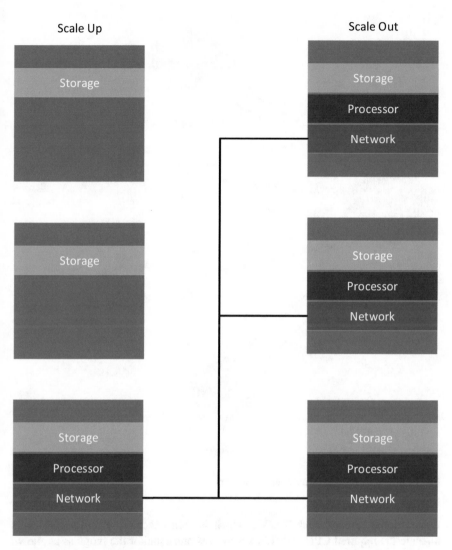

**Fig. 12.5**  Scale-up vs scale-out

The Master Node controls the process of distributing data and calculations between Worker Nodes. HDFS uses a default block size of 128 MB. In this scenario, each block is replicated three times (but can be scaled based on the number of Worker Nodes). When blocks are distributed between nodes fault tolerance is always maintained while smaller blocks increase parallelisation during processing as shown in Fig. 12.7.

MapReduce allows us to divide a complex computational task and map it to a set of distributed files such as HDFS. To achieve this the cluster uses a Job Tracker and multiple Task Trackers (one for each Worker Node). The Job Tracker sends code

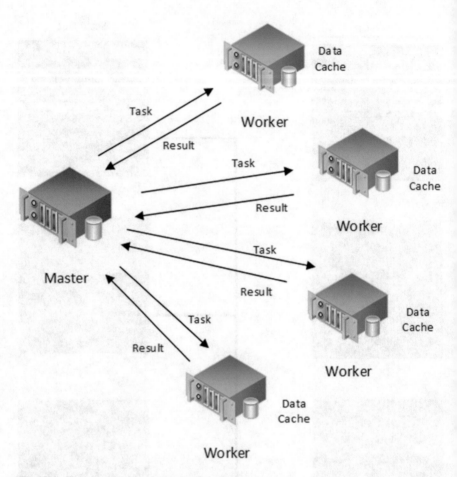

**Fig. 12.6** Cluster manager and associated workers

(instructions) to each Task Tracker which is then executed. The Task Trackers allocate the required CPU and RAM resources and monitor the progress as shown in Fig. 12.8.

With MapReduce, rather than sending data to where the application or logic resides, the logic is executed on the server where the data already resides, to expedite processing. Data access and storage is disk-based. The input is usually stored as files containing structured, semi-structured, or unstructured data, and the output is also stored in files. MapReduce was once the only method through which the data stored in the HDFS could be retrieved, but that is no longer the case. Today, there are other query-based systems such as Hive and Pig that are used to retrieve data from the HDFS using SQL-like statements. However, these usually run along with jobs that are written using the MapReduce model. That is because MapReduce has unique advantages. The process is shown in Fig. 12.9.

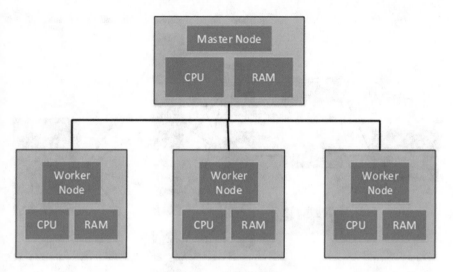

**Fig. 12.7**  Typical cluster setup for distributed frameworks

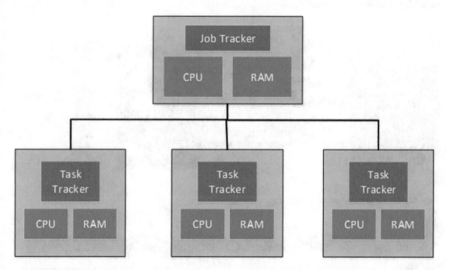

**Fig. 12.8**  Job tracker and associated task tracker configuration

Historically computational operations on large scale datasets were slow. This is due to restrictions in both CPU architecture and memory. The time it takes to process, and complete operations is called latency as shown in Fig. 12.10.

In most computations involving big data, most of the latency is due to the reading and writing of data. Storage latency varies depending on the underlying technology as shown in Fig. 12.11.

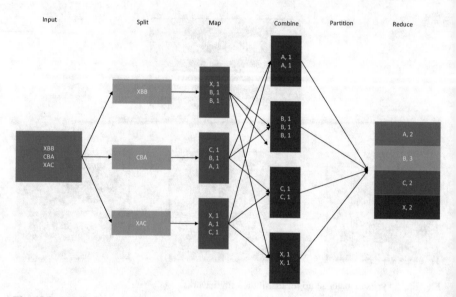

**Fig. 12.9**  MapReduce configuration

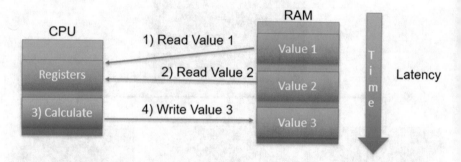

**Fig. 12.10**  CPU and memory latency

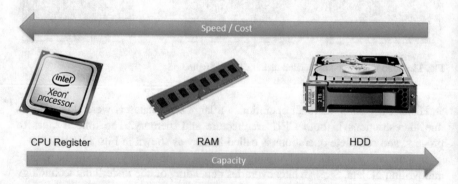

**Fig. 12.11**  Range of latency considerations dependent on hardware

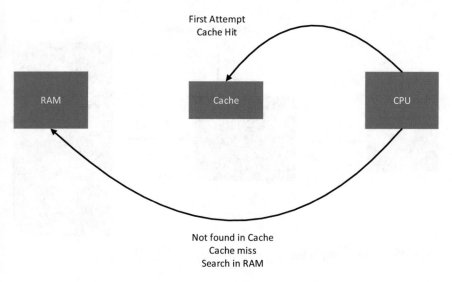

First Attempt
Cache Hit

RAM          Cache          CPU

Not found in Cache
Cache miss
Search in RAM

**Fig. 12.12**  Range of latency considerations dependent on hardware

Big data analytics provides methods for organising storage and computation in a way that maximises speed while reducing cost. This is archived through storage locality. Caching allows us to combine both slow and fast storage to reduce latency. When the CPU needs to access a particular memory address, it first checks the cache. If the memory location is in the cache the content can be retrieved and processed quickly. This is known as a cache hit. If the memory address is not in the cache, this is called a cache miss. Handling a cache miss increases latency as some of the cache must be cleared so data can be copied from the RAM as shown in Fig. 12.12.

A cache is effective if most accesses are cache hits (high cache hit rate). There are two main types of localities.

• Temporal Locality: Multiple accesses to the same addresses within a short time period.
• Spatial Locality: Multiple accesses to close-together addresses in a short time period.

Memory is partitioned into blocks. Moving a block of memory is quicker than moving each byte individually. Memory locations that are close to each other tend to reside within the same block. This results in more cache hits. Access locality is the ability for software to make use of the cache. Memory is divided into sections called pages. If software can use the same page or the same neighbouring pages, then it is said to have good access locality. Hardware is specifically designed to support software that has good access locality as shown in Fig. 12.13.

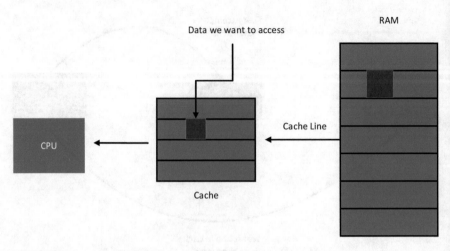

**Fig. 12.13**  Access locality in both the cache and RAM

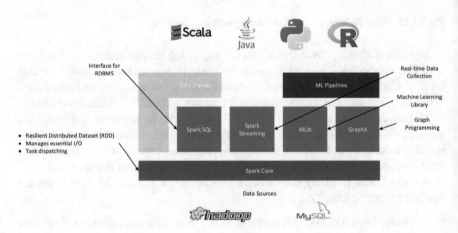

**Fig. 12.14**  Apache Spark framework

### 12.2.1.4   Apache Spark

Apache Spark improves how we perform distribution and computational tasks which are associated with big data [3]. Spark is one of the latest big data technologies used by industry and researchers to manage and process big data and is completely open-source (which is one of the main reasons for its popularity). The main five components of spark are shown in Fig. 12.14.

Spark was first released in 2013 and is a unified computing engine with a set of libraries for parallel data processing on computer clusters. Spark is more flexible than MapReduce and overcomes a variety of limitations. Spark can process data that

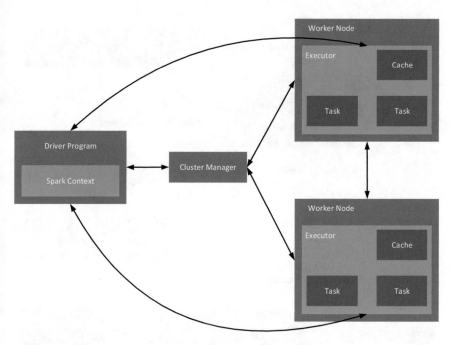

**Fig. 12.15** Spark context and its execution cycle

is stored in a variety of different formats including Amazon S3, HDFS, Structured Data and flat files.

With MapReduce (which distributes the calculations) files must be stored in HDFS. Spark does not have this requirement. Spark can perform operations up to $100\times$ faster than MapReduce which is a major benefit in the big data paradigm where Velocity is a key factor. As Spark is memory-oriented it can be a limiting factor due to cost. MapReduce writes most of the data to HDD after each map and reduce function meaning that it is disk oriented. Spark keeps all the data in memory after each transformation however it can use the HDD if the RAM becomes full.

Spark uses the concept of a Resilient Distributed Dataset (RDD). An RDD has several benefits which include distributed collection of data, fault tolerance, parallel operation, partitioned data, and the ability to use many data sources. Figure 12.15 shows the spark context and its execution cycle.

There are two types of operations in Spark which include:

- Transformations: which are lazily evaluated. The results are not computed till you apply an action that typically requires a result to be returned to the driver program. This design enables Spark to run more efficiently. A transformation is performed on an RDD which spawns another RDD (which creates a new dataset from an existing one).
- Actions: which are operations that trigger a computation that returns a value to the master.

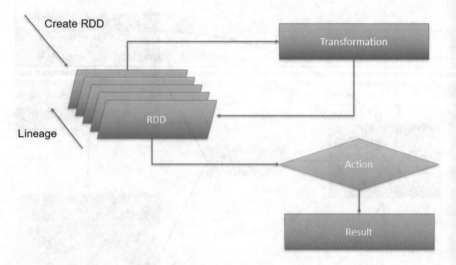

**Fig. 12.16**  Transformations and actions

**Fig. 12.17**  Spark execution process

Transformations and actions are shown in Fig. 12.16.

This philosophy can be seen when developing code used with Spark. When a method is called the result is not seen until the action is called e.g., show(). This is important as we do not want to keep calculating the transformations each time a change is made. In Spark the core data structures are immutable (cannot be changed). Data structures can only be changed by applying a transformation. Spark's language API allows Spark to be run using various programming languages:

- Scala: Spark's is primarily written in Scala (its default language)
- Java: code can be written and executed using Java
- Python: is universally supported in Spark using PySpark
- SQL: Spark supports a subset of the SQL standard. Particularly useful for DBA's
- R: Spark has two R libraries one which is part of the Spark core (SparkR) and a community-driven package (sparklyr)

The spark execution process is shown in Fig. 12.17.

Since the release of Spark 2.0, the framework has moved towards DataFrame usage. Although DataFrame syntax is used, the way files are distributed remains the same (RDDs). The use of Spark DataFrames is a prerequisite for using Sparks

```
In [7]: df.head()
```

Out[7]:

|   | country | continent | year | lifeExp | pop | gdpPercap |
|---|---------|-----------|------|---------|-----|-----------|
| 0 | Afghanistan | Asia | 1952 | 28.801 | 8425333 | 779.445314 |
| 1 | Afghanistan | Asia | 1957 | 30.332 | 9240934 | 820.853030 |
| 2 | Afghanistan | Asia | 1962 | 31.997 | 10267083 | 853.100710 |
| 3 | Afghanistan | Asia | 1967 | 34.020 | 11537966 | 836.197138 |
| 4 | Afghanistan | Asia | 1972 | 36.088 | 13079460 | 739.981106 |

**Fig. 12.18**  Spark DataFrame

Machine learning Library (MLib). As you will recall from earlier in the book a
DataFrame is a Dataset organised into named columns. They are conceptually
equivalent to a table in a relational database or an Excel spreadsheet. Spark
DataFrames hold data in a column and row format. Each column represents a
particular feature. Each row represents an individual data point (observation).
Spark DataFrames can input and output data from a wide variety of sources.
DataFrames facilitate different transformations on the data. A Spark DataFrame is
shown in Fig. 12.18.

## 12.3   Introduction to DASK

Processing gigabytes of data on a single laptop or computer is impractical and often
exceeds the computational limitations of the hardware. This problem can be overcome using DASK [4]. DASK is a flexible library for parallel computing in Python
that can be integrated with other open-source projects such as NumPy, Pandas,
scikit-learn and RAPIDS. DASK arrays are the equivalent of NumPy Arrays and
Dask DataFrames are equivalent of Pandas DataFrames. An example of how a
Pandas DataFrame is used in DASK is shown in Fig. 12.19. DASK-ML is the
equivalent of the sci-kit-learn library. Having these features makes the integration
of DASK into existing workflows easy for organisations to adopt.

The advantage of using DASK is that you can scale computations to multiple
cores on your computer. This enables you to process large datasets more quickly. It
also aids in speeding up computations that would ordinarily take a long time. The
DASK framework is shipped with schedulers designed for use on personal machines
as well as clusters. When loading large datasets, DASK reads in a sample of the data
to infer the data types. This will lead to issues when a given column has different data
types. To avoid type errors, it is good practice to declare the data types beforehand.

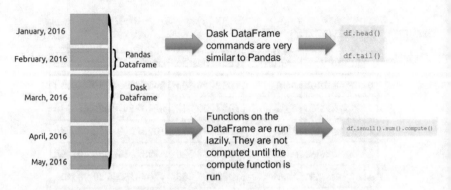

**Fig. 12.19** Pandas DataFrames in DASK

```
data_types ={'column1': str,'column2': float}
df = dd.read_csv("data,csv",dtype = data_types,blocksize=64000000 )
```

**Fig. 12.20** DASK chunks and the Blocksize parameter

**Fig. 12.21** DASK client

```
from dask.distributed import Client
client = Client()
```

**Fig. 12.22** DASK client and cluster configuration

| Client | Cluster |
|---|---|
| **Scheduler:** tcp://127.0.0.1:35493 | **Workers:** 8 |
| **Dashboard:** http://127.0.0.1:8787/status | **Cores:** 64 |
| | **Memory:** 535.16 GB |

DASK can load huge files by cutting them up into chunks using the blocksize parameter. as shown in Fig. 12.20.

DASK is designed for parallel computation and allows us to run computation on multiple cores and nodes. DASK provides a machine scheduler that works on a single node and offers a distributed scheduler that can scale to multiple nodes. Using dask.distributed requires a client as shown in Fig. 12.21. The dask.distributed package offers low latency, data locality, data sharing between workers, which is easy to set up.

Using dask.distributed is useful even on a single node because it provides diagnostic features and information via a dashboard. Failure to declare a Client will result in the usage of the single node scheduler by default. It provides parallelism on a single node by using processes or threads. A Client and associated Cluster configuration with eight workers is shown in Fig. 12.22.

## 12.3.1   DASK Arrays

DASK Array, DASK DataFrame, and DASK Bag generate task graphs where each node in the graph is a normal Python function. Edges between nodes are normal Python objects that are created by one task as outputs and used as inputs in another task. An example showing the relationship between NumPy Arrays and DASK Arrays are shown in Fig. 12.23.

An example of DASKs use of Collections (which include arrays), Task Graph and Schedulers are shown in Fig. 12.24.

DASK also supports bags. DASK bags are often used to parallelise simple computations on unstructured or semi-structured data like text data, log files, JSON records, and user-defined Python objects. Ideally, you should not load your data into Python and then load that data into a DASK bag. Instead, use DASK Bag to load data.

**Fig. 12.23**   Relation between NumPy Array and DASK array

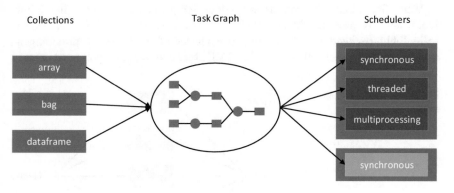

**Fig. 12.24**   Dask collections, task graph and schedulers

### 12.3.2   Scikit Learn and DASK Integration (DASK ML)

DASK provides the dask-ml function to allow machine learning training and pre-diction to be performed using parallelisation. The goal of dask-ml is to offer machine learning that is scalable. When you declare n_jobs = -1 in scikit-learn, you can run your computations in parallel. DASK utilises this capability to enable you to distribute this compute in a cluster. This is done using joblib, a package that allows for parallelism and pipelining in Python. Using DASK ML, you can implement scikit-learn models as well as other libraries such as XGBoost.

DASK is smaller and lighter than Spark. This means that it has fewer features and, instead, is used in conjunction with other libraries, particularly those in the numeric Python ecosystem. Spark is written in Scala with some support for Python and R. DASK is written in Python and only really supports Python. It interoperates well with C/C++/Fortran/LLVM, or other natively compiled code linked through Python.

Spark MLLib supports common operations that are easy to implement. People considering MLLib might also want to consider other JVM-based machine learning libraries like H2O, which may have better performance. DASK on the other hand relies on and interoperates with existing libraries like Scikit-Learn and XGBoost.

### 12.3.3   Scikit Learn Joblib

DASK is like Spark, but it is distinctly Python. This means that DASK uses existing Python APIs and data structures. The benefit of using DASK is that it is easy to switch between NumPy, Pandas, Scikit-learn and their DASK equivalents. Like Map Reduce, DASK maps a problem to a set of distributed nodes to compute and collate results as shown in Fig. 12.25.

Many Scikit-Learn algorithms are written for parallel execution using Joblib. Joblib natively provides thread-based and process-based parallelism. DASK can scale Joblib-backend algorithms out to a cluster of machines by providing an alternative Joblib backend. To use the DASK backend to Joblib you must create a

**Fig. 12.25** Dask and map reduce

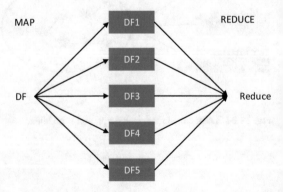

```
import numpy as np
from dask.distributed import Client

import joblib
from sklearn.datasets import load_digits
from sklearn.model_selection import RandomizedSearchCV
from sklearn.svm import SVC

client = Client(processes=False)              # create local cluster

digits = load_digits()

param_space = {
    'C': np.logspace(-6, 6, 13),
    'gamma': np.logspace(-8, 8, 17),
    'tol': np.logspace(-4, -1, 4),
    'class_weight': [None, 'balanced'],
}

model = SVC(kernel='rbf')
search = RandomizedSearchCV(model, param_space, cv=3, n_iter=50, verbose=10)

with joblib.parallel_backend('dask'):
    search.fit(digits.data, digits.target)
```

**Fig. 12.26** Example use of Dask parallelisation

Client and wrap your code with joblib.parallel_backend('dask'). For example, you might want to distribute a randomised cross-validated parameter search as shown in Fig. 12.26.

Note that the DASK joblib backend is useful for scaling out CPU-bound workloads; workloads with datasets that fit in RAM but have many individual operations that can be done in parallel.

## 12.4  GPU Computing

### 12.4.1  Introduction to GPU Hardware

Figure 12.27 shows a high-level overview of a GPU. As you can see the architecture is organised into an array of threaded streaming multiprocessors (SMs). Two or more SMs form a building block which often varies between different GPU models and architectures. Each SM has several streaming processors (SPs) that co-share the logic and instruction cache. GPU's have gigabytes of Graphics Double Data Rate

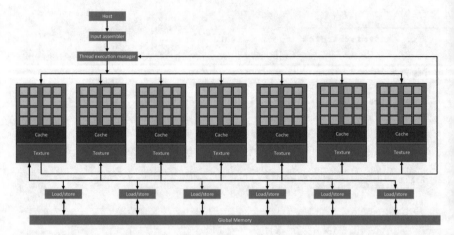

**Fig. 12.27** High-level view of GPU architecture

(GDDR) and synchronous DRAM (SDRAM) memory which is also referred to as Global Memory. The GPU's primary communication link to the CPU is over the PCI-Express which depending on generation offers speeds between 4 GB/s for Gen2 and 8–16 GB/s for Gen3 retrospectively. However, we can achieve much faster throughput using a direct link between GPU's known as NVLINK which offers up to 40 GB/s per channel. In recent years GPU's have seen a rapid expansion of onboard GPU memory which further decreases processing time as applications can keep more of their data local to the GPU. There are occasions where a GPU might have to access global memory (system RAM) where artefacts do not fit into GPU memory or where it is accessing libraries that are only compiled for CPU usage. The bandwidth between the GPU and CPU is expected to grow as bus bandwidth improves with the introduction of newer chipsets. A typical application can run between 5000 to 12,000 threads simultaneously in contrast to a CPU with can support 2–4 threads.

GPUs were first developed for computer games. However, their usage now spans a much larger group of domains, partially due to their use in machine learning, which include finance, simulation, engineering, and medicine.

### 12.4.2   Introduction to NVIDIA Accelerated Computing

Industrial leaders, large corporations, and researchers are creating new and innovative products while gaining unprecedented insights by utilising accelerated machine learning pipelines on GPUs. This approach allows machine learning practitioners to take advantage of cutting frameworks and hardware. This combination provides the capability to tackle today's most challenging scientific and commercial problems. This enables developers and data scientists alike to use popular languages such as C, C++, and Python to develop, optimise, and deploy applications.

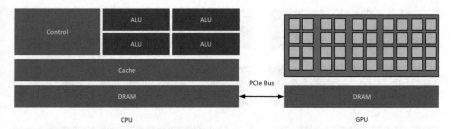

**Fig. 12.28** Multi-core CPU vs many-core GPU

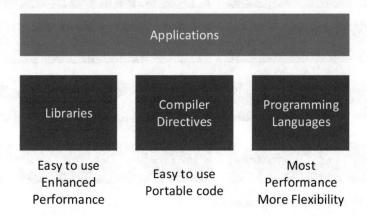

**Fig. 12.29** Three primary ways to accelerate applications using GPUs

At the time of writing, NVidia is one of the world's leaders in implementing end-to-end technologies to deploy large scale AI applications. Gaming has been heavily reliant on advancements in GPU technology since the 1970s. But they also make up a considerable proportion of computing within modern-day data centres. The demand for computing over the last several years has out-paced CPU provision, this is particularly true for AI applications. Where Moore's law is now failing to deliver the computational requirements, the rise of GPUs and accelerated computing now support our computational needs.

The demand for extra compute cycles has increased by 300,000x in the past 5 years. Moore's law has only given us approximately $1.1\times$ per year between the years 2010 and 2020 resulting in a significant shortfall for the needs of AI applications today. CPUs are heavyweight in the sense that they are designed for complex control logic and are optimised for sequential programs. On the other hand, GPUs are lightweight and are designed from simple control logic and are optimised for data-parallel tasks focusing on the throughput of parallel programs. Figure 12.28 shows the difference between a CPU and GPU.

There are three ways in which you can accelerate an application using GPU's which is shown in Fig. 12.29. An application can use one of the three methods for gaining access to and utilising GPU hardware. Libraries are typically written by

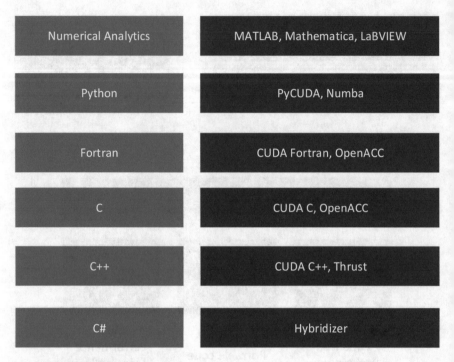

**Fig. 12.30** GPU programming languages

experts which can perform common computational tasks. Libraries are easy to use and should be utilised where possible. They are optimised and offer superior performance. Libraries offer:

- Ease of use: Using libraries enables GPU acceleration without in-depth knowledge of GPU programming
- Drop-in: Many GPU-accelerated libraries follow standard APIs, thus enabling acceleration with minimal code changes
- Quality: Libraries offer high-quality implementations of functions encountered in a broad range of applications

Compiler directives allow developers to annotate their sequential application which makes the compiler undertake the parallelisation and are available for C, C++, and FORTRAN. The third method is to utilise programming languages that are specially designed to utilise the GPU effectively. Although this approach provides the most performance and flexibility it requires significant effort from the developer.

There are several common libraries some of which you will already be familiar with such as cuDNN with is used by TensorFlow and Keras for DL. These libraries target a wide range of computing applications. Several different GPU programming languages can be used to exploit GPU computation as shown in Fig. 12.30. CUDA C and CUDA C++ are foundational languages of the CUDA platform, but they are not the only languages available for developing CUDA applications. PyCUDA and

Numba are widely used for GPU computation with Python. PyCuda is a collection of wrappers that expose the CUDA driver API.

### 12.4.3 CUDA

Compute Unified Device Architecture (CUDA) is a parallel computing platform that utilises GPUs for general-purpose computing [5]. CUDA was developed by NVIDIA in 2006 to assist with the development of image generation. However, today they have a broader application set especially around the parallel computing requirements in machine learning and DL. Parallel computing allows us to perform computations and associated operations simultaneously. GPUs are an example device that can perform parallel computation at scale. Although originally designed for computer games they have seen widespread use in accelerated computing, machine learning and DL and are commonly known as GPGPUs. Although CUDA development is undertaken in the C programming language, its functionality has been abstracted through drivers and API frameworks as previously discussed. The CUDA kernel is one of the most important concepts in CUDA development. Fundamentally the kernel is a function that can be executed in parallel by any number of different CUDA threads. When executing functions, the number of threads is specified when the kernel function is called. Note CPUs and GPUs are used in conjunction where device code is executed on the GPU and host code is executed on the CPU.

In 2007 CUDA was officially released by NVIDIA who altered their GPU to facilitate parallel programming. This meant that both software and hardware changes were made in the form of alterations to the chip. From the G80 onwards CUDA programs were no longer executed through the graphics interface. Instead, a new general-purpose parallel programming interface on the silicon chip serves the requests of CUDA programs. The general-purpose programming interface expands the types of applications that one can easily develop for GPUs. In addition, software frameworks were re-engineered so developers could use familiar programming tools.

### 12.4.4 CUDA Accelerated Computing Libraries

PyCUDA lets you access Nvidia's CUDA parallel computation API from Python. Python-based GPU code can reach elevated levels of performance and exploit the potential of GPU hardware but with much less effort on the part of the developer. This reduction in effort is achieved in many ways—for example, data types and resources are managed by the language itself instead of by the developer. In addition, closures and other high-level constructs are available. PyCUDA makes the entire functionality of the CUDA runtime framework available through Python which

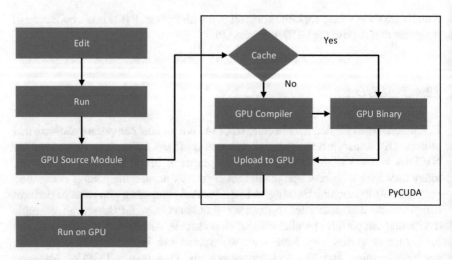

**Fig. 12.31** Process flow and interactions of PyCUDA

includes textures, pinned host memory, OpenGL interaction, and zero-copy host memory mapping. This is achieved using an object-oriented shell. Entities such as textures, code modules, and computing devices are reflected into Python using object-oriented terms, providing better abstraction than the low-level C interface. The process flow and interactions of PyCUDA are shown in Fig. 12.31.

Numba translates Python functions to optimised machine code at runtime using the industry-standard Low-Level Virtual Machine (LLVM) compiler library [6]. Primarily Numba is a just in time compiler for python which at the time of call converts your code into machine code that is run on your native machine. Numba allows you to speed up heavy calculations and computationally expensive python functions such as loops. Numba supports other libraries such as NumPy to speed up computation time. One of the major benefits of Numba is that you do not need to change or alter your underlying code. This can be achieved by adding a decorator around your existing functions. A wrapper class is also planned in future releases. The Numba workflow is shown in Fig. 12.32.

In the first step, the python function is optimised and converted into Numba's intermediate representation. After inference which is like Numpys type inference, it is later converted into LLVM interpretable code which is then passed to the LLVM's just in time compiler to generate the machine code. The machine code can be generated at runtime or during import time on either CPU (which is the default) or GPU. With Numba you can use @jit wrappers to run functions on CUDA/GPU by importing CUDA from Numba. Writing code and executing it on GPU using Numba still requires you to declare and manage a hierarchy of grids, blocks, and threads.

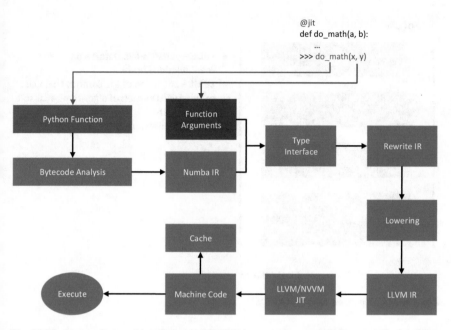

**Fig. 12.32** Process flow and interactions of PyCUDA

## 12.5   RAPIDS

RAPIDS is a suite of open-source software libraries and APIs which are grouped to provide machine learning partitioners with the ability to execute end-to-end data science and analytics pipelines entirely on GPUs [7]. Like many of the libraries previously discussed RAPIDS utilises NVIDIA CUDA primitives for low-level compute optimisation and exposes GPU parallelism and high-bandwidth memory speed through Python interfaces and Jupyter Notebooks.

The suite also focuses on common data preparation tasks for data science including a Pandas-esque DataFrame API that integrates with a variety of machine learning algorithms to limit associated serialisation costs. In addition, RAPIDS also includes support for multi-node, multi-GPU deployments, enabling vastly accelerated processing and training on much larger dataset sizes. Figure 12.33 shows the relevant components of the RAPIDS framework along with its set API libraries (cuDF, cuML and cuGraph). You can think of RAPIDS as a data science framework that benefits from the same compute capabilities as other DL frameworks described in this book such as Keras and TensorFlow.

RAPIDS accelerates the existing Scikit-Learn package to enable rapid modelling and the inclusion of larger datasets which until recently has hit computational limitations using traditional compute frameworks on CPU. To date, a wide variety of algorithms have been optimised for GPU accelerated computing as shown in Fig. 12.34.

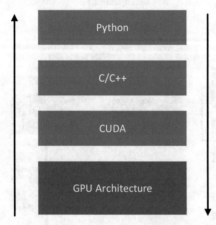

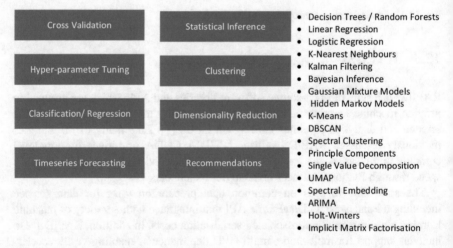

Fig. 12.33  Components used in RAPIDS

Fig. 12.34  GPU accelerated algorithms

cuDF, cuML, and cuGraph mimic well-known libraries and are the foundation to RAPIDS as shown in Fig. 12.35. While Pandas, Numpy, and sci-kit-learn packages are efficient, intuitive, and widely trusted they were not designed to run at scale - this limitation is addressed through the API's provided by RAPIDS. To facilitate parallelisation, RAPIDS uses Dask. Dask can distribute data and computation over multiple GPUs, either in the same system or in a multi-node cluster. Dask integrates with both RAPIDS cuDF, XGBoost, and RAPIDS cuML for GPU-accelerated data analytics and machine learning. The RAPIDS framework sits directly on top of the

**Fig. 12.35** RAPIDS framework

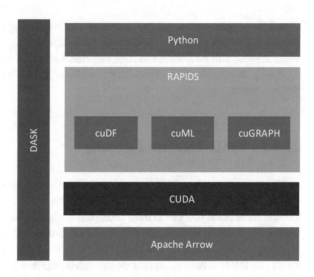

CUDA framework, therefore, exposing the power of underlying GPUs. Apache Arrow defines a language-independent columnar memory format for flat and hierarchical data, organised for efficient analytic operations on modern hardware like CPUs and GPUs. The Arrow memory format also supports zero-copy reads for lightning-fast data access without serialization overheads.

Figure 12.35 shows the top-down abstraction layers starting with python which links to the cuML algorithms through Cython, therefore, providing access to a high-level programming language bypassing the need for C which simplifies machine learning development.

### 12.5.1 cuDF Analytics

Most packages including Pandas only run-on CPUs and due to the limited number of cores available processing large DataFrames can be problematic. Large datasets can have millions, billions, or even trillions of data points that need to be processed promptly. Following on from the success of GPU acceleration in DL tech companies have created a variety of different frameworks to overcome this limitation. cuDF is a python based DataFrames library which allows you to perform a wide variety of pre-processing tasks such as loading, joining, aggregating and filtering data at scale. By using cuDF we gain access to a much wider array of graphics cores which dramatically speed up data processing tasks. cuDF's API is a mirror of Pandas and can in most cases be used as a direct replacement. As a result, it makes it easy for data scientists, analysts and engineers to integrate it into their existing workflows. The framework allows you to convert your existing Pandas DataFrames into a cuDF DataFrames which gives you instant access to the GPU.

cuDF supports most of the common DataFrame operations that Pandas does meaning that code can be accelerated with little effort. cuDF provides a pandas-like API that will be familiar to data engineers and data scientists, so they can use it to easily accelerate their workflows without going into the details of CUDA programming.

## 12.5.2  cuML Machine Learning

cuML is a suite of fast, GPU-accelerated machine learning algorithms designed for data science and analytical tasks. Its API is like scikit-learn's. This means you can use the same code you use to train scikit-learn's model to train cuML's model. cuML drastically reduces the amount of training time required to train traditional machine learning models. Although in many cases, you do not need to install cuDF to use cuML, cuDF is a nice complement for cuML since it is a GPU DataFrame. scikit-learn is a great library with a variety of machine learning models that you can use to train your algorithms. But if your data is big, it might take you a long time to train your model, especially when you experiment with different hyperparameters to find the best fit.

## 12.5.3  cuGraph Graph Analytics

While data engineering, statistical analysis, and machine learning are among the most known there are numerous cases where the focus of the analysis is on the relationship between data elements. In these cases, the data is best represented as a graph. Graph analysis, also called network analysis, is a collection of algorithms for answering questions posed against graph data. Graph analysis is not new. The application of graph analysis covers a wide variety of fields, including marketing, biology, physics, computer science, sociology, and cyber to name a few. RAPIDS includes the first official release of cuGraph.

RAPIDS cuGraph is a library of graph algorithms that seamlessly integrates into the RAPIDS data science ecosystem and allows the data scientist to easily call graph algorithms using data stored in a GPU DataFrame. One of the design goals of cuGraph is to have an API familiar to the data scientist which can be used to perform graph analytics. Therefore, a data scientist with experience with NetworkX will recognise the process of creating a graph object and then running analytics against that graph object.

### 12.5.4 Apache Arrow

Apache Arrow is an open-source, columnar, in-memory data representation that enables analytical systems and data sources to exchange and process data in real-time, simplifying and accelerating data access, without having to copy all data into one location [8]. Over the past few years, it has become increasingly difficult to physically consolidate all data into a single system as shown in Fig. 12.36.

Apache Arrow is an open-source project, initiated by over a dozen open-source communities, which provides a standard columnar in-memory data representation and processing framework. Arrow has emerged as a popular way to handle in-memory data for analytical purposes. At the time of writing, Arrow has been embedded into a broad range of open source (and commercial) technologies, including GPU databases, machine learning libraries and tools, execution engines and visualisation frameworks.

Arrow is a columnar in-memory representation which means data is represented column by column in memory as opposed to a row-based approach which is what most systems use. You can use a variety of different languages such as Java, C++, and Python, to access Arrow.

With Arrow data types are shared, meaning you don't have to convert between different data representations. Additionally, Apache Arrow can share data without having to serialize it or even copy it, delivering improved performance and efficiency to all these technologies. The Apache Arrow project uses the common data layer to create an ecosystem that was collaborative and widely adopted.

Most big data frameworks use a random strategy for assigning partitions to nodes. If each computation job uses one partition, this strategy results in a good division of computational load across a cluster. However, if a job needs multiple partitions, there is a big chance that it needs to fetch partitions from other nodes. Transferring data is always a performance penalty.

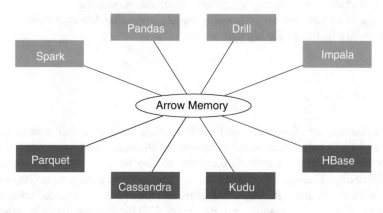

**Fig. 12.36** Arrow memory for data aggregation

Apache Arrow eliminates the need for serialization as data is represented by the same bytes on each platform and programming language. This generic format enables zero-copy data transfer in big data systems, to minimise the performance hit of transferring data. Typically, a data transfer consists of:

- Serialising data in a format
- Sending the serialized data over a network connection
- Deserializing the data on the receiving side

The big advantage here is that data can be transferred as-is from one environment to another environment without any translation because the data is understood as-is on both sides of the connection. In addition, in a big dataset, the number of rows can typically range from thousands to trillions of rows. Such a dataset may have thousands of columns. A typical analytics query on such a dataset references a handful of columns. Imagine for example a dataset of e-commerce transactions. You can imagine that a sales manager wants an overview of sales, of a specific region, grouped by item category. He does not want to see each individual sale. The average sale price is sufficient. Such a query can be provided in three steps:

- Traversing all values in the region column, keeping track of all the row/object ids of sales in the requested region
- Grouping the filtered ids based on the corresponding values in the item category column
- Computing aggregations for each group

Essentially, a query processor only needs to have one column in memory at any given time. By storing a collection in a columnar format, we can access all values of a single field/column separately. In well-designed formats, this is done in such a way that the layout is optimised for Single Instruction Multiple Data (SIMD) instructions on CPUs. For such analytics workloads, the Apache Arrow columnar layout is better suited than the FlatBuffers row-oriented layout. The key benefits are:

- Arrow features zero-copy data transfers for analytics applications
- Arrow enables in-memory, columnar format, data processing
- Arrow is a cross-platform, cross-language interoperable data exchange
- Arrow is a backbone for big data systems

## 12.6   Summary

In this chapter, we introduced accelerated machine learning which is cantered on CPU and GPU based accelerated computing. CPU distributed accelerated frameworks were introduced which support both scaling up and scaling out solutions. These included Hadoop and Apache Spark. This was contrasted with GPU-based computing which introduced GPU hardware and the NVidia accelerated computing platform. Within this section, we discussed CUDA and the recently released

RAPIDS framework that utilises the CUDA API's. RAPIDS itself was introduced and the three core libraries it provided to process data, implement machine learning and generate graphs (cuML, cuDF, cuGraph). The chapter was concluded with a discussion on Apache Arrow and its use of columnar-based data storage which provides in-memory data representation for big data systems.

# References

1. R. R. Schaller, "Moore's law: past, present and future," *IEEE Spectr.*, vol. 34, no. 6, pp. 52–59, 1997.
2. T. White, *Hadoop: The definitive guide.* " O'Reilly Media, Inc.," 2012.
3. M. Zaharia *et al.*, "Apache spark: a unified engine for big data processing," *Commun. ACM*, vol. 59, no. 11, pp. 56–65, 2016.
4. M. Rocklin, "Dask: Parallel computation with blocked algorithms and task scheduling," in *Proceedings of the 14th python in science conference*, 2015, vol. 130, p. 136.
5. J. Sanders and E. Kandrot, *CUDA by example: an introduction to general-purpose GPU programming*. Addison-Wesley Professional, 2010.
6. S. K. Lam, A. Pitrou, and S. Seibert, "Numba: A llvm-based python jit compiler," in *Proceedings of the Second Workshop on the LLVM Compiler Infrastructure in HPC*, 2015, pp. 1–6.
7. J. Zedlewski, "End-to-End Data Science on GPUs with \$\{\$RAPIDS\$\}\$," 2020.
8. G. Lentner, "Shared Memory High Throughput Computing with Apache Arrow™," in *Proceedings of the Practice and Experience in Advanced Research Computing on Rise of the Machines (learning)*, 2019, pp. 1–2.

# Chapter 13
# Deploying and Hosting Machine Learning Models

This is one of the most important chapters in the book as more machine learning models transition from research labs into real-world applications. Ultimately, of course, after you have finished experimenting, you will need to consider a more production-friendly environment than your laptop. With the widespread industrial support and investment, this has been made easier through a variety of different frameworks. Tech giants such as Google, Facebook and Microsoft provide access to compressive frameworks for free. In line with industrial automation, many businesses are looking towards the use of algorithms to solve complex and repetitive problems while streamlining existing processes [1]. This has led to the widespread utilisation of machine learning algorithms that are already integrated into many distinct aspects of our lives. This is apparent in many services such as social media, home entertainment, online shopping and even our healthcare. The advanced machine learning algorithms we see today are relatively new and consequently how we deploy these algorithms has not fully matured. Until recently this was only undertaken by large tech giants but as you will see in this chapter anyone can now deploy and utilise the machine learning algorithms they develop to solve many challenges they currently face. Figure 13.1 shows the overlap between development (training) and model deployment (inferencing).

So far in the book, we have focused on the training process outlined in Fig. 13.2. This section will be a logical extension of what we have already learned to leverage the power of machine learning to support business decision making and new insight generation.

An important thing to note is that a successful deployment strategy will likely require many different machine learning algorithms and techniques to solve complex problems. Figure 13.3 shows an example case study where a variety of different machine learning models are used to solve sub-problems to collectively address a much larger problem. For example, here we can see that marketing has been supported by chatbots (NLP), customer profiling (clustering), fraud (anomaly detection), image recognition for automated damage evaluation (CNNs) and claims forecasting (regression). Note that no single machine learning algorithm would be

© Springer Nature Switzerland AG 2022
P. Fergus, C. Chalmers, *Applied Deep Learning*, Computational Intelligence
Methods and Applications, https://doi.org/10.1007/978-3-031-04420-5_13

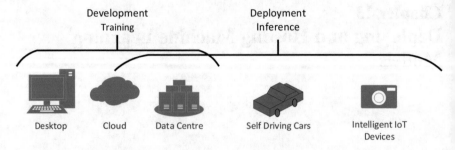

**Fig. 13.1** Overlap between development and model deployments

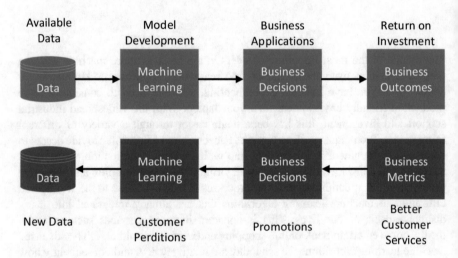

**Fig. 13.2** Machine learning and business decision making

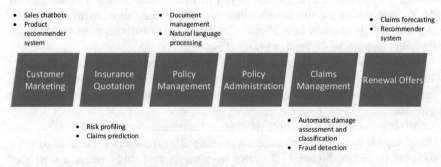

**Fig. 13.3** Workflow that uses different ML algorithms

capable of solving all these problems. By hosting models, the platform becomes the glue between each model to support generalised problem-solving at scale while fixed decision making uses logical code constructs and rule-based logic.

The remainder of this chapter will help you to devise a hosting and deployment strategy for your machine learning applications.

## 13.1   Introduction to Deployment

Now that we have fully trained our models the goal is to make them accessible to a much wider audience. Just like training a model, there are several ways of hosting it. For example, you may deploy and host models on dedicated servers or deploy them to edge devices, such as smartphones, home appliances, cars, and buildings. Once deployed models can be accessed using containers or services via interfaces (REST APIs, GRPC etc.).

An important consideration when deploying machine learning algorithms is how to assess and improve performance over time. In traditional software development, this is done through version upgrades based on user feedback. In machine learning this is achieved by continually presenting data to our deployed machine learning algorithms for ongoing learning. This constantly improves accuracy and the capability of machine learning algorithms to solve novel problems and is one of the key advantages over traditional software development. This end-to-end concept is illustrated in Fig. 13.4.

One of the key challenges in deploying machine learning models is to abstract the technical details from the user and provide common interfaces that allow users and enterprise systems to access and integrate core machine learning functionality into business processes and User Interfaces (UI).

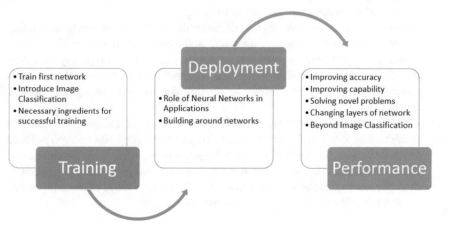

**Fig. 13.4**   Training, deployment and performance monitoring

## 13.1.1   Why Is Model Deployment Important

We are currently living in a massive information age where the torrent of data currently being transmitted has become impossible for humans alone to process and make sense of the acquired data. The frequency in which we are generating data and the continually developing technological advances designed to shift information from one place to another has led to increased computational and software requirements. Algorithms have been deployed within these data highways to quickly and automatically produce models that can analyse bigger and more complex data and deliver faster and more accurate results on a large scale. This has led to the ability to generate time-sensitive predictions. For example, Netflix's recommendation engines, Uber's arrival time estimation and LinkedIn connection suggestions. While this resides within the internal structure of Wide Area Networks (WANs) model deployment has become increasingly important on the edge of these infrastructures.

Trained models are primally hosted in three different settings. These include a) using cloud datacentres which are usually reserved for high throughput and high computation requirements, b) on-premise datacentre infrastructure and c) edge devices for low latency applications. When moving from proof of concept (POC) to production, there is a notable change in mindset. The machine learning model is no longer the product; the pipeline is.

- Datacentres and cloud infrastructure – Some of the big cloud providers offer machine learning compute as a service and support common machine learning and DL frameworks such as TensorFlow and CNTK. These are typically comprised of specialised hardware such as banks of NVidia DGX A100s which can be aggregated in large volumes so users can share GPUs in a manner better capable of supporting the data needs of AI applications.
- On-premise hosting – can range in diversity depending on the needs and budget of the organisation. Typically, hardware and associated frameworks are provisioned to support on-prem business processes. These servers typically host their models and support services within the organisation's local network and infrastructure. There may be reasons to do this due to data privacy and service sensitivity.
- Edge inferencing - There are scenarios where you need computation and data storage close to where the data is generated enabling betted data control, reduced costs, faster insights, and actions for continuous operations. At the far extreme of edge computing, it is more centred around simpler data processing tasks such as those for reading and processing sensor data. There are a range of capabilities that sit between edge computing and high-end data centres.

### 13.1.2   Enabling MLOps

MLOps is closely related to DevOps [2]. It is a combination of philosophies and practices designed to enable data science and IT teams to rapidly develop, deploy, maintain, and scale-out machine learning models and pipelines. MLOps is concerned with the following stages:

- Packaging models: to prepare them for execution in their designated runtime environments. This includes preparation for application integration, assessing scalability requirements and hardware considerations.
- Validate models: by measuring the performance of candidate models against Key Performance Indicators (KPI's). Deployment and application integration testing.
- Model deployment: identifying, targeting, and deploying models into a production environment. During deployment, services are implemented to support scalability and automation.
- Monitor model: track model performance to validate the desired KPIs. This can include measuring accuracy and response times. Logging this information enables model training (or retraining) based on experimental results.

The end-to-end MLOps workflow is shown in Fig. 13.5 which supports automating continuous integration (CI), continuous delivery (CD), and continuous training (CT) for machine learning systems.

Typically, teams of machine learning researchers and practitioners train models. However, it is the responsibility of the MLOPs team to expose and integrate models into work processes. The entire process is shown in Fig. 13.6.

### 13.1.3   MLOps Frameworks

In MLOPs there are a variety of different frameworks to support the deployment of models into production. A lot of these are underpinned by common technologies such as Docker and Kubernetes. There are open-source MLOps options as well as enterprise solutions. Some frameworks are focused on one step in the machine

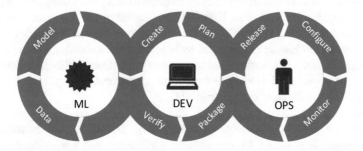

**Fig. 13.5**  MLOps workflow

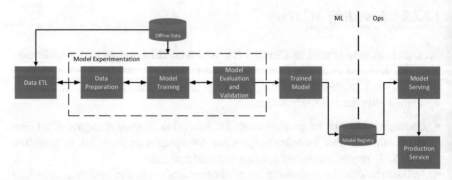

**Fig. 13.6** Exposing and integrating models using MLOps

learning model deployment workflow while others can manage the entire process (training and inferencing). Some of the most common MLOps frameworks you might encounter are:

- MLflow: which allows data professionals to automate sophisticated model tracking with ease. Through MLflow optimal models can be easily selected using a tracking server. Parameters, attributes, and performance metrics can be logged to this server and used to instantly search for models that fit a particular criterion. MLflow is quickly becoming an industry leader for automating the implementation, integration, and development of machine learning models. MLflow supports a wide variety of machine learning frameworks and technologies that include Azure ML, Fastai, H20, Keras, PyTorch and TensorFlow amongst many others. Although it is a powerful tool for sorting through logged models it does not answer the question of what models should be developed.
- Pachyderm: simplifies the process of managing your pipelines, datasets, and models. It combines end-to-end pipelines with data linage on Kubernetes. This platform works on an enterprise-scale to add the foundation for any machine learning project. The process starts with data versioning and data pipelining which provides data linage and results in deployed machine learning models.
- Kubeflow: is an machine learning platform that manages the deployment of workflows on Kubernetes. It is both scalable and portable and works well for deploying systems into different environments to carry out testing, development, and production-level services. Kubeflow was started by Google as an open-source platform for running TensorFlow. It was first designed to run TensorFlow jobs via Kubernetes but has since expanded to become a multi-cloud, multi-architecture framework that runs entire machine learning pipelines. With Kubeflow, data scientists do not need to learn new platforms or concepts to deploy their applications or deal with networking certificates, etc.
- DataRobot: is an AI automation tool that allows data scientists to automate the end-to-end process of deploying, maintaining, or building AI at scale. This framework is powered by open-source algorithms that are available on the cloud and on-premise.

Many of these frameworks are built on both Docker, Kubernetes, and model servers such as TensorFlow Serving which will be covered later in this chapter. Understanding these individual frameworks will allow you to move to other open-source or enterprise MLOps frameworks.

### 13.1.4   MLOps Application Programmable Interfaces API's

MLOPs separates the data scientists who generate a trained model and the engineers who serve the model as a production service. The model is handed over as an artefact to the MLOPs team who are responsible for the deployment of models on the API infrastructure. Engineers who deploy the model need to make the required features available in production for low-latency serving which if not done correctly can lead to training-serving skew. Training-serving skew is the difference between performance during training and performance during serving and can be caused by:

- A discrepancy between how you handle data in the training and serving pipelines
- A change in the data between when you train and when you serve
- A feedback loop between your model and your algorithm

When a model is deployed to a target environment to serve predictions is can be achieved using one of the following methods:

- Microservices with a REST API to serve online predictions
- An embedded model to an edge or mobile device
- Part of a batch prediction system

Certain types of frameworks are suited to particular processing tasks, so it is important to choose the correct type of API to avoid any bottlenecks in your production pipeline. Most software developers know there are two primary models for API design which includes gRPC and REST.

- gRPC: is a Remote procedure call platform developed by Google that provides high-performance, low latency and high-speed throughput. A gRPC channel provides a connection to a gRPC server on a specified port. The client invokes a method on the stub as if it is a local object; the server is notified of the client gRPC request as shown in Fig. 13.7.

  gRPC uses Protocol Buffers (PB) to exchange messages between client and server. There are multiple benefits in using gRPC which include:

  - gRPC uses binary payloads, which are efficient to create and parse and hence lightweight
  - Bi-directional streaming is possible in gRPC, which is not the case with a REST API
  - 10 times faster message transmission compared to REST API as gRPC uses serialised PB and HTTP/2
  - Loose coupling between client and server makes it easy to make changes

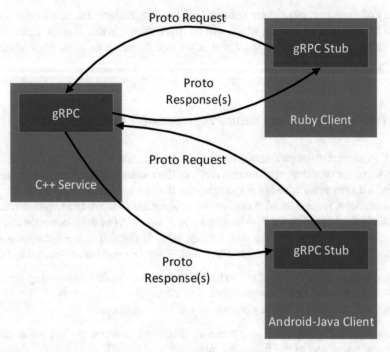

**Fig. 13.7** gRPC client-server requests

- gRPC allows for the integration of API's programmed in different languages
- REST uses JSON for exchanging messages between client and server, whereas gRPC uses PB which are compressed better than JSON, thus making gRPC transmit data over networks more efficiently

- REST: is fundamentally a request/response type relationship between the client and server. Something is requested, something is done, and then something is sent in return. This exchange is a conversation—for this reason, REST architectures are usually designed around the idea of providing highly modular micro-solutions for given use cases.

Streaming APIs are the exact opposite of the REST ethos. In its most basic state, Streaming APIs invert the conversational nature of REST, where a request is made and a response is given, and instead has the server send information to a client when an update is ready. While the client can, in theory, request an update, the streaming server should pre-empt this with updates as and when they are available. The differences are shown in Fig. 13.8.

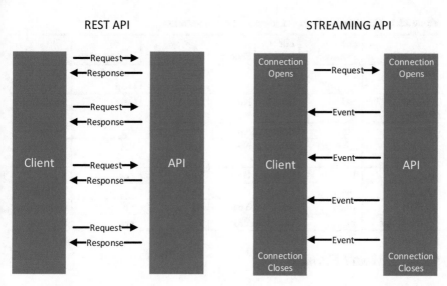

**Fig. 13.8** REST vs streaming APIs

## 13.2  Preparing a Model

Once a model has been trained and the desired performance has been achieved the first stage in the deployment process is to save the trained model in a format that can be accessed by the application. In machine learning the artefact created after training to make predictions is called a model. In the example of DL, the trained model is a file that contains the layers and learned weights in the DNN. Models are typically saved in a file that can be compressed. In this instance model files have a binary file format. There are a variety of different model formats which are usually dictated by the framework in which the training was undertaken. Some of the most common file formats and their associated frameworks are shown in Table 13.1.

Models are used to make predictions on new data by hosting them in an appropriate serving framework such as TensorFlow Severing which reads the model into memory (may contain multiple versions of a model for testing and versioning). There are also model formats that are designed to run on mobile and edge devices that lack access to an enterprise model server. For example, the .mlmodel file format is used to store models that are embedded in IOS applications while TensorFlow uses the .tflite model format for embedding models on Android and edge devices. Most models can be converted to run on different frameworks using tools such as TensorFlow converter.

**Table 13.1** Common file formats and associated frameworks

| File format | File extension | File type | Schema | Quantisation | Compression | Frameworks |
|---|---|---|---|---|---|---|
| Protobuf | .pd | Binary | Yes | Yes | Varint $ Gzip | TensorFlow |
| Pickled Python | .pkl | Binary | No | No | Gzip | Scikit-Learn |
| Mleap | .zip | Binary | No | No | Zip | PySpark |
| Apple ML Model | .mlmodel | Binary | No | Yes | Yes | iOS Core ML |
| H5 | .h5 | Binary | No | Yes | Yes | Keras |
| ONNX | .onnx | Binary | No | Yes | Yes | PyTorch |
| PMML | .pmml | XML | Yes | No | No | Scikit-Learn |
| Torch Script | .pt | Binary | Yes | Yes | Yes | PyTorch |

## *13.2.1  Model Formats*

In this section, we will cover each of the different model formats and the associated frameworks.

### 13.2.1.1  ProtoBuf (pb)

Googles Protobuf .pb files are served by TensorFlow Serving which can be accessed through both REST and gPRC calls. In TensorFlow, the protobuf file contains the graph definition as well as the weights of the model. Thus, a pb file is all you need to be able to run a given trained model. Once a graph has been loaded it can be used for inference and other tasks. A typical graph from a. pb file is shown in Fig. 13.8.

PB is like the Apache Thrift (used by Facebook), Ion (created by Amazon), or Microsoft Bond protocols, which all offer an RPC protocol stack (Fig. 13.9).

### 13.2.1.2  ONNX (.ONNX)

ONNX is a framework that uses an independent file format. The ONNX is used in Microsoft, Facebook, and Amazon frameworks. The idea behind ONNX is to provide greater interoperability between AI tools. Currently, developers are often locked into one framework therefore ONNX is a first step to enable more of these tools to work together through a shard model space. ONNX provides access to their own model zoo with a selection of pre-trained models for computer vision, language analysis, speech, and audio processing.

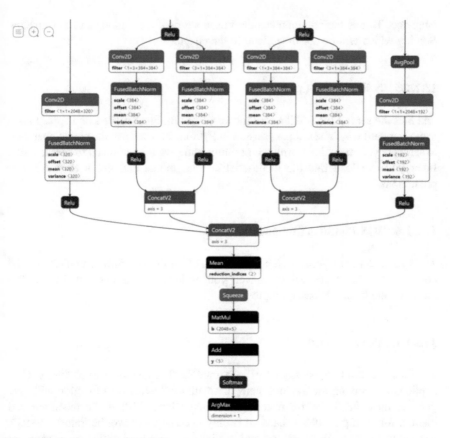

**Fig. 13.9** Graph contained in .pb file

### 13.2.1.3 Keras h5 (.h5)

Keras saves models natively as a .h5 file. Model weights are saved using the HDF5 format. This is a grid format that is ideal for storing multi-dimensional arrays of numbers. The model structure can be described and saved using two different formats: JSON and YAML.

### 13.2.1.4 TensorFlow SavedModel Format

SavedModel is TensorFlow's standard serialization format for trained models or model pieces. It stores the model's trained weights together with the exact TensorFlow operations to perform its computation. It can be used independently from the code that created it. It can be reused across different high-level model-building APIs like Keras because TensorFlow operations are their common basic language. This is the common standard used for deploying models to TensorFlow Serving which will be discussed later in the chapter.

#### 13.2.1.5 Scikit-Learn (.pkl)

.pkl files are served for Scikit-Learn models, often on Flask servers and apps. Pickle is the standard way of serialising objects in Python. You can use the pickle operation to serialise your machine learning algorithms and save the serialised format to a file. Later you can load this file to deserialise your model and use it to make new predictions.

#### 13.2.1.6 IOS Platform (.mlmodel)

To use a model with Core ML it needs to be in the .mlmodel format. You can use the coremltools Python package to convert your trained models into this format. The mlmodel file format is based on protobuf.

#### 13.2.1.7 PyTorch (.pt)

.pt. files are used to package PyTorch models that can be served inside C++ applications. Saving the model's state_dict with the torch.save() function will give you the most flexibility for restoring the model later. This is the recommended method for saving models because it is only necessary to save the trained model's learned parameters. When saving and loading an entire model, you save the entire module using Python's pickle module. Using this approach yields the most intuitive syntax and involves the least amount of code.

### 13.2.2 Freezing and Exporting Models

The process of freezing models results in a single file that contains all of the required information in a model. This includes graph and checkpoint variables which are saved as constants in a graph structure. This is in contrast to checkpoints that save the models gradients at each point so that the model can be reloaded for further training. These gradients are not required once training is completed therefore, they can be discarded before the model is moved into production. Typically, frozen models are serialised as a .pb file type.

A SavedModel is a directory containing serialised signatures and the state needed to run them, including variable values and vocabularies. The saved_model.pb file stores the actual TensorFlow program, or model, and a set of named signatures, each identifying a function that accepts tensor inputs and produces tensor outputs. The

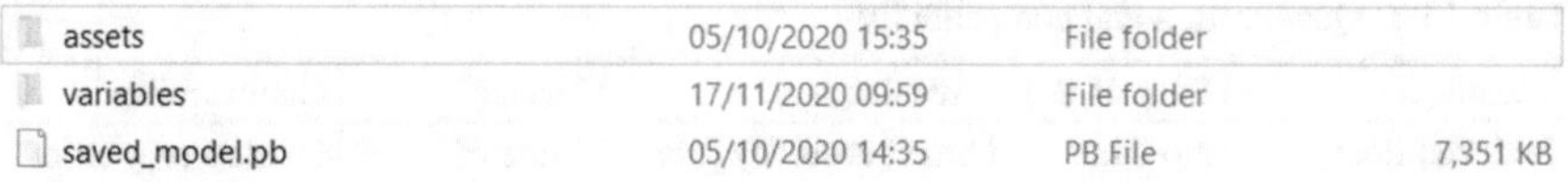

| assets | 05/10/2020 15:35 | File folder | |
| variables | 17/11/2020 09:59 | File folder | |
| saved_model.pb | 05/10/2020 14:35 | PB File | 7,351 KB |

**Fig. 13.10**  Saved model directory

variables directory contains a standard training checkpoint. The assets directory contains files used by the TensorFlow graph, for example, text files used to initialize vocabulary tables. The saved model format is shown in Fig. 13.10.

### 13.2.3  Model Optimisation

Depending on the task, you will need to make a trade-off between model complexity and size. If your task requires high accuracy, then you may need a large and complex model. For tasks that require less precision, it is better to use a smaller model because they not only use less disk space and memory but are also generally faster and more energy-efficient.

Model optimisation is used to:

- Reduce latency and inference costs for cloud and edge devices (e.g., mobile, IoT).
- Deploy models to edge devices with restrictions on processing, memory, power consumption, network usage, and model storage space.
- Enable execution on and optimise for existing hardware or new special-purpose accelerators.

The area of model optimisation can involve various techniques:

- Reduce parameter count with pruning and structured pruning.
- Reduce representational precision with quantization.
- Update the original model topology to a more efficient one with reduced parameters or faster execution. For example, tensor decomposition methods and distillation.

The solutions that you develop will utilise any number of these optimisation techniques to satisfy specific application requirements. In the remainder of this section, we will discuss some of these techniques in detail.

There are multiple ways in which you can deploy optimised models which includes:

- **Pre-optimised models for Edge Nodes and Mobile Devices:**

  - There are a variety of pre-optimised models which you can use that provide efficiency during inference. TensorFlow provides existing TensorFlow Lite pre-optimised models which drastically reduce computational requirements.

**Table 13.2** Quantization and compatibility

| Technique | Ease of use | Accuracy | Latency | Compatibility |
|---|---|---|---|---|
| Reduced float (post training) | No data required | Small accuracy loss | Same of faster than float32 | Float16 support or can fallback to float32 |
| Hybrid quantization (post training) | No data required | Small accuracy loss (accuracy $<=$float16) | Faster than float | Needs float and integer support |
| Integer quantization (post-training) | Unlabelled date | Accuracy $<=$hybrid quantization | Fastest | Integer only |
| Integer quantization (during training) | Labelled training data | Accuracy $>=$ integer post training | Fastest | Integer only |

- **Post-training tooling**
  - If you cannot use a pre-trained model for your application, try using TensorFlow Lite post-training quantization tools during TensorFlow Lite conversion, which can optimise your already-trained TensorFlow model. TensorFlow Lite is a framework that can convert a pre-trained TensorFlow model to optimise inference speed and reduce storage. This is primarily performed to support mobile and edge devices.

Models at the edge or on mobile devices need to be lightweight. This will allow the following:

- Optimised models reduce device storage requirements
- Improved latency when downloading new models over low bandwidth
- Smaller memory footprint for faster inference
- Techniques such as quantization reduce the latency of the model without impacting accuracy

TensorFlow Lite achieves optimisation using:

- **Quantization:** When a model is saved its parameters (functions and weights) are 32bit floating-point values. With quantization, we can reduce the precision of these values between 32bit and 8bit floating-point values or integers [3]. Simpler values also allow us to deploy the model on a broader range of hardware. Table 13.2 shows the different quantization techniques and their associated compatibility.
- **Weight Pruning:** Weight pruning removes parameters (synapses and neurons) within a model that do not enhance the performance of the model. Weight pruning allows sparse models to be compressed more efficiently. Figure 13.11 shows both synapses and neuron pruning.

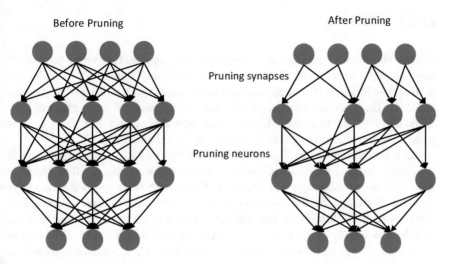

**Fig. 13.11** Synapses and neuron pruning

### 13.2.4   *Deploying the TFLite Model and Undertaking Inference*

A TFLite model is primarily used for inference on edge devices (Android, Raspberry PI). TensorFlow lite uses delegates to improve the performance of the TFLite model at the edge. TFLite delegate is a way to hand over parts of graph execution to other hardware accelerators such as a GPU or a DSP (Digital Signal Processor). TFLite uses several hardware accelerators for speed, accuracy, and optimising power consumption. Although post-training tooling offers good solutions for low powered devices, they are typically limited to lightweight models such as SSD-MobileNet and at the time of writing are incompatible with more complex models such as Faster-RCNNs.

## 13.3   Web Deployment

One of the easiest ways of deploying your trained model is through a website or web application. There are a wide variety of different frameworks for achieving this however it is dependent on whether the trained model will be accessed through the web app directly or by using a third-party inferencing mechanism such as TensorFlow serving. In this section, we introduce an extensible deployment pipeline that is capable of interfacing with trained TensorFlow models while making them accessible to end-users. Flask is a dynamic web application that uses Python and associated frameworks for seamless full-stack web development and provides easy integration for machine learning models.

### 13.3.1   Flask

Flask is one of many web frameworks available for python and is a micro-framework based on singular tasks [4]. Flask uses its extensible web framework to enable the flexible development of web applications using various web development libraries and tools. This provides experienced developers with the freedom to plug and play many libraries and databases. Unlike other web frameworks like Django, it is possible to integrate many different frameworks as shown in Fig. 13.12.

Flask is useful when developing machine learning projects. More importantly, it is a useful tool for educational purposes and those embarking on their machine learning journey. Although you could use Flask (with other tools) for enterprise solutions this could be time-consuming and, you would use more sophisticated solutions such as WordPress and ASP.NET linked to backend machine learning models. The benefit of Flask however is that it provides much more flexibility to developers. Flask and its associated machine learning pipeline are shown in Fig. 13.13.

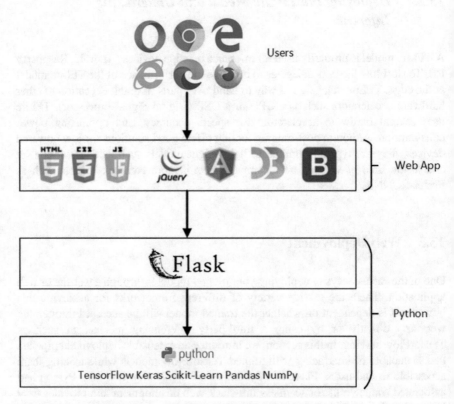

**Fig. 13.12**  Flask and the integration of different frameworks

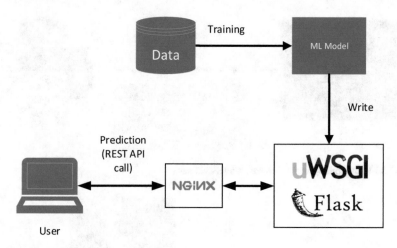

**Fig. 13.13** Flask and associated machine learning pipeline

## 13.3.2 Why Use Flask

Flask is a great tool for showing how front-end web interfaces can be linked with backend machine learning models for inference. One of the main advantages is that Flask uses Python to handle the backend of the web application (where our model will be run). This means that it is completely compatible with the Python code nativity provided by TensorFlow. While the Python code is used to handle the programming aspects of our website, we can interface with frontend components such as HTML and CSS.

## 13.3.3 Working and Developing in Flask

There are several ways in which we can send and receive data from our trained TensorFlow model. Firstly, we could use an API request which can send and receive information such as JSON to and from the Flask application. This works transmitting data to machine learning models for processing and receiving a response. For example, we could submit an image and it would return a set of binding box locations, classes, and probability scores. The process is shown in Fig. 13.14.

Another way of achieving this is to join the Flask application with a HTML form. In this method, the user interacts with the web front end like any other type of web page. In an object detection example, users could upload images through the web form which is then sent to the model for inference which returns the prediction as shown in Fig. 13.15.

This provides a basic overview and describes a powerful frontend framework that allows you to interface with your machine learning models.

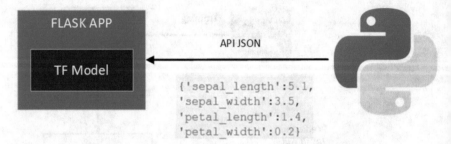

{'sepal_length':5.1,
'sepal_width':3.5,
'petal_length':1.4,
'petal_width':0.2}

**Fig. 13.14** Submitting request to ML models via flask

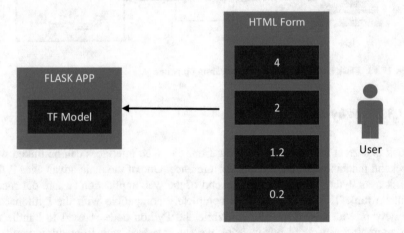

**Fig. 13.15** Submitting request to machine learning models via flask

## 13.4  Summary

This chapter covered the essential aspects of deploying and hosting machine learning models for inference. Within the machine learning pipeline, we discussed the deployment aspects of machine learning and how we can access the functionality through REST APIs and gRPC. The importance of model deployment was explained and how this can be achieved using an MLOps pipeline. This included a discussion on some of the more common MLOps frameworks and access through their common API interfaces. Within the MLOps pipeline, we discussed how models are prepared using a variety of different model formats. This also included how models are frozen, exported and optimised using optimisation tool kits which primarily focused on TFLite and edge nodes. The final stages in the MLOps pipeline are the deployment of models and how they can be accessed through web components. This section introduced Flask and the basic constructs needed to access model inference and undertake prediction.

# References

1. M. Treveil *et al.*, *Introducing MLOps.* " O'Reilly Media, Inc.," 2020.
2. S. Alla and S. K. Adari, "What Is MLOps?," in *Beginning MLOps with MLFlow*, Springer, 2021, pp. 79–124.
3. D. Lin, S. Talathi, and S. Annapureddy, "Fixed point quantization of deep convolutional networks," in *International conference on machine learning*, 2016, pp. 2849–2858.
4. M. Grinberg, *Flask web development: developing web applications with python.* " O'Reilly Media, Inc.," 2018.

# Chapter 14
# Enterprise Machine Learning Serving

In the previous chapter, we discussed the hosting of trained models and how we can use frameworks such as Flask to input and receive information that can be used in a business pipeline. Access to these models can be direct or through model servers to support enterprise solutions. In the previous chapter, we also discussed how models can be accessed directly through library imports. In this chapter, we will discuss component-based MLOps and how models can be packaged using Docker and distributed at scale using Kubernetes. The chapter will focus on enterprise-level solutions that containerise TensorFlow Serving for scalable model serving. Typically, to access GPUs through Docker using this configuration a Linux distribution is required. However, with new advances from Microsoft, the Linux Kernel can be embedded and accessed as a component directly within the OS using Windows Subsystem for Linux (WSL2). This overcomes the limitation of accessing GPUs with NVidia Docker runtime which is covered in this chapter. Currently, the only way to access the NVidia Docker runtime and GPU in Windows is to run WSL2.

## 14.1  Docker

In this section, we will introduce Docker and discuss why it is used in machine learning [1]. You will already have experience with installing software and packages on your machine. Figure 14.1 shows how this is typically undertaken. You would download an installer, run it and in some cases, you would get an error message (this could be due to a missing dependency or incorrect versions). Troubleshooting this can be both time consuming and challenging. This is what Docker is trying to fix. Docker aims to make it easy for you to install and run software on any given computer.

By using docker you abstract all the required system configurations and dependencies into a single runnable command. Docker makes it easy to install and run software without worrying about setup or dependencies. This is not the only reason

© Springer Nature Switzerland AG 2022
P. Fergus, C. Chalmers, *Applied Deep Learning*, Computational Intelligence Methods and Applications, https://doi.org/10.1007/978-3-031-04420-5_14

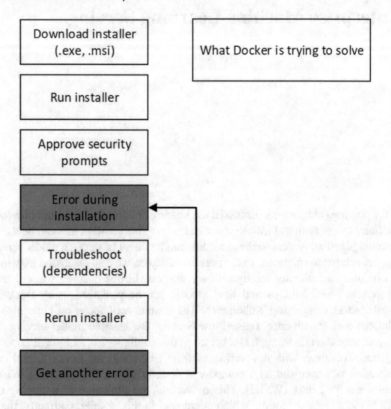

**Fig. 14.1**   Traditional software installation vs docker containerisation

you would use docker, but it does constitute one of the fundamental reasons within MLOps.

### 14.1.1   What Is Docker

Docker is better described as an ecosystem for creating and running containers. Figure 14.2 shows a Docker ecosystem and its residing tools. Collectively these tools allow us to create and run containers.

If we run the following command docker run -t tensorflow/serving:latest-gpu a series of actions occur. Firstly, the docker cli (command-line interface) connects to the Docker hub and it downloads a single file called an image. An image is a single file containing all the dependencies and all the configurations required to run that program (for example, TensorFlow serving). The image file is a single file that is stored locally on your hard drive. You can use this image to create containers. A

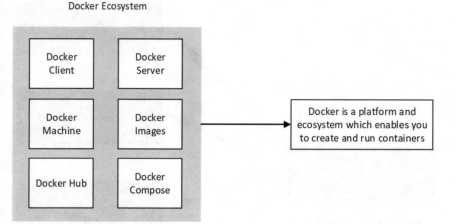

**Fig. 14.2**   Docker ecosystem

container is an instance of an image that you can think of as a running program as shown in Fig. 14.3. Note from this figure that a container is a program with its own isolated set of hardware resources. This includes its own memory space, network resources and its own section of hard drive space.

Images and containers are the backbone of any Docker project. This will be discussed throughout this chapter as we delve deeper into the subject.

### 14.1.2   Working with Docker

Docker is a cross-platform technology that can be run on Windows, Mac, and Linux. Before we can use Docker there are some pre-requisites on the host OS. The two tools that need to be installed include Docker Client (docker cli) which allows us to interface with docker using commands in the terminal. Commands issued to the Docker client interpret the commands and process them accordingly. The Docker client itself does not do anything with containers or images. Instead, the Docker client is simply a tool (or portal) to help us interact with another piece of software that is included in the package called the Docker server (Docker daemon). Docker server is the software that is responsible for creating containers, images, maintaining containers, uploading images, and everything else related to Docker. These two important components are shown in Fig. 14.4.

You interact with Docker directly as it runs independently as a service. Its functionality is accessed via the Docker client.

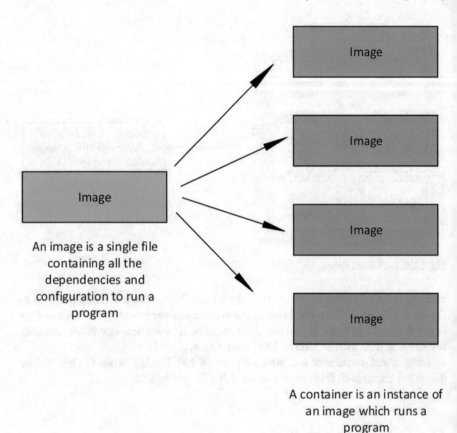

Fig. 14.3 Running instances of docker images

#### 14.1.2.1   Using Docker

In this section, we will focus on how to install Docker on Windows. An important note is that at the time of writing if you are a Windows Home/Sku you will not be able to install Docker for Windows desktop addition as it requires Hyper-V virtualisation which is only supported in Windows Professional and Enterprise additions (this does not affect Windows Server/Skus). This is a workaround, but this is not covered in the book. The later version of Docker uses WSL 2 to enable support for Linux containers.

Now we can run a simple hello world example. If we run the command "docker run hello-world" you will see in Fig. 14.5 below that we are unable to find the image "hello-world:latest" locally. This means we have not downloaded the image before. In this instance, we will retrieve the image from the Docker hub using the following command as shown in Fig. 14.5 "latest: Pulling from library/hello-world." This will result in several status commands before the "Hello from Docker!" message is sent. Figure 14.5 then provides a detailed discussion on the steps Docker took. In step

Docker for Windows/Mac

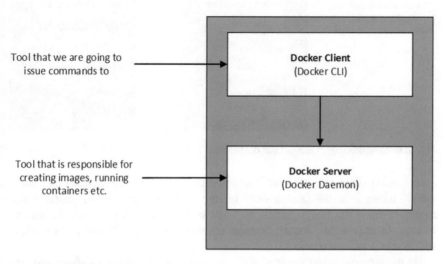

Tool that we are going to
issue commands to

**Docker Client**
(Docker CLI)

Tool that is responsible for
creating images, running
containers etc.

**Docker Server**
(Docker Daemon)

**Fig. 14.4** Docker client and docker server

```
C:\Users\Carl>docker run hello-world
Unable to find image 'hello-world:latest' locally
latest: Pulling from library/hello-world
0e03bdcc26d7: Pull complete
Digest: sha256:e7c70bb24b462baa86c102610182e3efcb12a04854e8c582838d92970a09f323
Status: Downloaded newer image for hello-world:latest

Hello from Docker!
This message shows that your installation appears to be working correctly.

To generate this message, Docker took the following steps:
 1. The Docker client contacted the Docker daemon.
 2. The Docker daemon pulled the "hello-world" image from the Docker Hub.
    (amd64)
 3. The Docker daemon created a new container from that image which runs the
    executable that produces the output you are currently reading.
 4. The Docker daemon streamed that output to the Docker client, which sent it
    to your terminal.

To try something more ambitious, you can run an Ubuntu container with:
 $ docker run -it ubuntu bash

Share images, automate workflows, and more with a free Docker ID:
 https://hub.docker.com/

For more examples and ideas, visit:
 https://docs.docker.com/get-started/
```

**Fig. 14.5** Docker hello world example

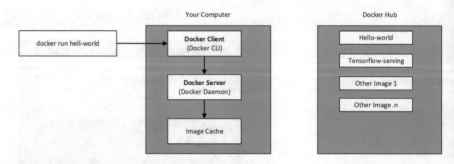

**Fig. 14.6** Downloading an image from docker hub

1 the Docker client contacted the Docker daemon which in step 2 pulled the "hello-world" image from the Docker Hub. In step 3 the Docker daemon creates a new container from the image which runs the executable that produces the output. Finally, in step 4 the Docker daemon streams that output to the Docker client which sent it to your terminal.

At the terminal when we executed the command "docker run hello-world" the Docker client is started. As stated above the Docker cli takes the commands from the user which in term passes the command to the Docker server. The Docker server oversees all the main aspects of running and hosting Docker containers containing the image. When we ran the command "docker run hello-world" it sends an instruction to start a new container using the image named hello-world. The hello world has a small program contained within it that prints out the generated messages shown in Fig. 14.5. When the command was received by the Docker server a series of actions occurred in the background. Docker server realised that we were trying to start up a new container using the image hello-world. The first thing the server does is check its local image cache to see if there is a local copy of the image. In this instance there is no image called hello-world, so a command is issued to the Docker Hub. In this instance, the hello-world image is downloaded from Docker Hub and stored in the local image cache. Once images are stored in the cache, they can be run at speed without having to be downloaded.

Once the image is cached locally Docker server uses it to create an instance of a Docker container. Remember a container is an instance of an image that is used to run a specific program with its own resources, I.e., memory, network resources, and hard drive space. The Docker server takes the image from the server image cache and loads it into memory and creates a container using the image. In our example, the programs' sole purpose is to print out the message "Hello from Docker." Figure 14.6 shows the process of downloading new images from Docker Hub if it is not present in the cache.

## 14.1.2.2 What's a Container

In this section, we will discuss what a container is and how it is created on your machine. To fully understand it is important for you to know some background concepts about the OS. OSs have a fundamental component known as the kernel which is a running software process that governs access between all the programs (I.e., executable pieces of software) which are running on the computer and all the physical hardware that is connected to your computer. In Fig. 14.7 we can see the top part of the diagram showing the individual processes running on the computer, such as Chrome, Terminal, or Spotify. It is important to know that none of these processes talks directly to the physical device. Instead, the process negotiates hardware access directly through the kernel. The kernel then requests and facilitates controlled access to the underlying hardware, such as the CPU, memory, or Hard Disk. Processes interact with the kernel through system calls which are simply function invocations. The kernel exposes different endpoints to offer hardware invocation functions.

Now, what happens if we have two programs as shown in Fig. 14.8 that want to use different versions of Python (v2 and v3). In this example let us say you cannot have two separate versions of python installed on the same computer. As shown in Fig. 14.8 Chrome would successfully execute but NodeJS would not because Chrome has access to Python v2 and NodeJS does not have access to Python V3.

To solve this issue one way would be to use namespaces as shown in Fig. 14.9 whereby installations reside within separate folder structures (segments). To ensure Chrome and NodeJS have access to the correct segment at any time either one will issue a system call, the kernel will interpret the incoming call and determine which process it is coming from and map it to the appropriate segment. Using this namespace (segment) feature we can ensure that both programs that reside on the same machine can gain access to the required dependencies.

Namespacing allows us to isolate processes. When a particular process asks for a resource, it will be directed to a specific area or set of resources on the underlying hardware. Namespacing can also be applied to software to restrict certain parts of the hardware. Namespacing allows us to limit the resources and communication to other processes. In addition, control groups can also be used to limit the number of

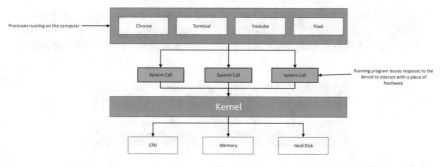

**Fig. 14.7** Processes running and interacting with hardware on a computer

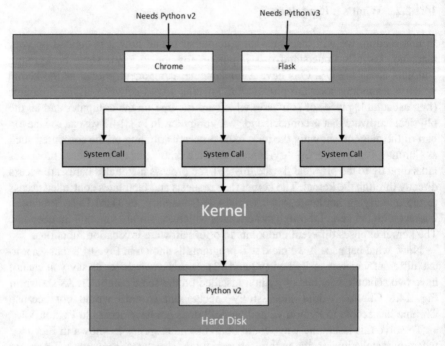

**Fig. 14.8** Running different versions of a program

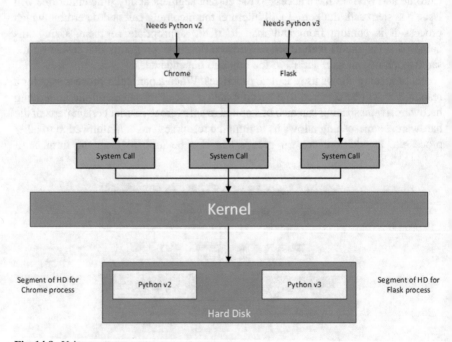

**Fig. 14.9** Using namespaces to segment processes

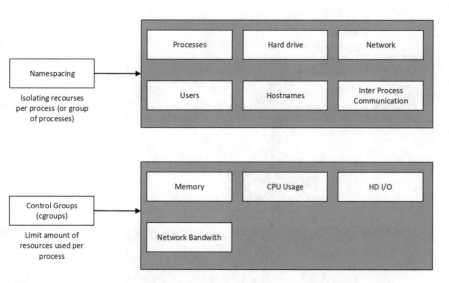

**Fig. 14.10** Using namespaces and control groups to isolate and limit resources

resources used by each process, such as the CPU and memory. Using these two together allows us to isolate a single process and limit the number of resources it can access and the amount of bandwidth it can use. Both the namespacing and control group mechanisms are shown in Fig. 14.10.

As shown in Fig. 14.11, the dotted line highlights the running process and the segment of resources it can access. This is known as a container. A container is a process or a set of processes that have a grouping of resources that are specifically assigned to it.

As Fig. 14.12 shows the container has a running process that sends a system call to the kernel which in turn analyses the incoming system call and directs it to a specific group of hardware resources (I.e., the RAM, CPU etc).

Now that we understand containers, we need to understand their relationship to images. So how does a single image file create a container? When we talk about an image, we are talking about a file system snapshot (Windows or Ubuntu). This is an image of the directories containing the source files. For example, looking at Fig. 14.13, an image may contain a snapshot of Flask and Python. Each image also contains a startup command for each program. The process of taking an image and hosting it in a container works in the following way:

- First the kernel isolates a proportion of the hard drive and makes it available to just that container. The filesystem snapshot is transferred to the proportion of the hard drive designated to the container.
- Second the start-up command is executed (for example Flask). When Flask is invoked a new instance of the process is created and that process is isolated to that specific set of resources inside the container.

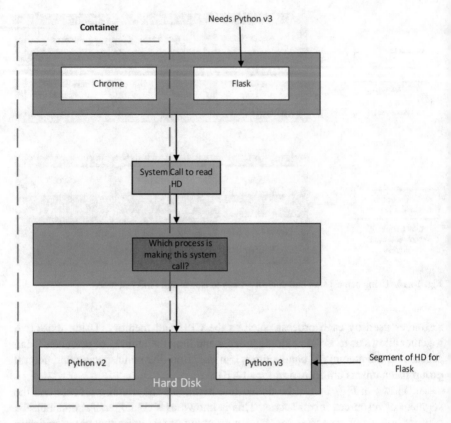

**Fig. 14.11** Docker container

Both namespacing and control groups are specific to Linux and are not included in Windows or Mac. When you install Docker for either Windows or Mac a Linux virtual machine is created (unless your system is running WSL 2) as shown in Fig. 14.14. In this instance, the containers are created inside the Linux virtual machine.

### 14.1.2.3   Docker Run

Running a Docker container is performed using the docker cli and referencing the docker run command. This command is used by referencing the image name as shown in Fig. 14.15.

Several different arguments can be executed with the run command. One of the main arguments commonly used allows you to override the default startup command. Figure 14.16 shows how the above process can be extended to provide inline commands to our image which is run in the container.

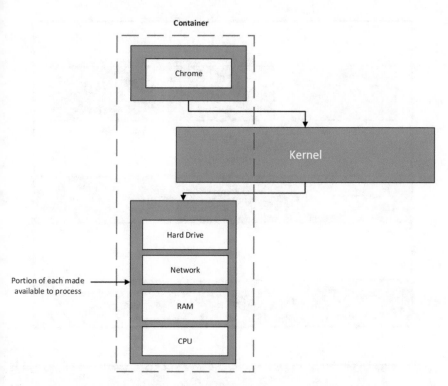

**Fig. 14.12** Sending system calls from a docker container

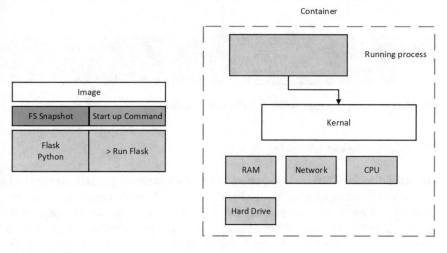

**Fig. 14.13** File system snapshot with associated startup command

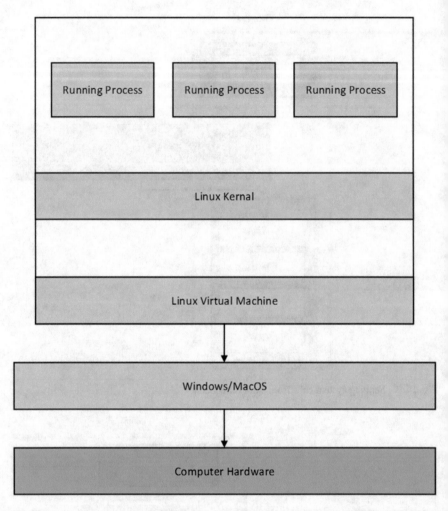

**Fig. 14.14**   Running processes hosted in Linux virtual machine

### 14.1.2.4   Container Lifecycle

Understanding the lifecycle is important to know when running docker services. As previously discussed by using the docker run command we can create our container. Creating and running a container are two separate steps. There are two additional commands in addition to docker run that can be used to start a new container. Docker run embodies two separate commands called "docker create" and "docker start" as shown in Fig. 14.17.

The create command creates the container using the image. While the start command starts the newly created container as shown in Fig. 14.18.

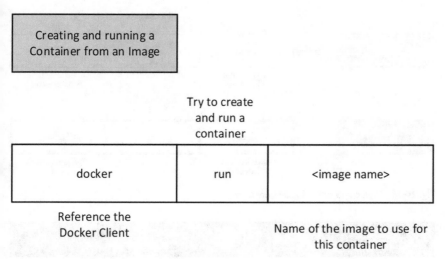

**Fig. 14.15** Running the docker command using the CLI

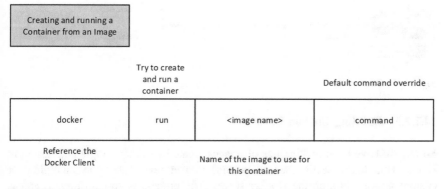

**Fig. 14.16** Docker Run command and associated arguments

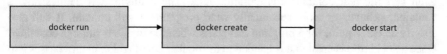

**Fig. 14.17** Docker commands: run, create and start

So, what is the difference between creating and starting a container. When we create a container the file system snapshot is configured within the hard drive segment. To start the container, we execute the startup command for the given image. We can create a container without running it as shown in Fig. 14.19. Once the container is created you can call the primary startup command with "docker start." (Fig. 14.19).

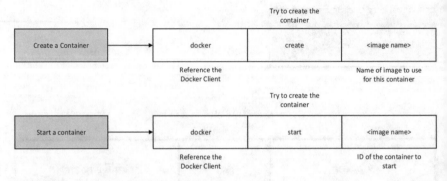

**Fig. 14.18** Create and run a docker container

**Fig. 14.19** Create container without running it

**Fig. 14.20** Dockerfiles

### 14.1.2.5   Building Custom Dockers

So far, we have been making use of images created by other people and hosted in Docker Hub. In this section, we will provide an overview of how you can build your custom images through the Docker server. The process is straightforward and is achieved through the creation of dockerfiles as shown in Fig. 14.20. A dockerfile is a plain text file that contains configuration data. The configuration defines how a container behaves or more specifically what programs it will contain. It will also specify an entry point for a program that starts when the image is run in a container. Once a dockerfile is created it is handed to the docker client which in turn passes it to the docker server. The docker server is responsible for processing the configuration file and building a usable image that can be used to start up a new container. The dockerfile is where the complexity of the image resides.

The process flow shown in Fig. 14.21 highlights the key stages that need to be undertaken to create a dockerfile. Firstly, we need to specify a base image. Secondly, we will run some commands to install additional programs and dependencies. The last step is to specify a startup command which is automatically run when the container is started. Once the dockerfile is created it can be used to build a docker image using the following command "docker build .". The dockerfile must be in the current working directory.

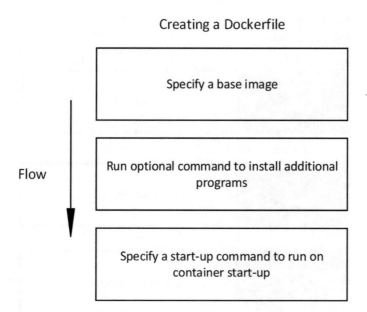

**Fig. 14.21** Docker creation workflow

An example of a dockerfile is shown in Fig. 14.22. Every line begins with a single word called an instruction which tells the docker server what to do. The instruction FROM is used to specify the docker image we wish to specify as an image. The RUN instruction is used to execute some command while we are preparing our custom image. Finally, the CMD instruction specifies what should be executed when our image is used in a container. Every line of configuration you will add to a dockerfile will always begin with an instruction. Figure 14.22 shows some of the most important instructions you will come across however there are many more. After each instruction we provide an instruction as shown below that customises how the instruction is executed. The process of creating a docker image works in the same fundamental way of installing an OS on a computer.

### 14.1.3 Docker Compose

It is possible to run multiple applications in a single container. However, this approach is less flexible, and you would encounter problems if the application became popular. As demand increases for your application, you would have to replicate each docker container with all the associated apps to accommodate increased traffic as shown in Fig. 14.23. The issue with this approach is that each of these servers will be completely disconnected from each other. In the example, in Fig. 14.23 the server visit counts would be independent of each other therefore giving different results depending on which Flask app accesses the key value.

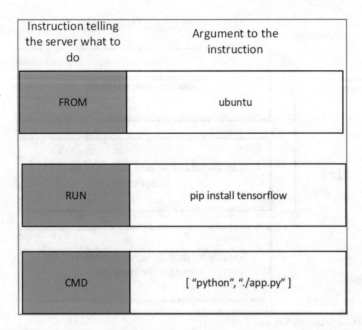

**Fig. 14.22** Docker build instructions

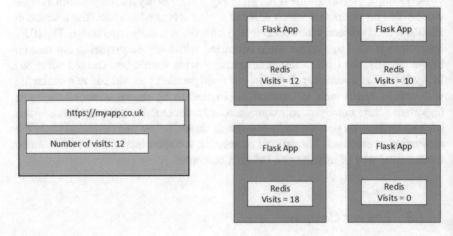

**Fig. 14.23** Running multiple applications in single container

Figure 14.24 would provide a much better solution as we can separate our Flask App and the Redis application (server counts) which are now both hosted in their own separate container.

To facilitate the above configuration, we would generate our docker images using the dockerfile but now we need to join them to form a complete application. By default, both containers once they are run do not have direct communications

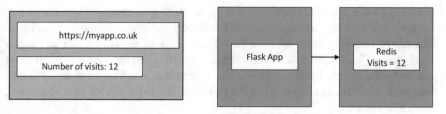

**Fig. 14.24**  Running applications in separate containers

**Fig. 14.25**  Docker
compose

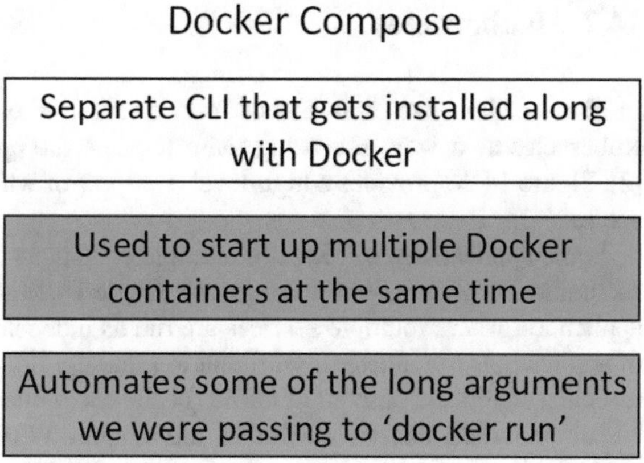

# Docker Compose

### Separate CLI that gets installed along with Docker

### Used to start up multiple Docker containers at the same time

### Automates some of the long arguments we were passing to 'docker run'

between the Flask App and the Redis server. They are both isolated, independent containers. We will need to set up networking infrastructure between them. To do this we could use dockers cli network feature. The problem however is that we would have to continually run these commands every time we wanted to run the containers. A better approach would be to use docker compose. This is a tool that is installed with Docker.

Docker compose is shown in Fig. 14.25 and can be run from the cli using "docker-compose". Docker-compose exists to minimise the number of commands that need to be run with the cli (i.e., Docker run, docker exec and so on). Docker-compose also allows us to start and run multiple containers and connect them to form a network.

## 14.1.4  Docker Volume and Mount

One of the final aspects of docker is the ability to share information within the host system and across relevant containers. There are two primary ways of achieving this. Firstly, using bind mounts allows you to bind the absolute path of a file or directory on the host machine which can then be mounted into the container. The second method is to use volumes which is a directory created within the docker storage directory on the host machine. With this approach, docker manages that directories contents and external access outside of the docker environment is now prohibited. The file or directory does not need to exist on the host already. It can be created on-demand if it does not exist. Bind mounts are performant but they rely on the host machines file system having a specific file system that is not required for volumes. However, when the container is run the paths specific to the OS are passed in using the "-v" switch.

## 14.2   Kubernetes

In this section, we will extend our discussion on containers and introduce Kubernetes as a way of reusing them to scale the applications you will develop [2]. Figure 14.26 provides a high-level overview of what Kubernetes is and why we use it.

Some applications will require multiple containers to be run at the same time to accommodate all functions and services. Figure 14.27 shows an example of a sample application where multiple services are run as independent containers. These types of applications are inherently difficult to scale up. So, for example, if we started to receive a significant amount of traffic (I.e., users of our system) one or more of these containers could exceed maximum throughput. What you would want to do is dynamically spawn new instances of specific services, (such as the worker process in the figure below). So, for example, if we had three users request the service in parallel, we would like to have three worker processes (containers). Rather than an individual container, some solutions will replicate the complete set of services (containers). This would mean that services, such as Nginx would be unnecessarily

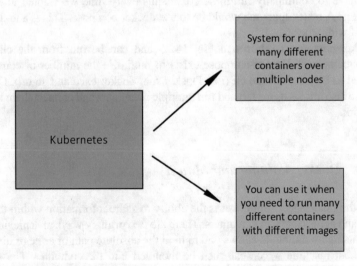

**Fig. 14.26**   Kubernetes

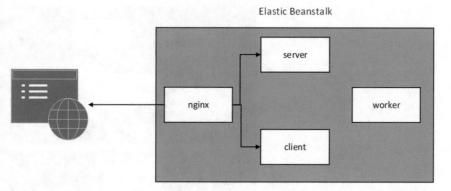

**Fig. 14.27** Scaling individual containers

duplicated as they can deal with many user requests. We only want to replicate those services that are computationally expensive and do scale well with increased numbers of user requests. So, if it is our worker container that is computationally expensive, we would only want to replicate the worker container not the Nginx, server or client containers.

The process of duplicating our worker containers is shown in Fig. 14.28. The approach shown is the one Kubernetes facilitates.

Figure 14.29 shows a typical Kubernetes cluster. A Kubernetes cluster consists of a master node that controls the work processes of each subsequent node in the Kubernetes cluster. Each node can be either a virtual machine or a physical computer. These worker nodes host the individual containers. The nodes can run one or more containers that are spread through the cluster. Developers manage the entire Kubernetes cluster through the master node. Users submit instructions to the master node on how many containers should be run throughout the cluster. Outside of the Kubernetes cluster, a load balancer regulates incoming traffic in the form of requests which are relayed to each worker node.

## 14.3 TensorFlow Serving

TensorFlow Serving is a flexible, high-performance serving system for machine learning models, designed for production environments [3]. TensorFlow Serving makes it easy to deploy new algorithms and experiments while keeping the same server architecture and APIs. TensorFlow Serving provides out-of-the-box integration with TensorFlow models but can be easily extended to serve other types of models and data. Typically, TensorFlow serving is provided as a docker image that can be hosted locally or on the cloud.

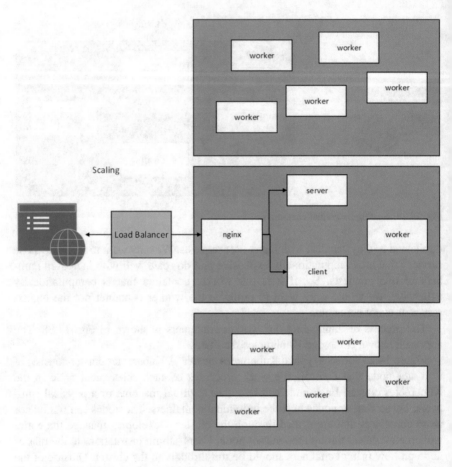

**Fig. 14.28**   Balancing containers using Kubernetes

## 14.3.1   Why Use TensorFlow Serving

TensorFlow Serving allows you to quickly host and serve your trained TensorFlow models in a production environment. TensorFlow Serving can manage model versioning making the management of models easier to maintain. The end-to-end workflow is shown in Fig. 14.30.

## 14.3.2   TensorFlow Serving on CPU and GPU (NVidia Runtime)

The NVIDIA Container Toolkit allows users to build and run GPU accelerated Docker containers. The toolkit includes a container runtime library to leverage

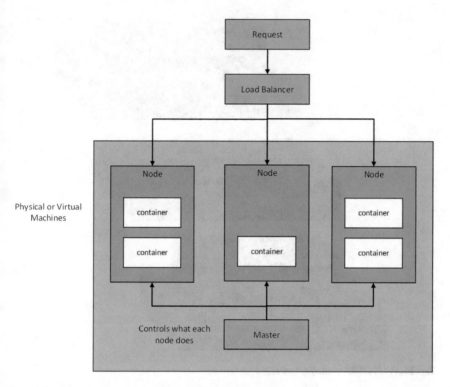

**Fig. 14.29** Large scale enterprise distributed Kubernetes cluster

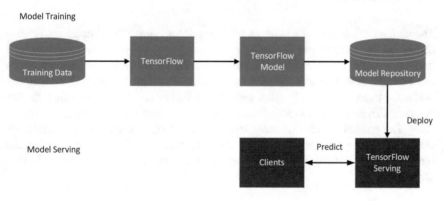

**Fig. 14.30** TensorFlow serving

NVIDIA GPUs as shown in Fig. 14.31. Before serving with a GPU, in addition to installing Docker, you will need to update NVIDIA drivers for your system. At the time of writing the Nvidia Container Toolkit is only supported on Linux. However, with the introduction of WSL2, the Nvidia Container Toolkit can now be run on Windows with GPU support [4] (Fig. 14.31).

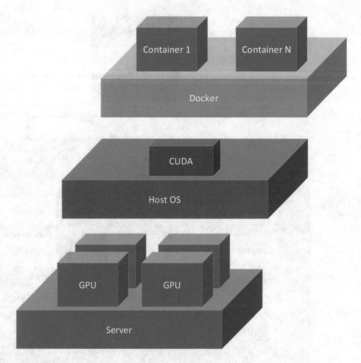

**Fig. 14.31** NVIDIA container runtime with docker

## 14.4    Summary

The chapter introduced the concept of enterprise serving. The chapter provided a discussion on Docker and how it can be installed, configured, and used to host images in containers. We highlighted the differences between images and containers and how the container lifecycle works. We also described the method for building custom images using dockerfiles and how services can be joined using docker compose. The chapter also introduced how we can load balance Docker instances using Kubernetes which facilitates rapid scale-out of containers using Kubernete clusters. The chapter was concluded with a discussion on TensorFlow Serving and how it can be utilised for hosting our trained models on both CPU and GPU hardware.

# References

1. I. Miell and A. Sayers, *Docker in practice*. Simon and Schuster, 2019.
2. B. Burns, J. Beda, and K. Hightower, *Kubernetes: up and running: dive into the future of infrastructure*. O'Reilly Media, 2019.
3. C. Olston *et al.*, "Tensorflow-serving: Flexible, high-performance ml serving," *arXiv Prepr. arXiv1712.06139*, 2017.
4. P. Singh, "Exploring WSL2," in *Learn Windows Subsystem for Linux*, Springer, 2020, pp. 75–98.

Printed in the United States
by Baker & Taylor Publisher Services